Wombat Goes Walkabout

Michael Morpurgo
Christian Birmingham

Collins

An imprint of HarperCollinsPublishers

For Alice and Lucie
MM

To Penny and Cathy
CB

The illustrator would like to thank Jackie French, Healesville Sanctuary,
Jirrahlinga Koala and Wildlife Sanctuary, HarperCollins Australia and Birdworld

Also published by HarperCollins:

Sam's Duck by Michael Morpurgo & Keith Bowen

The Magical Bicycle by Berlie Doherty & Christian Birmingham
The Sea Of Tranquility by Mark Haddon & Christian Birmingham
Windhover by Alan Brown & Christian Birmingham

First published
in hardback in Great Britain
by HarperCollins Publishers Ltd in 1999
First published in Picture Lions in 2000
5 7 9 10 8 6 4
ISBN: 0 00 771114 X

Text copyright © Michael Morpurgo 1999
Illustrations copyright © Christian Birmingham 1999
The author and illustrator assert the moral right
to be identified as the author and illustrator of this work.
A CIP catalogue record for this title is available from the British Library.

The HarperCollins website address is: www.**fire**and**water**.com
Manufactured in Thailand for Imago

One day Wombat woke up and thought, "I think I'll dig a hole today." Wombat loved digging holes. So off he went and dug a deep, deep hole. He crawled inside and sat there in the cool and the dark and began to think, because Wombat loved thinking too. He thought to himself, "Why is the sky blue? Why am I a wombat and not a kangaroo?"

Some time later, Wombat climbed out of his hole.

He looked around for his mother, but she wasn't there.

He was all alone.

"Who are you?" cried Kookaburra
from high in the sky.
"I'm Wombat," said Wombat.
"And what can you do, Wombat?"
"Not much. I dig a lot
and I think a lot."
"That's nothing," cackled Kookaburra.
"I can fly. Look at me."
And he looped the loop
and flew away.

Wombat went down to the creek
to look for his mother.
But she wasn't there either.
Just then Wallaby came hopping by.
"Who are you?" he asked, looking
down his nose at Wombat.
"I'm Wombat," said Wombat.
"And what can you do, Wombat?"
"Not much. I dig a lot
and I think a lot."
"That's nothing," laughed Wallaby.
"I can hop. I can skip. I can jump.
Look at me." And he hopped and
skipped and jumped away.

Wombat walked and walked,
and everywhere he walked he looked
for his mother. But he couldn't see her
anywhere. He sat down under a
stringy bark gum tree to get his
breath back. Just then Possum
popped up beside him.
"Who are you?" she asked, darting
her eyes this way and that.
"I'm Wombat," said Wombat.
"And what can you do?"
"Not much. I dig a lot
and I think a lot."
"That's nothing," laughed Possum.
"I can hang upside down.
I can swing by my tail. Look at me!"
And she swung away up the
stringy bark gum tree.

Wombat wandered sadly through the
bush, still looking for his mother.
Just then Emu came scampering by.
"Who are you?" he snapped.
"I'm Wombat," said Wombat.
"And what can you do?"
"Not much. I dig a lot
and I think a lot."
"That's nothing," laughed Emu.
"I can scamper. I can scoot
around in crazy circles. Look at me!"
And away he scampered, scooting
around in crazy circles.

Just then Boy came by,
hunting after Emu.
"Who are you?" he asked.
"I'm Wombat," said Wombat.
"And what can you do?"
"Not much. I dig a lot
and I think a lot."
"That's nothing," laughed Boy.
"I can do just about everything.
I can jump, I can run, I can swing.
I can even hunt. Look at me."
And off he went,
hunting after Emu.

It was baking hot now, and Wombat
shuffled into the shade of a great
eucalyptus tree. He hoped his mother
might be there. But she wasn't.
"Who are you?" called Koala from
way up in the tree above him.
"I'm Wombat," said Wombat.
"And what can you do?"
"Not much. I dig a lot
and I think a lot."
"That's nothing," laughed Koala.
"I can doze, I can snooze, I can snore.
Look at me." And very soon she was
dozing and snoozing and snoring away
high up in her eucalyptus tree.
By now Wombat was very, very tired.
So he lay down in the shade
and sang himself to sleep.

When Wombat woke up,
he looked around for his mother.
But she still wasn't there.
"I know," he thought. "I'll climb
the highest hill I can find.
Surely I'll be able to see her then."
So that's what he did.
He climbed and he climbed
and he climbed.

When he
reached the top
he looked about him.
Everywhere he looked there
were lots of cackling kookaburras,
hopping wallabies, swinging possums,
hunting boys, scampering emus, and
dozing koalas. But no matter how hard he
looked, he just couldn't see his mother anywhere.

But he did see something else.

He saw smoke. He saw fire.

It was leaping from tree to tree.

It was coming straight towards him.

Wombat thought hard, very hard.

Suddenly he knew what to do.

He ran down the hill as fast as

he could, and began to dig.

He dug and he dug and he dug.

Then Kookaburra came by, and Wallaby and Possum
and Emu and Boy and Koala. "Fire!" they all cried.
"Run, run, you silly Wombat. Fire! Fire!"
But Wombat just went on digging.

"What are you doing?"
they asked.
"I'm digging," replied Wombat.
"And I'm thinking too."
"What are you thinking?" they cried.
"I'm thinking that fire burns faster
than you can run or fly or hop or swing.
And I'm thinking that there's plenty of room
down in my hole if you want to join me.
We'll be quite safe."
They took just one look at all the crackling fire and
all the billowing smoke. One look was all they needed.

Down into Wombat's hole they jumped, until they were all sitting there, safe and snug. And to keep them all happy Wombat sang them the digging song that his mother had taught him.

When at last it was all over (the fire and the song) they climbed out into the evening air.

"I wish," sighed Wombat, looking around him sadly. "I just wish I could find my mother. I've lost her and she's lost me."

"Well, why didn't you ask?" they all said. "We'll find her for you." And away they went, flying and swinging, hopping and scampering, running around in all directions.

With so many of them looking, it wasn't
long before they found Wombat's mother,
and brought her back to him.

Wombat and his mother just hugged and
hugged and hugged.

"I've been looking everywhere for you," she cried.
"I was worried sick. What've you been up to?"

"Not much, Mum," Wombat said.
"I've just been thinking a lot,
and digging a lot.
That's all."

FIRST AID FOR THE

OBSTETRICS & GYNECOLOGY clerkship

THE STUDENT TO STUDENT GUIDE

SERIES EDITORS:

LATHA G. STEAD, MD
Assistant Professor of Emergency Medicine
Mayo Medical School
Rochester, Minnesota

S. MATTHEW STEAD, MD, PhD
Class of 2001
State University of New York—Downstate Medical Center
Brooklyn, New York

MATTHEW S. KAUFMAN, MD
Resident in Internal Medicine
Long Island Jewish Medical Center
Albert Einstein College of Medicine
New Hyde Park, New York

AUTHORS:

ROBERT L. FEIG
Resident in Ophthalmology
State University of New York—Downstate Medical Center
Brooklyn, New York

NICOLE C. JOHNSON, MD
Resident in Obstetrics and Gynecology
White Memorial Medical Center
Los Angeles, California

McGraw-Hill
Medical Publishing Division

New York   Chicago   San Francisco   Lisbon   London   Madrid
Mexico City   Milan   New Delhi   San Juan   Seoul
Singapore   Sydney   Toronto

McGraw-Hill

A Division of The McGraw·Hill Companies

First Aid for the Obstetrics & Gynecology Clerkship

1 2 3 4 5 6 7 8 9 0 CUS/CUS 0 9 8 7 6 5 4 3 2 1

ISBN 0-07-136423-4

Notice

Medicine is an ever-changing science. As new research and clinical experience broaden our knowledge, changes in treatment and drug therapy are required. The authors and the publisher of this work have checked with sources believed to be reliable in their efforts to provide information that is complete and generally in accord with the standards accepted at the time of publication. However, in view of the possibility of human error or changes in medical sciences, neither the authors nor the publisher nor any other party who has been involved in the preparation or publication of this work warrants that the information contained herein is in every respect accurate or complete, and they disclaim all responsibility for any errors or omissions or for the results obtained from use of the information contained in this work. Readers are encouraged to confirm the information contained herein with other sources. For example and in particular, readers are advised to check the product information sheet included in the package of each drug they plan to administer to be certain that the information contained in this work is accurate and that changes have not been made in the recommended dose or in the contraindications for administration. This recommendation is of particular importance in connection with new or infrequently used drugs.

This book was set in Goudy by Rainbow Graphics.
The editor was Catherine A. Johnson.
The production supervisor was Lisa Mendez.
Project management was provided by Rainbow Graphics.
The index was prepared by Oneida Indexing.
Von Hoffman Graphics was the printer and binder.

This book is printed on acid-free paper.

Library of Congress Cataloging-in-Publication Data

Feig, Robert.
 First aid for the obstetrics and gynecology clerkship / authors, Robert Feig, Nicole
Collette Johnson.
  p. ; cm. – (First aid for the clerkship)
 Includes index.
 ISBN 0-07-136423-4 (alk. paper)
  1. Obstetrics–Study and teaching (Graduate) 2. Gynecology–Study and teaching
(Graduate) 3. Clinical medicine–Study and teaching (Graduate) I. Johnson, Nicole
Collette. II. Title. III. Series.
 [DNLM: 1. Clinical Clerkship. 2. Career Choice. 3. Fellowships and Scholarships. 4.
Gynecology. 5. Obstetrics. W 18 F297f 2001]
RG141 .F45 2001
618–dc21
                                                    2001030600

Contents

Introduction

This clinical study aid was designed in the tradition of the *First Aid* series of books, formatted in the same way as the other titles in this series. Topics are listed by bold headings to the left, while the "meat" of the topic comprises the middle column. The outside margins contain mnemonics, diagrams, summary or warning statements, "pearls," and other memory aids. These are further classified as "exam tip" noted by the symbol and "ward tip" noted by the symbol.

The content of this book is based on the American Professors of Gynecology and Obstetrics (APGO) and the American College of Obstetricians and Gynecologists (ACOG) recommendations for the Ob-Gyn curriculum for third-year medical students. Each of the chapters contain the major topics central to the practice of obstetrics and gynecology and closely parallel APGO's medical student learning objectives.

The Ob-Gyn clerkship can be an exciting hands-on experience. You will get to deliver babies, assist in surgeries, and see patients in the clinic setting. You will find that rather than simply preparing you for the success on the clerkship exam, this book will also help guide you in the clinical diagnosis and treatment of the many interesting problems you will see during your obstetrics and gynecology rotation.

Acknowledgments

We would like to thank the following faculty for their help in reviewing the manuscript for this book:

Eugene C. Toy, MD
Assistant Course Director, Obstetrics-Gynecology Junior Clerkship
Department of Medical Education
Christus-St. Joseph Hospital
Houston, Texas

Patti Jayne Ross, MD
Clerkship Director
Department of Obstetrics and Gynecology
The University of Texas–Houston Medical School
Houston, Texas

How to Succeed in the Obstetrics & Gynecology Clerkship

Be on Time

Most OB/GYN teams begin rounding between 6 and 7 A.M. If you are expected to "pre-round," you should give yourself at least 10 minutes per patient that you are following to see the patient and learn about the events that occurred overnight. Like all working professionals, you will face occasional obstacles to punctuality, but make sure this is occasional. When you first start a rotation, try to show up at least 15 minutes early until you get the routine figured out.

Dress in a Professional Manner

Even if the resident wears scrubs and the attending wears stiletto heels, you must dress in a professional, conservative manner. Wear a *short* white coat over your clothes unless discouraged (as in pediatrics).

> **Men** should wear long pants, with cuffs covering the ankle, a long collared shirt, and a tie. No jeans, no sneakers, no short-sleeved shirts.
>
> **Women** should wear long pants or knee-length skirt, blouse or dressy sweater. No jeans, no sneakers, no heels greater than 1½ inches, no open-toed shoes.
>
> **Both men and women** may wear scrubs occasionally, during overnight call or in the operating room or birthing ward. Do not make this your uniform.

Act in a Pleasant Manner

The rotation is often difficult, stressful, and tiring. Smooth out your experience by being nice to be around. Smile a lot and learn everyone's name. If you do not understand or disagree with a treatment plan or diagnosis, do not "challenge." Instead, say "I'm sorry, I don't quite understand, could you please explain . . ."

Try to look interested to attendings and residents. Sometimes this stuff is boring, or sometimes you're not in the mood, but when someone is trying to teach you something, look grateful and not tortured.

Always treat patients professionally and with respect. This is crucial to practicing good medicine, but on a less important level if a resident or attending spots you being impolite or unprofessional, it will damage your grade and evaluation quicker than any dumb answer on rounds ever could. And be nice to the nurses. Really nice. Learn names; bring back pens and food from pharmaceutical lunches and give them out. If they like you, they can make your life a lot easier and make you look good in front of the residents and attendings.

Be Aware of the Hierarchy

The way in which this will affect you will vary from hospital to hospital and team to team, but it is always present to some degree. In general, address your questions regarding ward functioning to interns or residents. Address your medical questions to attendings; make an effort to be somewhat informed on your subject prior to asking attendings medical questions. But please don't ask a question just to transparently show off what you know. It's annoying to everyone. Show off by seeming interested and asking real questions that you have when they come up.

Address Patients and Staff in a Respectful Way

Address patients as Sir or Ma'am, or Mr., Mrs., or Miss. Try not to address patients as "honey," "sweetie," and the like. Although you may feel these names are friendly, patients will think you have forgotten their name, that you are being inappropriately familiar, or both. Address all physicians as "doctor," unless told otherwise.

Be Helpful to Your Residents

That involves taking responsibility for patients that you've been assigned to, and even for some that you haven't. If you've been assigned to a patient, know everything there is to know about her, her history, test results, details about her medical problems, and prognosis. Keep your interns or residents informed of new developments that they might not be aware of, and ask them for any updates as well.

If you have the opportunity to make a resident look good, take it. If some new complication comes up with a patient, tell the resident about it before the attending gets a chance to grill the resident on it. And don't hesitate to give credit to a resident for some great teaching in front of an attending. These things make the resident's life easier, and he or she will be grateful and the rewards will come your way.

Volunteer to do things that will help out. So what if you have to run to the lab to follow up on a stat H&H. It helps everybody out, and it is appreciated. Observe and anticipate. If a resident is always hunting around for some tape to do a dressing change every time you round on a particular patient, get some tape ahead of time.

Respect Patients' Rights

1. All patients have the right to have their personal medical information kept private. This means do not discuss the patient's information with family members without that patient's consent and do not discuss any patient in hallways, elevators, or cafeterias.
2. All patients have the right to refuse treatment. This means they can refuse treatment by a specific individual (you, the medical student) or of a specific type (no nasogastric tube). Patients can even refuse life-saving treatment. The only exceptions to this rule are a patient who is deemed to not have the capacity to make decisions or understand situations—in which case a health care proxy should be sought—or a patient who is suicidal or homicidal.
3. All patients should be informed of the right to seek advanced directives on admission. This is often done by the admissions staff, in a booklet. If your patient is chronically ill or has a life-threatening illness, address the subject of advanced directives with the assistance of your attending.

More Volunteering

Be self-propelled, self-motivated. Volunteer to help with a procedure or a difficult task. Volunteer to give a 20-minute talk on a topic of your choice. Volunteer to take additional patients. Volunteer to stay late. The more unpleasant the task, the better.

Be a Team Player

Help other medical students with their tasks; teach them information you have learned. Support your supervising intern or resident whenever possible. Never steal the spotlight, steal a procedure, or make a fellow medical student look bad.

Be Honest

If you don't understand, don't know or didn't do it, make sure you always say that. Never say or document information that is false (for example, don't say "bowel sounds normal" when you did not listen).

Keep Patient Information Handy

Use a clipboard, notebook, or index cards to keep patient information, including a miniature history and physical, lab, and test results at hand.

Present Patient Information in an Organized Manner

Here is a template for the "bullet" presentation:

"This is a [age]-year-old [gender] with a history of [major history such as abdominal surgery, pertinent OB/GYN history] who presented on [date] with [major symptoms, such as pelvic pain, fever], and was found to have [working diagnosis]. [Tests done] showed [results]. Yesterday the patient [state important changes, new plan, new tests, new medications]. This morning the patient feels [state the patient's words], and the physical exam is significant for [state major findings]. Plan is [state plan]."

The newly admitted patient generally deserves a longer presentation following the complete history and physical format (see below).

Some patients have extensive histories. The whole history can and probably should be present in the admission note, but in ward presentation it is often too much to absorb. In these cases, it will be very much appreciated by your team if you can generate a good summary that maintains an accurate picture of the patient. This usually takes some thought, but it's worth it.

Document Information in an Organized Manner

A complete medical student initial history and physical is neat, legible, organized, and usually two to three pages long (see Figure 1-1).

The main advantage to doing the OB/GYN clerkship is that you get to see patients. The patient is the key to learning, and the source of most satisfaction and frustration on the wards. One enormously helpful tip is to try to skim this book before starting your rotation. Starting OB/GYN can make you feel like you're in a foreign land, and all that studying the first two years doesn't help much. You have to start from scratch in some ways, and it will help enormously if you can skim through this book before you start. Get some of the terminology straight, get some of the major points down, and it won't seem so strange.

Select Your Study Material

We recommend:

- This review book, *First Aid for the Clinical Clerkship in Obstetrics & Gynecology*
- A full-text online journal database, such as *www.mdconsult.com* (subscription is $99/year for students)
- A small pocket reference book to look up lab values, clinical pathways, and the like, such as *Maxwell Quick Medical Reference* (ISBN 0964519119, $7)
- A small book to look up drugs, such as *Pocket Pharmacopoeia* (Tarascon Publishers, $8)

As You See Patients, Note Their Major Symptoms and Diagnosis for Review

Your reading on the symptom-based topics above should be done with a specific patient in mind. For example, if a postmenopausal patient comes to the office with increasing abdominal girth and is thought to have ovarian cancer, read about ovarian cancer in the review book that night.

Prepare a Talk on a Topic

You may be asked to give a small talk once or twice during your rotation. If not, you should volunteer! Feel free to choose a topic that is on your list; however, realize that this may be considered dull by the people who hear the lecture. The ideal topic is slightly uncommon but not rare. To prepare a talk on a topic, read about it in a major textbook and a review article not more than two years old, and then search online or in the library for recent developments or changes in treatment.

If you have read about your core illnesses and core symptoms, you will know a great deal about medicine. To study for the clerkship exam, we recommend:

2 to 3 weeks before exam: Read the entire review book, taking notes.
10 days before exam: Read the notes you took during the rotation on your core content list and the corresponding review book sections.
5 days before exam: Read the entire review book, concentrating on lists and mnemonics.
2 days before exam: Exercise, eat well, skim the book, and go to bed early.
1 day before exam: Exercise, eat well, review your notes and the mnemonics, and go to bed on time. Do not have any caffeine after 2 P.M.

Other helpful studying strategies include:

Study with Friends

Group studying can be very helpful. Other people may point out areas that you have not studied enough and may help you focus on the goal. If you tend to get distracted by other people in the room, limit this to less than half of your study time.

Study in a Bright Room

Find the room in your house or in your library that has the best, brightest light. This will help prevent you from falling asleep. If you don't have a bright light, get a halogen desk lamp or a light that simulates sunlight (not a tanning lamp).

Eat Light, Balanced Meals

Make sure your meals are balanced, with lean protein, fruits and vegetables, and fiber. A high-sugar, high-carbohydrate meal will give you an initial burst of energy for 1 to 2 hours, but then you'll drop.

Take Practice Exams

The point of practice exams is not so much the content that is contained in the questions but the training of sitting still for 3 hours and trying to pick the best answer for each and every question.

Tips for Answering Questions

All questions are intended to have one best answer. When answering questions, follow these guidelines:

Read the answers first. For all questions longer than two sentences, reading the answers first can help you sift through the question for the key information.
Look for the words "EXCEPT," "MOST," "LEAST," "NOT," "BEST," "WORST," "TRUE," "FALSE," "CORRECT," "INCOR-

RECT," "ALWAYS," and "NEVER." If you find one of these words, circle or underline it for later comparison with the answer.

Evaluate each answer as being either true or false. Example:

Which of the following is *least* likely to be associated with pelvic pain?

A. endometriosis **T**

B. ectopic pregnancy **T**

C. ovarian cancer **? F**

D. ovarian torsion **T**

By comparing the question, noting LEAST, to the answers, "C" is the best answer.

SAMPLE PROGRESS NOTES AND ORDERS

Terminology

G (gravidity) 3 = total number of pregnancies, including normal and abnormal intrauterine pregnancies, abortions, ectopic pregnancies, and hydatidiform moles (*Remember, if patient was pregnant with twins,* **G** = 1.)

P (parity) 3 = number of deliveries > 500 grams or ≥ 24 weeks' gestation, stillborn (dead) or alive (*Remember, if patient was pregnant with twins,* **P** = 1.)

Ab (abortion) 0 = number of pregnancies that terminate < 24th gestational week or in which the fetus weighs < 500 grams

LC (living children) 3 = number of successful pregnancy outcomes (*Remember, if patient was pregnant with twins,* **LC** = 2.)

Or use the "TPAL" system if it is used at your medical school:

T = number of term deliveries (3)

P = number of preterm deliveries (0)

A = number of abortions (0)

L = number of living children (3)

SAMPLE OBSTETRIC ADMISSION HISTORY AND PHYSICAL

Date

Time

Identification: 25 yo G3P2

Estimated gestational age (EGA): 38 5/7 weeks

Last menstrual period (LMP): First day of LMP

Estimated date of confinement: Due date (*specify how it was determined*) by LMP or by _____ wk US (*Sonograms are most accurate for dating EGA when done at < 20 weeks.*)

Chief complaint (CC): Uterine contractions (UCs) q 7 min since 0100

History of present illness (HPI): 25 yo G3P2 with an intrauterine pregnancy (IUP) at 38 5/7 wks GA, well dated by LMP (10/13/99) and US at 10 weeks GA, who presented to L&D with CC of uterine contractions q 7 min. Prenatal care (PNC) at Highland Hospital (12 visits, first visit at 7 wks GA), uterine size = to dates, prenatal BP range 100–126/64–83. Problem list includes H/o + group B *Streptococcus* (GBS) and a +PPD with subsequent negative chest x-ray in 5/00. Pt admitted in early active labor with a vaginal exam (VE) 4/90/–2.

Past Obstetric History

'92 NSVD @ term, wt 3,700 g, no complications

'94 NSVD @ term, wt 3,900 g, postpartum hemorrhage

Allergies: NKDA

Medications: PNV, Fe

Medical Hx: H/o asthma (asymptomatic × 7 yrs), UTI × 1 @ 30 wks s/p Macrobid 100 mg × 7 d, neg PPD with subsequent neg CXR (5/00)

Surgical Hx: Negative

Social Hx: Negative

Family Hx: Mother—DM II, father—HTN

ROS: Bilateral low back pain

PE

General appearance: Alert and oriented (A&O), no acute distress (NAD)

Vital signs: T, BP, P, R

HEENT: No scleral icterus, pale conjunctiva

Neck: Thyroid midline, no masses, no lymphadenopathy (LAD)

Lungs: CTA bilaterally

Back: No CVA tenderness

Heart: II/VI SEM

Breasts: No masses, symmetric

Abdomen: Gravid, nontender

Fundal height: 36 cm

Estimated fetal weight (EFW): 3,500 g by Leopold's

Presentation: Vertex

Extremities: Mild lower extremity edema, nonpitting

Pelvis: Adequate

VE: Dilatation (4 cm)/effacement (90%)/station (−2); sterile speculum exam (SSE)? (Nitrazine?, Ferning?, Pooling?); membranes intact

US (L&D): Vertex presentation confirmed, anterior placenta, AFI = 13.2

Fetal monitor: Baseline FHR = 150, reactive. Toco = UCs q 5 min

Labs

Blood type: A+

Antibody screen: Neg

Rubella: Immune

HbsAg

VDRL: Nonreactive

FTA

GC

Chlamydia

HIV: See prenatal records

1 hr GTT: 105

3 hr GTT

PPD: + s/p neg CXR

CXR: Neg 5/00

AFP: Neg x 3

Amnio

PAP: NL

Hgb/Hct

Urine: + blood, − protein, − glucose, − nitrite, 2 WBCs

GBS: +

Assessment

1. Intrauterine pregancy @ 38 5/7 wks GA in early active labor
2. Group B strep +
3. H/o + PPD with subsequent – CXR 5/00
4. H/o UTI @ 30 wks GA, s/p Rx—resolved
5. H/o asthma—stable × 7 yrs, no meds

Plan

1. Admit to L&D
2. NPO except ice chips
3. H&H, VDRL, and hold tube
4. D5 LR TRA 125 cc/hr
5. Ampicillin 2 g IV load, then 1 g IV q 4 hrs (*for GBS*)
6. External fetal monitors (EFMs)
7. Prep and enema

SAMPLE DELIVERY NOTE

Always sign and date your notes.

NSVD of viable male infant over an intact perineum @ 12:35 P.M., Apgars 8&9, wt 3,654 g without difficulty. Position LOA, bulb suction, nuchal cord × 1 reducible. Spontaneous delivery of intact 3-vessel cord placenta @ 12:47 P.M., fundal massage and pitocin initiated, fundus firm. 2nd-degree perineal laceration repaired under local anesthesia with 3-0 vicryl. Estimated blood loss (EBL) = 450 cc. Mom and baby stable. Doctors: Johnson & Feig.

SAMPLE POSTPARTUM NOTE

S: Pt ambulating, voiding, tolerating a regular diet
O: *Vitals*
Heart: RR without murmurs
Lungs: CTA bilaterally
Breasts: Nonengorged, colostrum expressed bilaterally
Fundus: Firm, mildly tender to palpation, 1 fingerbreadth below umbilicus
Lochia: Moderate amount, rubra
Perineum: Intact, no edema
Extremities: No edema, nontender
Postpartum Hgb: 9.7
VDRL: NR
A: S/p NSVD, PP day # 1—progressing well, afebrile, stable
P: Continue postpartum care

SAMPLE POST-NSVD DISCHARGE ORDERS

1. D/c pt home
2. Pelvic rest × 6 weeks
3. Postpartum check in 4 weeks
4. D/c meds: FeSO$_4$ 300 mg 1 tab PO tid, #90 (*For Hgb < 10; opinions vary on when to give FE postpartum*)
   Colace 100 mg 1 tab PO bid PRN no bowel movement, #60

SAMPLE POST-CESAREAN SECTION NOTE

S: Pt c/o abdominal pain, no flatus, minimal ambulation

O: *Vitals*

I&O (urinary intake and output): Last 8 hrs = 750/695

Heart: RR without murmurs

Lungs: CTA bilaterally

Breasts: Nonengorged, no colostrum expressed

Fundus: Firm, tender to palpation, 1 fingerbreadth above umbilicus; incision without erythema/edema; C/D/I (clean/dry/intact); normal abdominal bowel sounds (NABS)

Lochia: Scant, rubra

Perineum: Intact, Foley catheter in place

Extremities: 1+ pitting edema bilateral LEs, nontender

Postpartum Hgb: 11

VDRL: NR

A: S/p primary low-transverse c/s secondary to arrest of descent, POD # 1– afebrile, + flatus, stable

P:
1. D/c Foley
2. Strict I&O—Call HO if UO < 120 cc/4 hrs
3. Clear liquid diet
4. Heplock IV once patient tolerates clears
5. Ambulate qid
6. Incentive spirometry 10×/hr
7. Tylenol #3 2 tabs PO q 4 hrs PRN pain

SAMPLE DISCHARGE ORDERS POST-CESAREAN SECTION

1. D/c patient home
2. Pelvic rest × 4 weeks
3. Incision check in 1 week
4. Discharge meds:
   Tylenol #3 1–2 tabs PO q 4 hrs PRN pain, #30
   Colace 100 mg 1 tab PO bid, #60

High-Yield Facts in Obstetrics

Normal Anatomy

VULVA

The vulva consists of the labia majora, labia minora, mons pubis, clitoris, vestibule of the vagina, vestibular bulb, and the greater vestibular glands. Basically, it is the external female genitalia (see Figure 2-1).

Blood Supply

From branches of the external and internal pudendal arteries

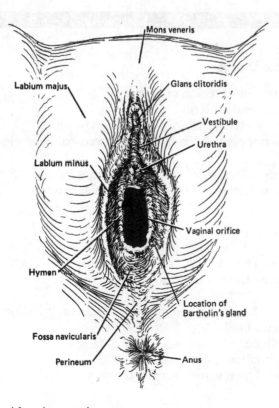

FIGURE 2-1. External female genitalia.

(Reproduced, with permission, from Pernoll ML. *Handbook of Obstetrics and Gynecology,* 10th ed. New York: McGraw-Hill, 2001: 22.)

Lymph

Medial group of superficial inguinal nodes

Nerve Supply

Anterior parts of vulva: Ilioinguinal nerves and the genital branch of the genitofemoral nerves
Posterior parts: Perineal nerves and posterior cutaneous nerves of the thigh

Blood Supply

- **Vaginal branch of the uterine artery** is the primary supply of the vagina.
- **Middle rectal and inferior vaginal branches of the hypogastric artery** (internal iliac artery) are secondary blood supplies.

Nerve Supply

- **Hypogastric plexus**—sympathetic innervation
- **Pelvic nerve**—parasympathetic innervation

Components of the Uterus

- **Fundus:** Uppermost region of uterus
- **Corpus:** Body of the uterus
- **Cornu:** Part of uterus that joins the fallopian tubes
- **Cervix:** Inferior part of cervix that connects to the vagina via the *cervical canal*
  - **Internal os:** Opening of cervix on the uterine side
  - **External os:** Opening of cervix on the vaginal side

Histology

Mesometrium: The visceral layer of the peritoneum reflects against the uterus and forms this outmost layer of the organ (the side that faces the viscera).
Myometrium: The smooth muscle layer of uterus. It has three parts:
1. Outer longitudinal
2. Middle oblique
3. Inner longitudinal
Endometrium: The mucosal layer of the uterus, made up of columnar epithelium

Blood Supply

Uterine arteries—arise from internal iliac artery
Ovarian arteries

Nerve Supply

- Superior hypogastric plexus
- Inferior hypogastric plexus
- Common iliac nerves

LIGAMENTS OF THE PELVIC VISCERA

Broad ligament: Extends from the lateral pelvic wall to the uterus and adnexa. Contains the fallopian (uterine) tube, round ligament, uterine and ovarian blood vessels, lymph, utererovaginal nerves, and ureter (see Figure 2-2).

Round ligament: The remains of the gubernaculum; extends from the corpus of the uterus down and laterally through the inguinal canal and terminates in the labia majora.

Cardinal ligament: Extends from the cervix and lateral vagina to the pelvic wall; functions to support the uterus.

FALLOPIAN (UTERINE) TUBES

The fallopian tubes extend from the superior lateral aspects of the uterus through the superior fold of the broad ligament laterally to the ovaries.

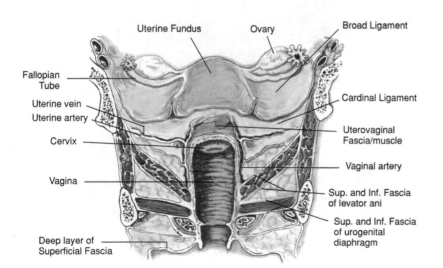

FIGURE 2-2. Supporting structures of the pelvic viscera.
(Reproduced, with permission, from Lindarkis NM, Lott S. *Digging Up the Bones: Obstetrics and Gynecology.* New York: McGraw-Hill, 1998: 2.)

Parts, from Lateral to Medial

- **Infundibulum:** The lateralmost part the uterine tube. The free edge is connected to the fimbriae.
- **Ampulla:** Widest section
- **Isthmus:** Narrowest part
- **Intramural part:** Pierces uterine wall

Blood Supply

From uterine and ovarian arteries

Nerve Supply

Pelvic plexus (autonomic) and ovarian plexus

OVARIES

The ovaries lie on the posterior aspect of the broad ligament, and are attached to the broad ligament by the mesovarium. They are not covered by peritoneum.

Blood Supply

Ovarian artery, which arises from the aorta at the level of L1. Veins drain into the vena cava on the right side and the left renal vein on the left.

Nerve Supply

Derived from the aortic plexus

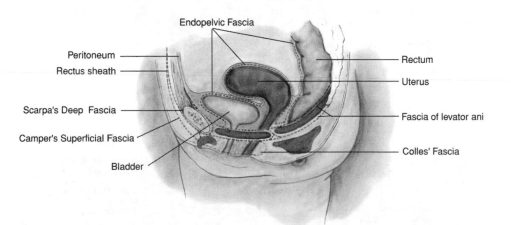

FIGURE 2-3. Fascia of the pelvis.

(Reproduced, with permission, from Lindarkis NM, Lott S. *Digging Up the Bones: Obstetris and Gynecology*. New York: McGraw-Hill, 1998: 2.)

Histology

Ovaries are covered by tunica albuginea, a fibrous capsule. The tunica albuginea is covered by germinal epithelium.

Diagnosis of Pregnancy

History

The majority of women have amenorrhea from the last menstrual period (LMP) until after the birth of their baby.

Symptoms

Although not specific to pregnancy, these symptoms may alert the patient to the fact that she is pregnant:

- Breast enlargement and tenderness from about 6 weeks' gestational age (GA)
- Areolar enlargement and increased pigmentation after 6 weeks' GA
- Colostrum secretion may begin after 16 weeks' GA
- Nausea with or without vomiting, from about the date of the missed period
- Urinary frequency, nocturia, and bladder irritability due to increased bladder circulation and pressure from the enlarging uterus

Signs

Some clinical signs can be noted, but may be difficult to quantify:

- Breast enlargement, tension, and venous distention—particularly obvious in the primigravida
- Bimanual examination reveals a soft, cystic, globular uterus with enlargement consistent with the duration of pregnancy (see Table 3-1)
- Chadwick's sign: Bluish discoloration of vagina and cervix, due to congestion of pelvic vasculature

PREGNANCY TESTING

How?

The beta subunit of human chorionic gonadotropin (hCG) is detected in maternal serum or urine.

- hCG is a glycoprotein produced by the developing placenta shortly after implantation

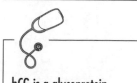

Some women experience vaginal bleeding in pregnancy, and therefore fail to recognize their condition.

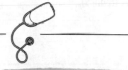

Nausea and/or vomiting occurs in approximately 50% of pregnancies, most notably at 2 to 12 weeks' GA, and typically in the A.M.

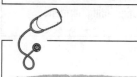

Hyperemesis gravidarium—persistent vomiting that results in weight loss, dehydration, acidosis from starvation, alkylosis from loss of HCl in vomitus, and hypokalemia.

hCG is a glycoprotein hormone composed of alpha and beta subunits.

TABLE 3-1. Fundal Height During Pregnancy

Weeks Pregnant	Fundal Height
12	Barely palpable above pubic symphysis
15	Midpoint between pubic symphysis and umbilicus
20	At the umbilicus
28	6 cm above the umbilicus
32	6 cm below the xyphoid process
36	2 cm below xyphoid process
40	4 cm below xiphoid process[a]

[a] Due to engagement and descent of the fetal head, the fundal height at 40 weeks is typically less than the fundal height at 36 weeks.

> hCG is similar in structure and function to luteinizing hormone (the beta subunits are similar in both hormones).

- A monoclonal antibody to the hCG antigen is utilized → the hCG–antibody complex is measured qualitatively

Pregnancy tests not only detect hCG produced by the syncytiotrophoblast cells in the placenta, but also in:
- Hydatidiform mole
- Choriocarcioma
- Other germ cell tumors
- Ectopically producing breast cancers and large cell carcinoma of the lung

> The hCG alpha subunit is identical to that in luteinizing hormone (LH), follicle-stimulating hormone (FSH), and thyroid-stimulating hormone.

When?
- Blood levels become detectably elevated 8 to 10 days after fertilization (3 to 3.5 weeks after the LMP)
- hCG rises in a geometric fashion during T1, producing different ranges for each week of gestation:

Duration of Pregnancy (from Time of Ovulation)	Plasma hCG (mU/mL)
1 week	5–50
2 weeks	50–500
3	100–10,000
4	1,000–30,000
5	3,500–115,000
6–8	12,000–270,000
8–12	15,000–220,000
20–40	3,000–15,000

> Plasma hCG levels in early pregnancy should double every 48 hours.

Urine hCG

- Preferred method to recognize normal pregnancy
- Total urine hCG closely parallels plasma concentration
- First morning specimens have less variability in relative concentration and generally higher levels, improving accuracy
- Assays detecting 25 mU/mL recognize pregnancy with 95% sensitivity by 1 week after the first missed menstrual period

- False negatives may occur if:
  - The test is performed too early
  - The urine is very dilute
- False positives may occur if:
  - Proteinuria (confirm with plasma hCG)
  - Urinary tract infection (UTI)

Plasma hCG

Used when quantitative information is needed:
- Diagnosing ectopic pregnancy
- Monitoring trophoblastic tumors
- Screening for fetal abnormalities

Do not provide additional information in diagnosing routine pregnancy since they are positive < 1 week before urine hCG.

INDICATIONS

Women of reproductive age with:
- Pain
- Amenorrhea

Do not assay for hCG before a woman has missed a menstrual period because of low test sensitivity before this time.

FETAL HEART TONES (FHTs)

The electronic Doppler device can detect fetal heart tones as early as 8 weeks' GA, albeit with difficulty.

If FHTs are not auscultated by 11 weeks' GA, an ultrasonic evaluation should be performed to document a viable intrauterine pregnancy.

ULTRASONIC SCANNING (US)

Not generally used to diagnose pregnancy, but can do so once a gestation sac is present within the uterus.

When?
- To confirm an intrauterine pregnancy (if it is suspected to be ectopic)
- To confirm the presence of a fetal heartbeat in a patient with a history of miscarriage
- To diagnose multiple pregnancy
- To estimate gestational age
- To screen for fetal structural anomalies

Scan dating is useful up to 20 weeks' GA when menstrual data is unreliable or conflicts with clinical findings.

Limitations

Scan dating becomes progressively less accurate and should be utilized only up to 20 weeks' GA:
- US measures the size of the fetus, not the gestational age.
- Biologic variation in size increases as gestation advances.

Physiology of Pregnancy

TERMS TO KNOW

Aldosterone: Enhances Na$^+$ reabsorption at the collecting duct of the kidney

Aneuploidies: Abnormal numbers of chromosomes that may occur as a consequence of abnormal meiotic division of chromosomes in gamete formation

Antidiuretic hormone (arginine vasopressin): Acts to conserve water by increasing the permeability of the collecting duct of the kidney

Blastocyst: At the 8- to 16-cell stage, the blastomere develops a central cavity and becomes a blastocyst. The cells on the outer layer differentiate to become *trophoblasts*.

Blastogenic period: The first 4 weeks of human development

Blastomere/morula: In 2 to 4 days after fertilization, a fertilized oocyte undergoes a series of cellular divisions and becomes a blastomere or morula

BMI: A calculation that relates patient's height to weight:
   Weight(kg)/height(m^2)
   Obese = ≥ 30
   Overweight = 25 to 29.9
   Norm = 18.5 to 24.9
   Does not consider lean body mass or percentage of body fat

Conception: The fertilization of an ovum by sperm

Decidua: The name given to the endometrium or lining of the uterus during pregnancy and the tissue around the ectopically located fertilized ovum

Embryonic period: Begins with the folding of the embryonic disk (which is formed from the inner cell mass) in week 2 of development

Erythrocyte sedimentation rate (ESR): A nonspecific laboratory indicator of infectious disease and inflammatory states. An anticoagulant is added to a tube of blood, and the distance the red blood cells fall in 1 hour is the rate.

Fetus: The term given to the conceptus after 8 weeks of life; it has a crown–rump length of 30 mm and a gestational age of 10 weeks. The fetal period continues until birth.

Gestational age: The time calculated from the last menstrual period and by convention exceeds the developmental age by 2 weeks

Oocyte: The primitive ovum before it has completely developed
Primary: The oocyte at the end of the growth period of oogonium and before the first maturation division has occurred
Secondary: The larger of two oocytes resulting from the first maturation division
Oogenesis: Formation and development of the ovum
Oogonium: The primordial cell from which an oocyte originates
Organogenesis: Occurs between 4 and 8 weeks after conception
Polar body: The small cell produced in oogenesis resulting from the divisions of the primary and secondary oocytes
Preembryonic period: The first 2 weeks after fertilization
Pregenesis: The time period between the formation of germ cells and the union of sperm and egg
Puerperium: The period of up to 6 weeks after childbirth, during which the size of the uterus decreases to normal
Residual volume (RV): The volume of gas contained in the lungs after a maximal expiration
Tidal volume (TV): The volume of air that is inhaled and exhaled during normal quiet breathing
Total lung capacity (TLC): The volume of gas contained in the lungs after a maximal inspiration
Vital capacity (VC): The volume of gas that is exhaled from the lungs in going from TLC to RV
Zona pellucida: Inner, solid, thick membranous envelope of the ovum (vitelline membrane, zona radiata)

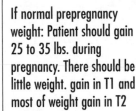

Joint changes (i.e., pubic symphysis) + postural changes secondary to change in center of gravity results in backaches and other aches that are common in pregnancy.

If normal prepregnancy weight: Patient should gain 25 to 35 lbs. during pregnancy. There should be little weight. gain in T1 and most of weight gain in T2 and T3.

Ideal weight gain:
T1: 1.5 to 3 lbs. gained
T2 and T3: 0.8 lbs./wk

GENERAL EFFECTS OF PREGNANCY ON THE MOTHER

Table 4-1 summarizes maternal physiologic changes during pregnancy.

Total Body Water

Increases by an average of 8.5 L and is composed of:

- Fetal water
- Amniotic fluid
- Placental tissue
- Maternal tissue
- Edema
- Increased hydration of connective tissue ground substance → laxity and swelling of connective tissue → changes in joints that mainly occur in T3.
- Generalized swelling → corneal swelling, intraocular pressure changes, gingival edema, increased vascularity of cranial sinuses, tracheal edema

Energy Requirements

Energy requirements increase gradually from 10 weeks to 36 weeks by 50 to 100 kcal/day. In the final 4 weeks, requirements increase by 300 kcal/day.

TABLE 4-1. Summary of Changes in the Body During Pregnancy

	T1 (1–14 wks)	T2 (14–28 wks)	T3 (28 wks–term) Term = 37–42 wks	During Labor	9-Month Period
Body water					↑ by 8.5 L
Energy requirements		↑ by 50–100 kcal/d	↑ by 300 kcal/d		
Body weight	↑ (primarily reflects maternal growth)	↑ (primarily reflects maternal growth)	↑ (primarily reflects fetal growth)		↑ by 25–35 lb
Tidal volume	↑				↑ by 200 mL
Vital capacity	↑				↑ by 100–200 mL
Cardiac output	↑ by 60%			↑ by 30% during each contraction May ↑ further in second stage of labor	↑
Blood pressure (BP)		↓		↑ by 10–20 mm Hg during each contraction May ↑ further in second stage of labor	
Systolic BP	↔				
Diastolic BP	↓	↓ by 15 mm Hg at 16–20 wks	↑ to T1 level		
Heart rate	↑ by 10–15%/min			↔	
Stroke volume	↑ by 10%			↑ During each contraction	
Central venous pressure	↔			↑ of 3–5 mm Hg during each contraction	
Systemic vascular resistance	↓ from pre-pregnancy level	↓↓ from pre-pregnancy level	↑, but not to prepregnancy level	↑ with each contraction	
Glomerular filtration rate (GFR)	↑	↑ to 60% above nonpregnant levels by 16 wks			↑
Renal plasma flow	↑	↑ to 30–50% above nonpregnant levels by 20 wks	Peaks at 30 wks		↑
Plasma aldosterone	↑ w/in 2 wks of conception	↑ 3–5 times the nonpregnant level	↑ 8–10 times the nonpregnant level		↑

(Continued)

TABLE 4-1. Summary of Changes in the Body During Pregnancy (continued)

	T1 (1–14 wks)	T2 (14–28 wks)	T3 (28 wks–term) Term = 37–42 wks	During Labor	9-Month Period
Serum alkaline phosphatase					↑
Plasma prolactin	↑				↑ 10–20 times nonpregnant level
Cortisol and other corticosteroids	↑ from 12 wks	↑	↑		↑ to 3–5 times nonpregnant levels
Glucagon					↑
Insulin sensitivity	↑	↓ at 20 wks	↓		
Fasting insulin levels		↑ at 20 wks	Peak at 32 wks		
Plasma volume	↑	↑	↑		↑ by 50%
Red blood cell (RBC) mass	↑	↑	↑		↑ by 18–30%
Mean corpuscular volume (MCV)	↔ or ↑ from 82–84 fL		↑ from 86–100 fL or more		
Neutrophils	↑	↑	↑ to 30 wks		
Erythrocyte sedimentation rate (ESR)	↑				↑
Albumin blood levels	↓	↓ from 3.5–2.5 g/100 mL	↓ by 22%		
Total globulin		↑ by 0.2 g/100 mL			
Total proteins		↓ by 20 wks from 7–6 g/100 mL			
Thyroxine-binding globulin					↑ (Thyroxine-binding globulin levels double)
Total plasma cholesterol	↓ by 5%	↑	↑		↑ by 24–206%
Low-density lipoprotein (LDL)					↑ by 50–90%
Very low-density lipoprotein (VLDL)			Peaks at 36 wks		↑ by 36%
High-density lipoprotein (HDL)		↑ by 30%	Decreases from T2		↑ by 10–23%
Triglycerides			Reach 2–4 times nonpregnant level at 36 wks		↑ by 90–570%
Lipoprotein (a)	↑	↑ until 22 wks	↓ to nonpregnant levels		↔
Uterine contractions		Begin at 20 wks	↑		

Metabolism

- Metabolic modifications begin soon after conception and are most marked in the second half of pregnancy when fetal growth requirements increase.
- The uterus and placenta require carbohydrate, fat, and amino acids.

CARBOHYDRATE

The placenta is freely permeable to glucose, which increases availability to fetus.

Goal in pregnancy is to increase the availability of glucose for the fetus, while the mother utilizes lipids.

First 20 Weeks

Insulin sensitivity increases in first half of pregnancy.
- Fasting glucose levels are lower.
- This favors glycogen synthesis and storage, fat deposition, and amino acid transport into cells.

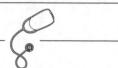

Pregnancy is an anabolic state.

After 20 weeks

After 20 weeks, insulin resistance develops and plasma insulin levels rise.
- A carbohydrate load produces a rise in plasma insulin 3 to 4 times greater than in the nonpregnant state, but glucose levels also are higher.
- This reduces maternal utilization of glucose and induces glycogenolysis, gluconeogenesis, and maternal utilization of lipids as energy source.
- Despite these high and prolonged rises in postprandial plasma glucose, the fasting level in late pregnancy remains less than nonpregnant levels.

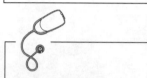

The optimal time to screen for glucose intolerance/ diabetes mellitus (DM) in the pregnant female is at 26 to 28 weeks' GA.

AMINO ACIDS

- Plasma concentration of amino acids falls during pregnancy due to hemodilution.
- Urea synthesis is reduced.

LIPIDS

- All lipid levels are raised, with the greatest increases being in the triglyceride-rich component.
- Lipids cross the placenta.
- Hyperlipidemia of pregnancy is *not* atherogenic, but may unmask a pathologic hyperlipidemia.

Normal pregnancy is a hyperlipemic, as well as a glucosuric, state.

Fat

- Early in pregnancy, fat is deposited.
- By midpregnancy, fat is the primary source of maternal energy.
- Postpartum, lipid levels return to normal.
- May take 6 months

The increase in cholesterol excretion results in increased risk of gallstones.

Cholesterol

- There is an increased turnover of cholesterol from lipoproteins, creating an increased supply to most tissues and increased supply for steroid production.
- Total cholesterol is raised postpartum in all mothers, but can be reduced by dieting after delivery.

Triglycerides, very low-density lipoprotein (VLDL), low-density lipoprotein (LDL), and high-density lipoprotein (HDL) increase during pregnancy.

DRUGS/OTHER SUBSTANCES

- Plasma levels of phenytoin fall during pregnancy.
- The half-life of caffeine is doubled.
- Antibiotics are cleared more rapidly by the kidney.

Central Nervous System

Syncope may occur from multiple etiologies:

1. Venous pooling in lower extremities → dizziness/light-headedness especially with abrupt positional changes
2. Dehydration
3. Hypoglycemia
4. Postprandial shunting of blood flow to the stomach
5. Overexertion during exercise

Emotional and psychiatric symptoms may result from:
- Hormonal changes of pregnancy
- Progesterone → tiredness, dyspnea, depression
- Euphoria secondary to endogenous corticosteroids

Respiratory System

Fetal PCO_2 must be greater than maternal PCO_2; thus, the maternal respiratory center must be reset. This is done in several ways:
- During pregnancy, progesterone reduces the carbon dioxide threshold at which the respiratory center is stimulated and increases the respiratory center sensitivity. This may lead to hyperventilation of pregnancy.
- Tidal volume (TV) increases by 200 mL.
- Vital capacity (VC) increases by 100 to 200 mL.

Cardiovascular System

CARDIAC OUTPUT

- Cardiac output (CO) increases by 40% by week 10, due to a 10% increase in stroke volume and increase in pulse rate by 10 to 15% per minute.
- Generalized enlargement of the heart and enlargement of left ventricle
- Heart is displaced anterolaterally secondary to rise in level of diaphragm → alters electrocardiogram (ECG) and may produce changes that mimic ischemia.

Physical Exam
- At end of T1—both components of S_1 become louder, with exaggerated splitting.
- After midpregnancy—90% of pregnant women demonstrate a third heart sound or S_3 gallop.
- **Systolic ejection murmurs** along the left sternal border occur in 96% of pregnant patients (due to increased flow across aortic and pulmonic valves).
- **Diastolic murmurs** are *never normal*, and their presence warrants evaluation by a cardiologist.

Healthy women must be treated as potential cardiac patients during pregnancy and the puerperium until functional murmurs resolve and the cardiovascular system returns to baseline status.

During Labor

- CO increases by 30% during each contraction with an increase in stroke volume, but no increase in heart rate.

VENOUS SYSTEM

Venous dilation results from:
- Relaxation of vascular smooth muscle
- Pressure of enlarging uterus on inferior vena cava and iliac veins

Gastrointestinal System

Reflux esophagitis (heartburn):
- Enlarging uterus displaces the stomach above the esophageal sphincter and causes increased intragastric pressure.
- Progesterone causes a relative relaxation of the esophageal sphincter.
- There may also be reflux of bile into the stomach due to pyloric incompetence.
- **Constipation** may occur secondary to progesterone, which relaxes intestinal smooth muscle and slows peristalsis.

GALLBLADDER

- Increases in size
- Empties more slowly
- **Cholestasis,** probably due to a hormonal effect since it also occurs in some users of oral contraceptives (OCs) and hormone replacement therapy (HRT)

LIVER

- Hepatic function increases.
- Plasma globulin and fibrinogen concentrations increase.
- Synthetic rate of albumin increases → total albumin mass increases by 19%, plateauing at 28 weeks.
- Velocity of blood flow in hepatic veins decreases.
- Serum alkaline phosphatase increases largely due to placental production

Genitourinary System

- **Urinary stasis** secondary to decreased ureteral peristalsis and mechanical uterine compression of the ureter at pelvic brim as pregnancy progresses
- **Asymptomatic bacteriuria** occurs in 5 to 8% of pregnant women.
- **Urinary frequency increases:**
  - During first 3 months of pregnancy due to bladder compression by enlarging uterus
  - During last week of pregnancy as the fetal head descends into pelvis
- **Nocturia:**
  - Physiologic after T1
  - Passing urine four times per night is normal
  - Fetal movements and insomnia contribute to the nocturia
- **Stress incontinence:**
  - Occurs frequently during normal pregnancy

Patients with hypertensive heart disease or cardiac disease may develop progressive or sudden deterioration.

Increased distensibility and pressure of veins → predisposition to development of varicose veins of legs, vulva, rectum, and pelvis.

Decreased GI motility may be responsible for the increased absorption of water, Na+, and other substances.

The superior rectal vein is part of the portal system and has no valves, hence the high pressure within the system is communicated to the pelvic veins and produces **hemorrhoids.**

The increase in cholestasis plus increase in lipids and cholesterol lead to higher incidence of gallstones, cholecystitis, and biliary obstruction.

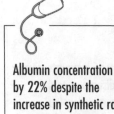

Albumin concentration falls by 22% despite the increase in synthetic rate due to hemodilution.

Bacteriuria + urinary stasis predispose patients to pyelonephritis, the most common nonobstetric cause for hospitalization during pregnancy.

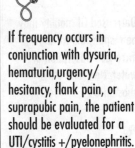

If frequency occurs in conjunction with dysuria, hematuria,urgency/ hesitancy, flank pain, or suprapubic pain, the patient should be evaluated for a UTI/cystitis +/pyelonephritis.

In pregnancy, the increased rate of renal clearance → reduced effective dose of antibiotics.

GFR increases → quantity of glucose filtered in urine is greater than in nonpregnant state → tubular threshold for glucose is exceeded → glycosuria is detected in 50% of pregnant women.

- Due to relaxation of the bladder supports
- The urethra normally elongates during pregnancy, but not in those who develop stress incontinence.

BLADDER

Bladder tone decreases, but bladder capacity increases progressively during pregnancy.

URETERS

Ureters undergo progressive dilatation and kinking in > 90% of pregnant women at ≥ 6 weeks
- Accompanied by a decreased urine flow rate
- Dilatation is greater on right secondary to dextrorotation of the uterus, and does not extend below the pelvic brim.
- Dilatation is secondary to the physical obstruction by the pregnant uterus and the effects of pregnancy hormones.
- Ureteric dilatation extends up to the calyces → increased glomerular size and increased interstitial fluid → enlarged kidneys (length increases by 1 cm and weight increases by 20%).

RENAL FUNCTION

- Renal plasma flow increases from T1, reaching 30 to 50% above non-pregnant levels by 20 weeks. Flow remains elevated until 30 weeks and then slowly declines to nonpregnant levels postpartum.
- Glomerular filtration rate (GFR) increases soon after conception. It reaches 60% above nonpregnant level by 16 weeks and remains elevated for remainder of pregnancy.

RENAL TUBULE CHANGES

Tubular function changes:
- Tubules lose some of their resorptive capacity—amino acids, uric acid, and glucose are not as completely absorbed in the pregnant female.
- Results in an increase in protein loss of up to 300 mg/24 hr

Renal retention of Na+ results in water retention. Mother and conceptus increase their Na+ content by 500 to 900 nmol (due to increased reabsorption by renal tubules).

Hematologic

PLASMA VOLUME

Plasma volume increases by 50% during pregnancy due to increase in both red blood cells (RBCs) and plasma, but proportionately more plasma. This results in hemodilution.
- Greater in multigravids than primigravids
- Greater in multiple pregnancies than in single pregnancies
- Positively correlated with birth weight
- Increase in plasma volume is less in patients with recurrent abortions.
- Advantage of increased circulating volume:
  - Helps to compensate for increased blood flow to uterus and kidneys
  - Reduces viscosity of blood and increases capillary blood flow

RED BLOOD CELLS

- Circulating RBC mass increases progressively during pregnancy:
  - By 18% in women not given Fe supplements
  - By 30% in women on Fe supplementation
- Reticulocyte count increases by ≥ 2%.
- Mean corpuscular volume (MCV) usually increases.

HEMOGLOBIN

- Fetal Hgb (HbF) concentration increases 1 to 2% during pregnancy, secondary to an increase in the number of RBCs with HbF

ERYTHROCYTE SEDIMENTATION RATE

Erythrocyte sedimentation rate (ESR):
- Rises early in pregnancy due to the increase in fibrinogen and other physiologic changes
- An ESR = 100 mm/hr is not uncommon in normal pregnancy.

WHITE BLOOD CELLS

Neutrophils
- Neutrophil count increases in T1 and continues to rise until 30 weeks.
- Neutrophilic metabolic activity and phagocytic function increases.

Lymphocytes
- Counts remain unchanged, but function is suppressed.

PLATELETS

- Platelet reactivity is increased in T2 and T3 and returns to normal at 12 weeks postpartum
- In 8 to 10% of normal pregnancies, the platelet count falls below 150×10^3 without negative effects on the fetus.

Endocrine System

In general, the endocrine system is modified in the pregnancy state by the addition of the fetoplacental unit. The fetoplacental unit produces human chorionic gonadotropin (hCG) and human placental lactogen (hPL) among other hormones.
- hCG (luteotropic): Coregulates and stimulates adrenal and placental steroidogenesis. Stimulates fetal testes to secrete testerone. Possesses thyrotrophic activity.
- hPL (also called human chorionic somatomammotropin [hCS]): Anti-insulin and growth hormone-like effects → impaired maternal glucose and free fatty acid release.

PITUITARY GLAND

Pituitary gland increases in weight and sensitivity.

Prolactin
- Plasma levels rise within a few days postconception.
- At term, levels are 10- to 20-fold higher than nonpregnant state.

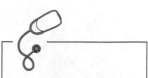

Tubules are presented with increased quantities of urine because of the increased GFR.

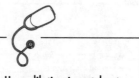

Progesterone increases Na+ excretion, but its increase is balanced by effects of increased aldosterone, mineralocorticoids, and prostaglandins.

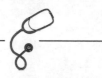

Hemodilution is *not* due to a fall in total circulating hemoglobin.

An apparent anemia may be a sign of good physiologic adaptation to pregnancy, while an elevated hemoglobin may represent pathology (i.e., hemoconcentration in pregnancy-induced hypertension).

Follicle-Stimulating Hormone
- Blunted response to gonadotropin-releasing hormone (GnRH)
- Shows a progressive decreased response → no response at 3 weeks after ovulation

Luteinizing Hormone
- Response to GnRH diminishes and finally disappears.

ADRENAL GLAND

- Plasma cortisol and other corticosteroids increase progressively from 12 weeks to term and reach 3 to 5 times nonpregnant levels.
- Half-life of plasma cortisol is increased, while its clearance is reduced.

THYROID GLAND

The following changes are thought to be due to the increase in estrogen during pregnancy:
- Increases in size during pregnancy
- Total thyroxine levels and thyroxine-binding globulin increase. The result is that *free thyroxine remains normal and the mother remains euthyroid.*

PARATHYROID GLANDS

- Parathyroid hormone levels increase in pregnancy, which increases maternal calcium absorption, to offset maternal losses across the placenta to the fetus.
- At term, serum parathyroid hormone levels are higher in the mother, but calcitonin is higher in the fetus. This results in fetal bone deposition.

PLASMA PROTEINS

Concentrations of proteins in maternal serum fall markedly by 20 weeks, mostly due to a fall in serum albumin. This fall reduces the colloid osmotic pressure in the plasma → edema in pregnancy.

PANCREAS

- Size of islets of Langerhans increases during pregnancy.
- The number of beta cells increases during pregnancy.
- The number of insulin receptor sites increases during pregnancy.

Insulin
- Serum levels rise during second half of pregnancy, but insulin resistance increases as well.
- This insulin resistance may be due to presence of hPL, prolactin, or other pregnancy hormones that have anti-insulin activity.

Glucagon
- Levels are slightly raised in pregnancy, but not as much as insulin levels.

Integumentary System/Skin

Many physiologic changes in the skin can occur during gestation. Some are believed to result from changes in the hormonal milieu of pregnancy (see Table 4-2).

> The pregnant female is more susceptible to viral infections, malaria, and leprosy.

> The fetoplacental unit produces hCG and hPL.

> Pregnancy andcombinations of estrogen and progestational agents (i.e., OCs and HRT) are the most frequent causes of melasma (often called the **"mask of pregnancy"**).

TABLE 4-2. Pruritic Dermatologic Disorders Unique to Pregnancy

Disease	Onset	Pruritis	Lesions	Distribution	Incidence	Increased Incidence Fetal Morbidity/ Mortality	Intervention
Pruritic urticarial papules and plaques of pregnancy (PUPPP)	T2–T3	Severe	Erythematous urticarial papules and plaques	Abdomen, thighs, buttocks, occasionally arms and legs	Common (0.25–1%)	No	Topical steroids, antipruritic drugs (hydroxyzine, phenhydramine)
Papular eruptions (prurigo gestationis and papular dermatitis)	T2–T3	Severe	Excoriated papules	No area of predilection	Uncommon (1:300–1:2,400)	Unlikely	Systemic/topical corticosteroids, antipruritics
Pruritis gravidarum	T3	Severe	Excoriations common	Generalized	Common (1–2%)	Yes	Antipruritics, cholestyramine
Impetigo herpetiformis	T3	Minimal	Pustules	Genitalia, medial thighs, umbilicus, breasts, axillae	Rare	Yes (maternal sepsis common)	Systemic corticosteroids and antibiotics for secondary infection
Herpes gestationis	T2–postpartum	Severe	Erythematous papules, vesicles, bullae	Abdomen, extremities, generalized	Rare (1:10,000)	Yes	*Mild*—topical steroids, antihistamines *More severe*—systemic corticosteroids

MELANOCYTE-STIMULATING HORMONE EFFECTS

Melanocyte-stimulating hormone increases can result in the following:

- **Linea nigra:** Black line/discoloration of the abdomen that runs from above the umbilicus to the pubis; may be seen during the latter part of gestation
- **Darkening of nipple and areola**
- **Facial cholasma/melasma:** A light- or dark-brown hyperpigmentation in exposed areas such as the face. More common in persons with brown or black skin color, who live in sunny areas, and who are taking OCs.
- A suntan acquired in pregnancy lasts longer than usual.

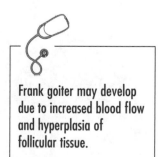

Frank goiter may develop due to increased blood flow and hyperplasia of follicular tissue.

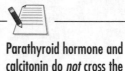

Thyroid-stimulating hormone, iodide, thyroid-releasing hormone, and T⁴ cross the placenta. TSH does not.

Parathyroid hormone and calcitonin do *not* cross the placenta.

ESTROGEN EFFECTS

- Spider nevi are common (branched growths of dilated capillaries on the skin).
- Palmar erythema

CORTICOSTEROID EFFECTS

Striae on the abdomen, breasts, etc., develop in response to increased circulating corticosteroids.

FINGERNAILS

Grow more rapidly during pregnancy

HAIR

- The rate at which hair is shed is reduced.
- The excess retained hair is often lost in the puerperium, secondary to maternal emotional stress.

NORMAL ANATOMICAL ADAPTATIONS IN PREGNANCY

Vagina

- Vaginal epithelium hypertrophies and quantity of glycogen-containing cells shed into vagina increase.
- Connective tissue decreases in collagen content and there is an increase in water content (like the cervix—*see below*).
- Vagina becomes more acidic (pH = 4 to 5) → hinders growth of most pathogens and favors growth of yeasts.

Uterus

- Hypertrophy and hyperplasia of myometrial smooth muscle secondary to:
  - Action of steroid hormones
  - Uterine distention and wall thinning with the growing fetus, placenta, amniotic fluid
- Term uterus weighs 1,100 g with a 20-fold increase in mass (nonpregnant, parous uterus weighs 70 g).

ROUND LIGAMENT

Round ligament increases in length, muscular content, and diameter:
- During pregnancy, the ligaments may contract spontaneously or in response to uterine movement.
- In labor, contractions of the ligaments pulls the uterus forward → expulsive force is directed as much into the pelvis as possible.

VASCULAR SUPPLY OF THE UTERUS

- In the nonpregnant state, the uterine artery is most important blood source

- During pregnancy, the ovarian arteries contribute 20 to 30% of the blood supply in 70% of women.
- Uterine arteries dilate to 1.5 times their nonpregnant diameter.

UTERINE CERVIX

- Amount of collagen within cervix is reduced to one third of nonpregnant amount.
  - The duration of spontaneous labor is inversely proportional to cervical collagen concentration at the beginning of dilation.

Accumulation of glycosaminoglycans and increase in water content and vascularity in the cervix results in **softening** and cyanosis = characteristic cervix of gravid female:
- Results in increased compliance to stretch
- This process is called **"cervical ripening"** and takes place gradually over the last few weeks of gestation.
- In early T1, squamous epithelium of ectocervix becomes hyperactive, endocervical glands become hyperplastic, and endocervical epithelium proliferates and grows out over the ectocervix.
- The resulting secretions within the endocervical canal create the **antibacterial mucous plug of the cervix.**

UTERINE ISTHMUS

- The uterine isthmus is normally a small region of the uterus that lies between the uterine corpus and cervix.
- Beginning at 12 weeks of pregnancy, the isthmus enlarges and thins secondary to hormonal influences of pregnancy and uterine distention.
- During labor, the isthmus expands and is termed the *lower uterine segment.*

CONCEPTION

Ovulation

- Ovulation is necessary for normal fertilization to occur:
  - The ovum must leave the ovary and be carried into the fallopian tube.
  - The unfertilized ovum is surrounded by its zona pellucida.
  - This oocyte has completed its first meiotic division and carries its first polar body.

Fertilization

- Fertilization typically occurs within 24 hours after ovulation in the third of the fallopian tube adjacent to the ovary (ampulla):
  - The sperm penetrates the zona pellucida and fuses its plasma membranes with those of the ovum.
  - The sperm nucleus and other cellular contents enter the egg's cytoplasm.
  - Fertilization signals the ovum to complete meiosis II and to discharge an additional polar body.

The uterus is composed of smooth muscle, whose myometrial cells contain estrogen and progesterone receptors.

Cervical effacement and dilation occur in the already ripened cervix.

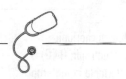

Cervical effacement causes expulsion of the **mucous plug** as the cervical canal is shortened during labor.

Preimplantation

- Fertilized ovum remains in the ampulla for 80 hours after follicular rupture and travels through isthmus of fallopian tube for 10 hours.
- The fertilized egg divides to form a multicellular blastomere.
- The blastomere passes from the fallopian tube into the uterine cavity.
- The embryo develops into a **blastocyst** as it freely floats in endometrial cavity 90 to 150 hours after conception (see Table 4-3).

Implantation

- On day 5 to 6 of development, the blastocyst adheres to the endometrium with the help of adhesion molecules on the secretory endometrial surface.
- After attachment, the endometrium proliferates around the blastocyst.

Placentation

- During week 2, cells in the outer cell mass differentiate into **trophoblasts.**

	TABLE 4-3. Embryology
Weeks	***Embryo* Development**
1	Early morula; no organ differentiation.
3	Double heart recognized.
4	Initial organogenesis has begun.
6	*Genetic* sex determined.
8	Sensory organ development and nondifferentiated gonadal development.
	***Fetal* Development**
12	Brain configuration rougly complete, internal sex organs now specific, uterus now no longer bicornuate, and blood forming in marrow. *External* genitalia forming (9–12 weeks).
16	Fetus is active now, sex determination by visual inspection (ultrasound) is possible due to the formed external genitalia. Myelination of nerves, heart muscle well developed, vagina and anus open, and ischium ossified.
20	Sternum ossifies.
24	Primitive respiratory movements.
28	Nails appear and testes at or below internal inguinal ring.
36	Earlobe soft with little cartilage, testes in inguinal canals, and scrotum small with few rugae.
40	Earlobes stiffen by thick cartilage, and scrotum well developed.

Reproduced, with permission, from Lindarkis NM, Lott S. *Digging Up the Bones: Obstetrics and Gynecology.* New York: McGraw-Hill, 1998: 6.

Human chorionic gonadotropin (hCG) is detectable in maternal serum after implantation has taken place, approximately 8 to 11 days after conception.

Trophoblasts (trophoectoderm) are the precursor cells for the placenta and membranes.

- A trophoblastic shell forms the initial boundary between the embryo and the endometrium.
- The trophoblasts nearest the myometrium form the placental disk; the other trophoblasts form the chorionic membranes.

Postimplantation

- The endometrium or lining of the uterus during pregnancy is termed *decidua*.
- Maternal RBCs may be seen in the trophoblastic lacunae in the second week postconception.

> The decidua produces maternal steroids and synthesizes proteins that are related to the maintenance and protection of the pregnancy from immunologic rejection.

The Placenta

The placenta continues to adapt over T2 and T3. It is the **primary producer of steroid hormones** after 7 weeks' gestational age.

BLOOD SUPPLY

Flow in the arcuate and radial arteries during normal pregnancy is high with low resistance (resistance falls after 20 weeks).

Developmental Ages

Postconception Day	Tissue/Organ Formation
4	Blastula
7–12	Implantation
13	Primitive streak
16	Neural plate
19–21	First somite
23–25	Closure of anterior neuropore
25–27	Arms bud
	Closure of posterior neuropore
28	Legs bud
44	Sexual differentiation

Multiple Gestation (Figure 4-1)

- Division of embryos before differentiation of trophoblast (between days 2 and 3) → 2 chorions, 2 amnions
- Division of embryos after trophoblast differentiation and before amnion formation (between days 3 and 8) → 1 placenta, 1 chorion, 2 amnions
- Division of embryos after amnion formation (between days 8 and 13) → 1 placenta, 1 chorion, 1 amnion

PREGNANCY PROTEINS

hCG (Human Chorionic Gonadotropin)
Source: Placenta
Function:
- Maintains the corpus luteum
- Stimulates adrenal and placental steroidogenesis

Dizygotic Twins
Nonidentical or Fraternal Twins
(Always have 2 chorions and 2 amnions,

and sexes may be different.)

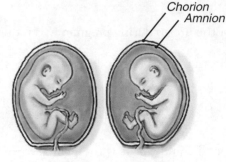
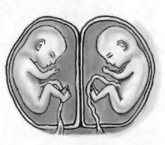

Chorion
Amnion

Dichorionic Diamnionic (1/3)
Separate development

Dichorionic Diamnionic (1/3)
Fused development

Monozygotic Twins
Identical or Maternal Twins

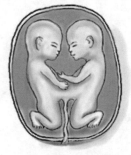
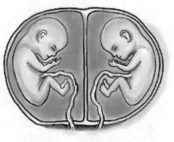

**Monochorionic
Monoamnionic (rare)**
(Siamese twins)
Twins share single cavity

**Monochorionic
Diamnionic (< 1/3)**
Twins are in separate cavities

FIGURE 4-1. Multiple gestation.
(Reproduced, with permission, from Lindarkis NM, Lott S. *Digging Up the Bones: Obstetrics and Gynecology.* New York: McGraw-Hill, 1998: 56.)

ACTH (Adrenocorticotropic Hormone)
Source: Trophoblasts
Function: Stimulates an increase in circulating maternal free cortisol

hPL (Human Placental Lactogen)
Source: Trophoblasts
Function: Antagonizes insulin → maternal glucose intolerance, lipolysis, and proteolysis

CRH (Corticotropin-Releasing Hormone)
Source: Placental tissue and decidua
Function: Stimulates placental ACTH release and participates in the surge of fetal glucocorticoids associated with late T3 fetal maturation

Prolactin

Source: Decidualized endometrium
Function: Regulates fluid and electrolyte flux through the fetal membranes

Alpha-Fetoprotein (AFP)

Source: Yolk sac, fetal gastrointestinal tract, and fetal liver
Function: Regulates fetal intravascular volume (osmoregulator)

- MSAFP peaks between 10 and 13 weeks' gestational age, then declines thereafter.
- Detectable as early as 7 weeks' gestation

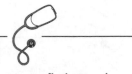

Amniotic fluid AFP and maternal serum (MSAFP) are elevated in association with neural tube defects and low in trisomy 21.

PREGNANCY STEROIDS

Estrogens

Function: Estrogens affect uterine vasculature, placental steroidogenesis, and parturition.

Estradiol
Source:
- Maternal ovaries for weeks 1 through 6 of gestation
- Subsequently, the placenta secretes increasing quantities of estradiol synthesized from the conversion of circulating maternal and fetal DHEA-S.
- After T1, the placenta is the major source of circulating estradiol.

MSAFP is decreased in pregnancies with Down's syndrome.

Estrone
Source:
- Maternal ovaries, adrenals, and peripheral conversion in the first 4 to 6 weeks of pregnancy
- The placenta subsequently secretes increasing quantities.

In women with threatened T1 abortions, estradiol concentrations are abnormally low for gestational age.

Estriol
Source:
- Placenta
- Continued production is dependent on the presence of a living fetus.

Progesterone
Source:
- Corpus luteum before 6 weeks' gestational age
- Thereafter, the placenta produces progesterone from circulating maternal low-density lipoprotein (LDL) cholesterol.

During T3, low estradiol levels are associated with poor obstetrical outcomes.

Function:
- Affects tubal motility, the endometrium, uterine vasculature, and parturition
- Inhibits T lymphocyte–mediated tissue rejection

Cortisol
Source: Decidual tissue
Function: Suppresses the maternal immune rejection response of the implanted conceptus

Abortion will occur in 80% of women with progesterone levels under 10 ng/mL.

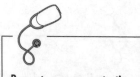

Progesterone concentrations of < 5 ng/mL are diagnostic of fetal death in T1. Prompt diagnostic studies should be performed to distinguish between ectopic pregnancy and intrauterine fetal demise.

Protesteronr concentrations are significantly elevated in: women with hydratidiform mole complications of Rh isoimmunization.

LDL Cholesterol
Source: Fetal adrenal gland
Function:

- Principal regulatory precursor of corpus luteum progesterone production
- Principal lipoprotein utilized in fetal adrenal steroidogenesis

Antepartum

Goal

To increase the probability of a healthy baby without maternal compromise

When and How Often

- < 28 weeks—every month
- 28 to 36 weeks—every 2 to 3 weeks
- 36 weeks to delivery—once per week until delivery

See Table 5-1.

Definitions

Gravidity: The number of times a woman has been pregnant
Parity: The number of times a woman has had a pregnancy that led to a birth after 20 weeks' gestation or an infant > 500 g

Terminology of Reproductive History

The mother's pregnancy history is described in terms of gravidity (G) and parity (P), in which parity includes term births, preterm births, abortions, and living children. The order expressed is as follows:
Total number of times pregnant
(Gravidity); Term births; Preterm births;
Abortuses; Living Children

The terminology is written as in the following example: **G3P1201.**

The above indicates that a woman has been pregnant 3 times, has had 1 term birth, 2 preterm births, 0 abortions, and has 1 live child.

TABLE 5-1. Prenatal Visits

First Visit	6–8 Weeks	16–18 Weeks	26–28 Weeks
1. History and physical (H&P) 2. Labs: ■ Hct/Hgb ■ Rh factor ■ Blood type ■ Antibody screen ■ Pap smear ■ *Gonorrhea* and *Chlamydia* cultures ■ Urine analysis (glucose, proteins, ketones) and culture, microscopic exam for sediment ■ Infection screen: Rubella, syphilis, hepatitis B, human immunodeficiency virus (HIV), tuberculosis (TB) 3. Genetic screen 4. Patient education	1. H&P 2. Fetal exam: ■ **Fetal heart tones** 3. Urine analysis and culture 4. HIV testing (if repeat is warranted)	1. H&P 2. Fetal exam: ■ Fetal heart ■ Fundal height 3. **Pelvic sonogram (optional)** 4. Amniocentesis (if indicated) 5. **Triple screen (serum alpha-fetoprotein, estriol, beta-hCG)** 6. Urine analysis and culture	1. H&P 2. Fetal exam: ■ Fetal heart ■ Fundal height ■ Fetal position 3. Labs: ■ Complete blood count ■ Ab screen ■ *Gonorrhea* and *Chlamydia* cultures (optional) ■ **Diabetes screen** ■ Urine analysis/culture ■ Syphilis screen (optional) 4. Give Rhogam if nonsensitized Rh negative patient

Week 32	Week 36	Week 38	Week 39	Week 40
1. H&P 2. Fetal exam: ■ Fetal heart ■ Fundal height ■ Fetal position 3. Urine analysis/culture	1. H&P 2. Fetal exam: ■ Fetal heart ■ Fundal height ■ Fetal position 3. Urine analysis/culture 4. **Group B strep culture**	1. H&P 2. Fetal exam: ■ Fetal heart ■ Fundal height ■ Fetal position 3. Urine analysis/culture 4. **Cervical exam (frequency is controversial)**	1. H&P 2. Fetal exam: ■ Fetal heart ■ Fundal height ■ Fetal position 3. Urine analysis/culture	1. H&P 2. Fetal exam: ■ Fetal heart ■ Fundal height ■ Fetal position 3. Urine analysis/culture 4. **Fetoplacental functional tests (if indicated)**

Important Hallmarks in Prenatal Visits

- Pap smear—first visit
- Rh screen—first visit
- *Gonorrhea* and *Chlamydia*—first visit
- First sonogram—week 16 to 18
- Amniocentesis—week 16 to 18
- Triple screen—week 16 to 18
- Diabetes screen—week 26 to 28
- Group B strep culture—week 36

Definitions

Gestational age (GA): The time of pregnancy counting from the first day of the last menstrual period

Developmental age: The time of pregnancy counting from fertilization

First trimester: 0 to 14 weeks

Second trimester: 14 to 28 weeks

Third trimester: 28 weeks to birth

Embryo: Fertilization to 8 weeks

Fetus: 8 weeks until birth

Previable: Before 24 weeks

Preterm: 24 to 37 weeks

Term: 37 to 42 weeks

Nägele's Rule

- Nägele's rule is used to calculate the estimated date of confinement (i.e., due date) +/– 2 weeks
- First day of patient's last normal menstrual period – 3 months + 7 days + 1 year

Abdominal Exam and Fundal Height

As the fetus grows, the location of the uterus, or fundal height, grows superiorly in the abdomen, toward the maternal head. The location in the abdomen that the fetus and uterus are located is described in terms of weeks (see Figure 5-1).

Fetus at the level of umbilicus: 20 weeks

Fetus at level of pubic symphysis: 12 weeks

Fetus between pubic symphysis and umbilicus: 16 weeks

Maternal Serum Alpha-Fetoprotein (MSAFP)

- Normally, MSAFP begins to rise at 13 weeks and peaks at 32 weeks. It is produced in the placenta.
- MSAFP screening is most accurate between 16 and 18 weeks.
- **An inaccurate gestational age is the most common reason for an abnormal screen.**

High levels are associated with:
- Neural tube defects (NTDs)
- Abdominal wall defects (gastrochisis and omphalocele)
- Fetal death
- Placental abnormalities (i.e., abruption)
- Multiple gestations

Low levels are associated with:
- Down's syndrome (Trisomy 21)
- One third to one fifth of Down's syndrome fetuses exhibit low MSAFP

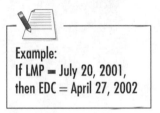

Nägele's rule assumes two things:
1. A normal gestation is 280 days.
2. Patients all have a 28-day menstrual cycle.

Example:
If LMP = July 20, 2001, then EDC = April 27, 2002

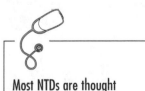

The first step in the workup of an abnormal triple screen should be an ultrasound for dating.

Most NTDs are thought to be polygenic or multifactorial.

HIGH-YIELD FACTS

Antepartum

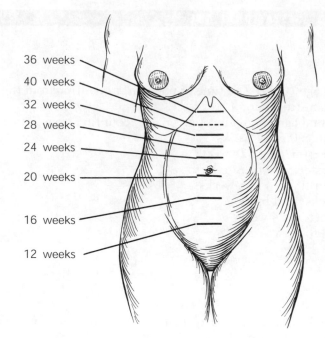

FIGURE 5-1. Fundal height.

(Reproduced, with permission, from Pearlman MD, Tintinalli JE, eds. *Emergency Care of the Woman.* New York: McGraw-Hill, 1998: 91.)

Estradiol

Low levels are associated with:
- **Trisomy 21** (Down's syndrome)
- **Trisomy 18** (Edward's syndrome)
- Possibly low in **trisomy 13** (Patau's syndrome)

Human Chorionic Gonadotropin (hCG)

High levels are associated with:
- Trisomy 21

Low levels are associated with:
- Trisomy 18
- Anencephaly

Rh INCOMPATIBILITY AND PREGNANCY

What Is Rh?

- The surface of the human red blood cell (RBC) may or may not contain a Rhesus (Rh) antigen. If so, that person is said to be Rhesus + (for example, if someone with blood type A has a Rhesus antigen, the blood type is A+. If that person has no Rhesus antigen, he is A–).
- Half of all antigens in a fetus come from the father, and half come from the mother.

The Problem with Rh Sensitization

The parental combination you must worry about: Mother Rh– and father Rh+.

- If the pregnant female is Rh– and her fetus is Rh+, then she may become sensitized to the Rh antigen and develop antibodies (Figure 5-2).
- These antibodies cross the placenta and attack the fetal RBCs → fetal RBC hemolysis.

Sensitization

Sensitization may occur during:
- Amniocentesis
- Miscarriage/threatened abortion
- Vaginal bleeding
- Placental abruption/previa
- Delivery
- Abdominal trauma
- Cesarean section
- External version

Scenario of Fetal Danger

Rh– mother becomes sensitized during an earlier pregnancy in which the child was Rh+. She is exposed to Rh+ blood during that pregnancy and/or delivery and develops antibodies. Then, in a later pregnancy, her immune system, already primed to recognize Rh+ blood, crosses the placenta and attacks Rh+ fetal blood.

Screening

In each pregnancy, a woman should have her Rh type determined and an antibody screen performed at the initial visit with an **indirect Coombs' test.**

RhoGAM: Treatment for Exposure

If the Rh– mother is exposed to fetal blood, **RhoGAM** is given. RhoGAM is RhIgG (IgG that will attach to the Rh antigen) and prevent immune response by the mother.

Erythroblastosis fetalis

Hemolytic disease of the newborn/fetal hydrops occurs when the mother lacks an antigen present in the fetus → fetal RBCs trigger an immune response when they reach the mother's circulation → maternal antibodies cause fetal RBC hemolysis and anemia → fetal hyperbilirubinemia → kernicterus → heart failure, edema, ascites, pericardial effusion.

After Rh sensitization, a **Kleihauer–Bettke** test is done to determine the amount of fetal RBCs in the maternal circulation. Adjustments in the amount of RhIgG are given to mother accordingly (see RhoGAM below).

FIGURE 5-2. Rh incompatibility.

(Reproduced, with permission, from DeCherney AH, Pernoll ML. *Current Obstetric & Gynecologic Diagnosis & Treatment.* Norwalk, CT: Appleton & Lange, 1994: 339.)

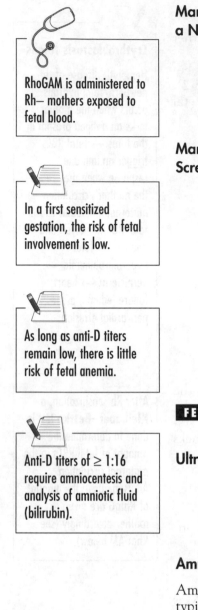

RhoGAM is administered to Rh– mothers exposed to fetal blood.

In a first sensitized gestation, the risk of fetal involvement is low.

As long as anti-D titers remain low, there is little risk of fetal anemia.

Anti-D titers of ≥ 1:16 require amniocentesis and analysis of amniotic fluid (bilirubin).

Managing the Unsensitized Rh– Patient (The Rh– Patient Who Has a Negative Antibody Screen)

1. Antibody screen should be done at 0, 24 to 28 weeks.
2. If negative, give 300 µg of RhIgG to prevent maternal development of antibodies.
3. At birth, determine if baby is Rh+; if so, give postpartum RhIgG.

Management of the Sensitized Rh– Patient (If on Initial Visit the Antibody Screen for Rh Is Positive)

1. Perform antibody screen at 0, 12 to 20 weeks.
2. Check the antibody titer.
   - If titer remains stable at < 1:16, the likelihood of hemolytic disease of the newborn is low.
   - If the titer is > 1:16 and/or rising, the likelihood of hemolytic disease of the newborn is high.
3. Amniocentesis begins at 16 to 20 weeks' GA.
   - Fetal cells are analyzed for Rh status.
   - Amniotic fluid is analyzed by spectrophotometer, which measures the light absorbance by bilirubin. Absorbance measurements are plotted on the **Liley curve,** which predicts the severity of disease.

FETAL IMAGING

Ultrasound

- Intrauterine pregnancy seen via vaginal ultrasound (US) when beta-hCG > 1,500
- Intrauterine pregnancy seen via abdominal US when beta-hCG > 6,000

Amniocentesis

Amniocentesis is the most extensively used fetal sampling technique and is typically performed at 15 weeks' GA when the amniotic fluid is 200 mL.

Indications
- Fetal anomaly suspected on US
- Abnormal MSAFP
- Family history of congenital abnormalities
- Offered to all patients ≥ 35 years of age

Procedure
- Thirty milliliters of amniotic fluid is removed via a 20- to 22-gauge needle using a transabdominal approach with US guidance.
- Biochemical analysis is performed on the extracted fluid:
  - Amniotic fluid AFP levels
  - Fetal cells can be grown for karyotyping or DNA assays.

Risks
- Pain/cramping
- Vaginal spotting/amniotic fluid leakage in 1 to 2% of cases

- Symptomatic amnionitis in < 1/1,000 patients
- **Rate of fetal loss ≤ 0.5%**

Chorionic Villus Sampling (CVS)

Chorionic villus sampling is a diagnostic technique in which a small sample of chorionic villi is taken transcervically or transabdominally and analyzed.
- Typically done between 9 and 12 weeks' GA
- Allows for chromosomal status, fetal karyotyping, and biochemical assays or DNA tests to be done earlier than amniocentesis

Risks
- 0.5% rate of complications
- Preterm delivery
- Premature rupture of membranes
- Fetal injury

Cordocentesis

Cordocentesis is a procedure in which a spinal needle is advanced transplacentally under US guidance into a cord vessel to sample fetal blood. Typically performed after 17 weeks.

Indications
- Fetal karyotyping because of fetal anomalies
- To determine the fetal hematocrit in Rh isoimmunization or severe fetal anemia
- To assay fetal platelet counts, acid–base status, antibody levels, blood chemistries, etc.
- **Fetal abdominal measurements:** Taken to determine their proportionality to the fetal head (head-to-abdominal circumference ratio) and assess fetal growth.
- **Amniotic fluid index (AFI):** Represents the total of linear measurements (in centimeters) of the largest amniotic fluid pockets in each of the four quadrants of the amniotic fluid sac.
  - Reduced amniotic fluid volume (AFI < 5) = **oligohydramnios**
  - Excessive fluid (AFI > 20) = **polyhydramnios**

Genetic Testing

Genetic testing, if indicated, is performed with the following techniques:

FISH (fluorescent *in situ* hybridization): A specific DNA probe with a fluorescent label that binds homologous DNA → allows identification of specific sites along a chromosome

Karyotyping: Allows visualization of chromosome size, banding pattern, and centromere position

Indications
- Advanced maternal age
- Previous child with abnormal karyotype
- Parental chromosome rearrangements
- Fetal structural abnormality on sonogram
- Unexplained intrauterine growth retardation (IUGR)
- Abnormally low MSAFP

The fetal head is normally larger than the body in T2 and early T3.

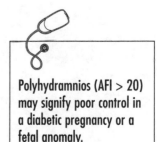

Oligohydramnios (AFI < 5) may suggest possible fetal compromise due to umbilical cord compression.

Polyhydramnios (AFI > 20) may signify poor control in a diabetic pregnancy or a fetal anomaly.

Weight Gain

- Weight gain for normal BMI = **25 to 35 lb**
- Optimal weight gain for an underweight teenager carrying a singleton pregnancy = 40 lb or 5 lb every 4 weeks in second half of pregnancy
- An obese woman may need to gain only 15 lb.

Diet

- The average woman must consume an additional **300 kcal/day** beyond baseline needs.

Vitamins

- **400 µg/day folic acid** is required.
- **30 mg elemental iron per day is recommended in T2 and T3.**
  - Total of 1 g Fe is needed for pregnancy (500 mg for increase RBC mass, 300 mg for fetus, 200 mg for GI losses).
  - The recommended dietary allowance (RDA) for calcium is increased in pregnancy to 1,200 mg/day and may be met adequately with diet alone.
  - The RDA for zinc is increased from 15 to 20 mg/day.

Vegetarians

- *Lactoovovegetarians* in general have no nutritional deficiencies, except possibly Fe and Zn.
- *Vegans* must consume sufficient quantities of vegetable proteins to provide all essential amino acids normally found in animal protein.
  - Due to decreased protein density of most vegetables, patients may gain a greater than average amount of weight.
  - Supplementation of Zn, vitamin B_{12}, and Fe is necessary.

Pica

Occasionally seen in pregnancy, pica is the compulsive ingestion of nonfood substances with little or no nutritional value:
- Ice
- Clay (geophagia)
- Starch (amylophagia)

ANSWERS TO COMMONLY ASKED QUESTIONS

Caffeine in Pregnancy

- Contained in coffee, tea, chocolate, cola beverages
- Currently no studies have shown deleterious fetal effects with customary amounts

- Adverse maternal effects include:
  - Insomnia
  - Acid indigestion
  - Reflux
  - Urinary frequency

Exercise

- No data exist to indicate that a pregnant woman must decrease the intensity of her exercise or lower her target heart rate.
- Women who exercised regularly before pregnancy should continue:
  - Exercise may relieve stress, decrease anxiety, increase self-esteem, and shorten labor.
- The form of exercise should be one with low risk of trauma, particularly abdominal.
- Exercise that requires prolonged time in the supine position should be avoided in T2 and T3.
- Exercise should be stopped if patient experiences oxygen deprivation → extreme fatigue, dizziness, or shortness of breath.
- Contraindications to exercise include:
  - Evidence of IUGR
  - Persistent vaginal bleeding
  - Incompetent cervix
  - Risk factors for preterm labor
  - Rupture of membranes
  - Pregnancy-induced hypertension

Nausea and Vomiting (N&V)

- Recurrent N&V in T1 occurs in 50% of pregnancies.
- If severe, can result in dehydration, electrolyte imbalance, and malnutrition
- Management of mild cases includes:
  - Avoidance of fatty or spicy foods
  - Eating small, frequent meals
  - Inhaling peppermint oil vapors
  - Drinking ginger teas
- Management of severe cases includes:
  - Discontinuation of vitamin/mineral supplements until symptoms subside
  - Antihistamines
  - Promethazine
  - Metoclopramide
  - Intravenous droperidol

"Morning sickness" can occur day or night.

Heartburn

- Common in pregnancy
- Treatment consists of:
  - Elimination of spicy/acidic foods
  - Small, frequent meals
  - Decrease amount of liquid consumed with each meal
  - Limit food and liquid intake a few hours prior to bedtime

- Sleep with head elevated on pillows
- Utilize liquid forms of antacids and H_2-receptor inhibitors

Constipation

- Common in pregnancy
- Management includes:
  - Increase intake of high-fiber foods
  - Increase liquids
  - Psyllium-containing products

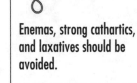

Enemas, strong cathartics, and laxatives should be avoided.

VARICOSITIES

- Common in pregnancy, particularly in lower extremities and vulva
- Can lead to chronic pain and superficial thrombophlebitis
- Management includes:
  - Avoidance of garments that constrict at the knee and upper leg
  - Use of support stockings
  - Increased periods of rest with elevation of the lower extremities

Hemorrhoids

- Varicosities of the rectal veins are common in pregnancy
- Management includes:
  - Cool sitz baths
  - Stool softeners
  - Increase fluid and fiber intake to prevent constipation

If thrombosis of a hemorrhoid occurs, clot excision should be attempted to alleviate pain and swelling.

Leg Cramps

- Occur in 50% of pregnant women, typically at night and in T3
- Most commonly occur in the calves
- Massage and stretching of the affected muscle groups is recommended.

Backache

- Typically progressive in pregnancy
- Management includes:
  - Minimize time standing.
  - Wear a support belt over the lower abdomen.
  - Acetaminophen
  - Exercises to increase back strength
  - Supportive shoes and avoidance of high heels

Rhythmic cramping pains originating in the back may signify preterm labor.

Round Ligament Pain

- Sharp, bilateral or unilateral groin pain
- Frequently occurs in T2
- May increase with sudden movement/change in position
- May be alleviated by patient getting on hands and knees with head on floor and buttocks in air

Sexual Relations

- There are no restrictions during the normal pregnancy.
- Nipple stimulation, vaginal penetration, and orgasm may → release of oxytocin and prostaglandins → uterine contractions.
- Contraindications:
  - If membranes have ruptured
  - If + placenta previa

Employment

- Work activities that increase risk of falls/trauma should be avoided.
- Exposure to toxins/chemicals should be avoided.

Travel

- If prolonged sitting is involved, the patient should attempt to stretch her lower extremities and walk for 10 minutes every 2 hours.
- The patient should bring a copy of her medical record.
- Wear seat belt when riding in car.
- Airplane travel in pressurized cabin presents no additional risk to the pregnant woman.
- In underdeveloped areas or when traveling abroad, the usual precautions regarding ingestion of unpurified water and raw foods should be taken.

Hypercoaguable state and mechanical compression of venous blood flow to extremities → increased risk of thrombosis.

Immunizations

There is no evidence of fetal risk from inactivated virus vaccines, bacterial vaccines, toxoids, or tetanus immunoglobulin, and they should be administered as appropriate. Safe vaccines:

- Yellow fever
- Oral polio
- Hepatitis B
- Diphtheria
- Tetanus

Three immunizations should be **avoided** during pregnancy:

- Measles
- Mumps
- Rubella

Viral vaccinations may be safely given to the children of pregnant women.

Immune globulin is recommended for pregnant women exposed to measles, hepatitis A and B, tetanus, chickenpox, or rabies.

Vaccines safe in pregnancy:
- Hep B
- Oral polio
- Tetanus
- Yellow fever
- Diphtheria

Vaccines *unsafe* in pregnancy:
- Measles
- Mumps
- Rubella

Give immune gloublin in pregnancy for exposure to:
- Hepatitis A and B
- Tetanus
- Chickenpox
- Rabies

WHEN TO CALL THE PHYSICIAN

- Vaginal bleeding
- Leakage of fluid from the vagina
- Rhythmic abdominal cramping of > 6/hr

- Progressive and prolonged abdominal pain
- Fever and chills
- Dysuria
- Prolonged vomiting with inability to hold down liquids or solids for > 24 hours
- Progressive, severe headache, visual changes, or generalized edema
- Pronounced decrease in frequency or intensity of fetal movements

Intrapartum

THREE STAGES OF LABOR

The successive stages of labor are illustrated in Figure 6-1.

First Stage

The first stage of labor begins with onset of **labor** (uterine contractions of sufficient frequency, intensity, and duration to result in effacement and dilation of the cervix), and ends when the cervix is fully/completely dilated to 10 cm.

The first stage of labor consists of two phases:

1. **Latent phase:** Begins with the onset of labor and ends at approximately 4 cm cervical dilatation.

   Average Duration
   - Nulliparous—20 hours
   - Multiparous—14 hours

2. **Active phase:** Rapid dilation. Begins at 4 cm dilation and ends at 10 cm.

Active phase is further classified according to the rate of cervical dilation: **Acceleration phase, phase of maximum slope,** and **deceleration phase.**

Fetal descent begins at 7 to 8 cm of dilation in nulliparas and becomes most rapid after 8 cm.

Average duration of cervical dilation from 4 to 10 cm:
- Nulliparous: 1.2 cm/hr
- Multiparous: 1.5 cm/hr

Second Stage

The second stage of labor is the stage of **fetal expulsion.** It begins when the cervix is fully dilated and ends with the delivery of the fetus.

Average Pattern of Fetal Descent
- Nulliparous: 1 cm/hr
- Multiparous: 2 cm/hr

Duration of labor is typically shorter in the multiparous woman than in nulliparous women.

There are **three stages of labor,** and **two phases of stage 1.**

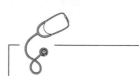

Remember the three "Ps" that affect the duration of the Active Phase:
- **Power** (strength and frequency of contractions)
- **Passenger** (size of the baby)
- **Pelvis** (size and shape of mother's pelvis)

If progress during the active phase is slower than these figures, evaluation for adequacy of uterine contractions, fetal malposition, or cephalopelvic disproportion should be done.

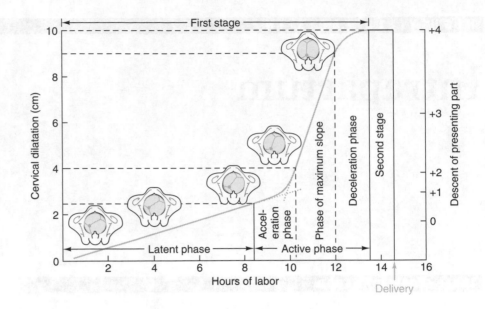

FIGURE 6-1. Schematic illustration of progress of rotation of occipitoanterior presentation in the successive stages of labor.

(Reproduced, with permission, from DeCherney AH, Pernoll ML. *Current Obstetric & Gynecologic Diagnosis & Treatment.* Norwalk, CT: Appleton & Lange, 1994: 211.)

Third Stage

The main event of the third stage is placental separation. It begins immediately after the delivery of the fetus and ends with the delivery of the fetal and placental membranes.

Abnormalities of the second stage may be either protraction or arrest of descent (the fetal head descends < 1 cm/hr in a nullip and < 2 cm/hr in a multip).

Duration
- Usually under 10 minutes; considered prolonged if more than 30 minutes

The three signs of placental separation are:

1. Gush of blood from vagina
2. Umbilical cord lengthening
3. Fundus of the uterus rises up and becomes firm

If 30 minutes have passed without placental extrusion, manual removal of the placenta may be required.

TRUE LABOR VERSUS FALSE LABOR

False Labor (Braxton Hicks Contractions)	True Labor
Occur at irregular intervals	Occur at regular intervals that shorten
Intensity remains the same	Increase in intensity
Discomfort in lower abdomen	Discomfort in back and lower abdomen
Cervix is not dilated	Dilated cervix
Relieved by medications	NOT relieved by medications

- Blood supply to the uterus—uterine and ovarian arteries
- Normal blood flow to nonpregnant uterus—100 cc/min
- Normal blood flow to 17-week uterus—500 cc/min (intrauterine growth retardation occurs if flow is less)
- Normal blood loss for normal vaginal delivery—300 to 500 mL
- Normal blood loss for normal C-section—800 to 1,000 mL

What are the three signs of placental separation?
1) gush of blood
2) umbilical cord lengthening
3) fundus of uterus rises and firms

CLINICAL SIGNS OF LABOR

Bloody Show

Discharge of small amount of blood-tinged mucus from vagina (mucous plug)

Rupture of Membranes (ROM)

ROM is characterized by sudden gush of nearly colorless fluid. ROM can be diagnosed with pool, nitrazine, and fern tests (described in PROM section).

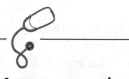

Spontaneous rupture of membranes (SROM) most often occurs during the course of active labor.

ASSESSMENT OF THE LABORING PATIENT

Initial Assessment

History and Physical
- Patients without prenatal care require a complete H&P and those with prenatal care require an update and focused physical. Prenatal record should be obtained when possible.

Labs
- Patients without prenatal care require:
  - Complete blood count (CBC)
  - Blood typing
  - Rh determination
  - Urine testing
- Patients who have had antepartum care require:
  - Urine test for protein or glucose
  - CBC
  - A specimen of blood in the event that subsequent crossmatching is required

Crucial Information for a Laboring Patient

The following information should always be obtained from a laboring patient:
- Time of onset and frequency of contractions
- Status of fetal membranes
- Presence/absence of vaginal bleeding
- Notation of fetal activity

- History of allergies
- How long ago did patient consume food or liquids and how much
- Use of medications
- Risk status assignment (high or low)

Vaginal Exam (VE)

A sterile speculum exam if:
- Suspect rupture of membranes
- Preterm labor
- Signs of placenta previa

Otherwise, a digital VE may be performed

The following must be assessed:

STATUS OF AMNIOTIC FLUID AND MEMBRANES

A sterile speculum is used to look for fluid in the posterior vaginal fornix **(pool test),** which determines if ROM has occurred.

Fluid may be collected on a swab for further study if the source of fluid is unclear:
- **Ferning test** (high estrogen content of amniotic fluid causes fern pattern on slide when allowed to air dry):
  - Crystallization/arborization is due to interaction of amniotic fluid proteins and salts.
  - Confirms ROM in 85 to 98% of cases
- **Nitrazine test**—nitrazine paper is pH sensitive and turns blue in presence of amniotic fluid:
  - Amniotic fluid (pH = 7.15) is more alkaline than vaginal secretions.
  - 90 to 98% accurate

Fluid should also be examined for vernix or meconium.
- The presence of meconium in the amniotic fluid may indicate fetal stress.
- Meconium staining is more common in term and postterm pregnancies than in preterm pregnancies.
- Meconium aspiration syndrome (MAS) can occur → infant tachypnea, costal retractions, cyanosis, coarse breath sounds, etc.
- Prevent MAS via amnioinfusion intrapartum and DeLee suction postpartum

CERVICAL EXAM

There are four parameters of the cervix that are examined: effacement, consistency, dilation, and position.

EFFACEMENT

Effacement describes the **length of the cervix.** With labor, the cervix thins out and softens, and the length is reduced. The normal length is 3 to 4 cm.
- *Terminology:* When the cervical length shrinks by 50% (to around 2 cm), it is said to be 50% effaced. When the cervix becomes as thin as the adjacent as the lower uterine segment it is 100% effaced.

- *Determination of effacement:* Palpate with finger and estimate the length from the internal to external os.

DILATION

Dilation describes the size of the opening of the cervix at the external os.
- *Ranges:* Ranges from closed or zero to fully dilated (10 cm). The presenting part of a term-sized infant can usually pass through a cervix that is fully dilated.
- *Determination of dilation:* The examining finger is swept from the margin of the cervix on one side to the opposite side.

CERVICAL POSITION

Position describes the location of cervix with respect to the fetal presenting part. It is classified as one of the following:
- *Posterior*—difficult to palpate because it is behind the fetus, and usually high in the pelvis
- *Midposition*
- *Anterior*—easy to palpate, low down in pelvis

During labor, the cervical position usually progresses from posterior to anterior.

CERVICAL CONSISTENCY

Consistency ranges from firm to soft. Soft indicates onset of labor.

Bishop Score

- A scoring system that helps determine the status of the cervix—is it favorable or unfavorable for successful delivery?
- If induction of labor is indicated, the status of the cervix must be evaluated to help determine the method of labor induction that will be utilized.

See Table 6-1 and section on Labor Induction.

A score of ≥ 8 indicates that the probability of vaginal delivery after labor induction is similar to that after spontaneous labor.

Vaginal prostaglandins are inserted for ripening of cervix.
IV pictocin is used to increase and intensify contractions.

TABLE 6-1. Bishop Scoring System

Factor	0 Points	1 Point	2 Points	3 Points
Dilation (cm)	Closed	1–2	3–4	5–6
Effacement (%)	0–30	40–50	60–70	80
Station[a]	−3	−2	−1 to 0	+1 to +2
Consistency	Firm	Medium	Soft	—
Position	Posterior	Midposition	Anterior	—

[a] Station reflects −3 to +3 scale.

Leopold Maneuvers

Leopold maneuvers are begun in midpregnancy through labor to assess the fetus and maternal abdomen (Figure 6-2). Consist of four parts:

First maneuver answers the question: "What fetal part occupies the fundus?"

Second maneuver answers the question: "On what side is the fetal back?"

Third maneuver answers the question: "What fetal part lies over the pelvic inlet?"

Fourth maneuver answers the question: "On which side is the cephalic prominence?"

Five aspects of the fetus are described from the Leopold maneuvers:

- Station
- Lie
- Presentation
- Position
- Attitude

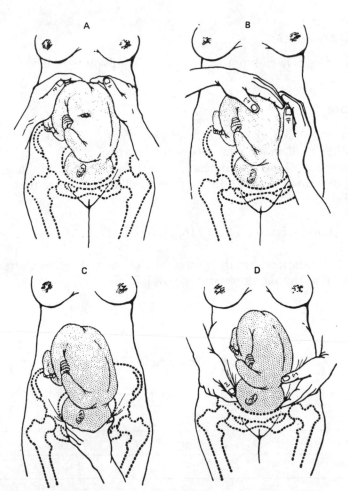

FIGURE 6-2. Leopold maneuvers. Determining fetal presentation (A and B), position (C), and engagement (D).

(Reproduced, with permission, from Pernoll ML. *Benson & Pernoll's Handbook of Obstetrics and Gynecology*, 10th ed. New York: McGraw-Hill, 2001: 159.)

STATION

Station describes the degree of descent of the fetal head (or presenting part) in relation to ischial spines.

Terminology (Two Systems)
1. The ischial spine is zero station, and the areas above and below are divided into thirds. Above the ischial spines are stations −3, −2, and −1, with −3 being the furthest above the ischial spines and −1 being closest. Positive stations describe fetal descent below the ischial spines. +3 station is at the level of the introitus, and +1 is just past the ischial spines.
2. Very similar except that the areas above and below the ischial spines are divided by centimeters, up to 5 cm above and 5 cm below. Above are five stations or centimeters: −5, −4, −3, −2, and −1, with −5 being the 5 cm above the ischial spines and −1 being 1 cm above. Positive stations describe fetal descent below the ischial spines. +5 station is at the level of the introitus, and +1 is 1 cm past the ischial spines.

LIE

Lie describes the relation of the long axis of the fetus to that of the mother. Can be either:
- **Longitudinal** (99% of term or near term births). This can be vertex (head first) or breech (buttocks first).
- **Transverse** (0.4% of term or near term births)

PRESENTATION/PRESENTING PART

Presentation describes the portion of the fetus that is foremost within the birth canal. It is normally determined by palpating through the cervix on vaginal examination.
- If the lie is longitudinal, the presentation is either the head (cephalic) or buttocks (breech). One type of cephalic presentation is the **vertex presentation** in which the posterior fontanel is the presenting part. This is considered normal.
- If the lie is transverse, the shoulder is the presenting part.

THE FETAL SKULL

The top of the fetal skull is composed of five bones: two frontal, two parietal, and one occipital. The anterior fontanel lies where the two frontal and two parietal meet, and the posterior fontanel lies where the two parietal meet the occipital bone.

FETAL POSITIONS

Position refers to the relation of the presenting part to the right (R) or left (L) side of the birth canal and its direction anteriorly (A), transversely (T), or posteriorly (P).

For a cephalic occipital presentation, the position can be described in the following ways:
Occipital anterior (OA)
Occipital posterior (OP)
Left occipital anterior (LOA)
Left occipital posterior (LOP)

HIGH-YIELD FACTS

Intrapartum

> *Interpreting Fetal Positions:*
> Imagine the mother lying in the anatomical position and the baby's occiput in relation to her body. You are at the end of the bed looking between mom's legs. Figure 6-3 represents the mother's birth canal with the fetal head inside in various positions as you look at the fetal head.

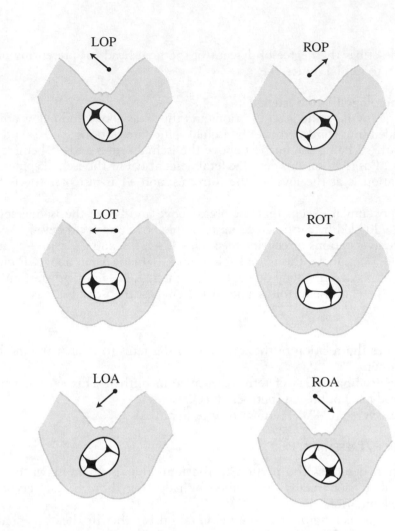

FIGURE 6-3. Vertex presentations.
(Reproduced, with permission, from Lindarkis NM, Lott S. *Digging Up the Bones: Obstetrics and Gynecology.* New York: McGraw-Hill, 1998: 28.)

Left occipital transverse (LOT)
Right occipital anterior (ROA)
Right occipital posterior (ROP)
Right occipital transverse (ROT)

FETAL ATTITUDE AND POSTURE

In the later months of pregnancy, the fetus assumes a characteristic posture ("attitude/habitus"), which typically describes the position of the arms. Examples include arms folded over thorax or parallel to the sides.

Normal Presentation

VERTEX PRESENTATION (OCCIPITAL PRESENTATION)

Vertex presentation is usual (96% of at or near term presentations). The head is flexed so that the chin is in contact with the chest. The **posterior fontanel** is the presenting part.

Malpresentations

FACE PRESENTATION

In face presentation (0.3% of presentations at or near term), the fetal neck is sharply extended so the occiput is in contact with the fetal back. The face is the presenting part. Diagnosis is made by palpation of the fetal face on vaginal exam.

SINCIPUT PRESENTATION

The fetal head assumes a position between vertex presentation and face presentation so that the anterior fontanel presents first.

BROW PRESENTATION

The fetal head assumes a position such that the eyebrows present first. This forces a large diameter through the pelvis; usually, vaginal delivery is possible only if the presentation is converted to a face or vertex presentation.

BREECH PRESENTATIONS

In breech presentations, the presenting fetal part is the buttocks. Normally, the delivery is C-section. Incidence: 3.5% at or near term but much greater in early pregnancy (14%). Those found in early pregnancy will often spontaneously convert to vertex as term approaches.

Risk Factors
- Low birth weight (20 to 30% of breeches)
- Congenital anomalies such as hydrocephalus or anencephaly
- Uterine anomalies
- Multiple gestation
- Placenta previa

Diagnosis can be made by:
- Leopold maneuvers
- Ultrasound

Types of Breech
- **Frank breech (65%):** The thighs are flexed (bent forward) and the legs are extended (straight) over the anterior surfaces of the body (feet are in front of the head or face).
- **Complete breech (25%):** The thighs are flexed (bent) on the abdomen and the legs are flexed (folded) as well.
- **Incomplete (footling) breech (10%):** One or both of the hips are not flexed so that a foot lies below.

Management
- Normally, **C-section** is the form of delivery.
- **External cephalic version:** This is maneuvering the infant to a vertex position. Can be done only if breech is diagnosed before onset of labor and the GA > 37 weeks. The success rate is 75%, and the risks are placental abruption or cord compression.
- **Trial of breech vaginal delivery:** This is the attempt at a vaginal delivery. It can be done only in a frank breech, GA > 36 weeks, fetal weight 2,500 to 3,800 g, fetal head flexed, and favorable pelvis. Risks are greater for birth trauma (especially brachial plexus injuries) and prolapsed cord that entraps the aftercoming head.

Vaginal delivery is possible only if the fetus is mentum anterior; mentum posterior cannot deliver vaginally → cesarean section.

Sinciput and sinciput presentation are usually transient and almost always convert to vertex or face.

Why is pelvimetry and head position so important in frank breech vaginal delivery? Because the head doesn't have time to mold in order to fit through the birth canal.

Shoulder dystocia occurs when, after the fetal head has been delivered, the fetal shoulder is impacted behind the pubic symphysis.

Risk Factors
- Macrosomia
- Gestational diabetes
- Maternal obesity
- Post-term delivery
- Prolonged stage 2 of labor

Complications
- Fetal humeral/clavicular fracture
- Brachial plexus nerve injuries
- Hypoxia/death

Treatment
Several maneuvers can be done to displace the shoulder impaction:
- **Suprapubic pressure** on maternal abdomen
- **McRoberts maneuver:** Maternal thighs are sharply flexed against maternal abdomen. This decreases the angle between the sacrum and spine and may dislodge fetal shoulder.
- **Woods corkscrew maneuver:** Pressure is applied against scapula of posterior shoulder to rotate the posterior shoulder and "unscrew" the anterior shoulder.
- **Posterior shoulder delivery:** Hand is inserted into vagina and posterior arm is pulled across chest, delivering posterior shoulder and displacing anterior shoulder from behind pubic symphysis.
- **Break clavicle or cut through symphysis**
- **Zavanelli maneuver:** If the above measures do not work, the fetal head can be returned to the uterus. At this point, a C-section can be performed.

CARDINAL MOVEMENTS OF LABOR

The cardinal movements of labor are changes in the position of the fetal head during passage through the birth canal. The movements are as follows: engagement, flexion, descent, internal rotation, extension, and external rotation.

Engagement

Engagement is the descent of the biparietal diameter (the largest transverse diameter of the fetal head, 9.5 cm) to the plane of the pelvic inlet (Figure 6-4):
- Often occurs before the onset of true labor, especially in nulliparas

Descent

Descent is the fetal head passing down into the pelvis. It occurs in a discontinuous fashion. The greatest rate of descent occurs in the deceleration phase of the first stage of labor and during the second stage of labor (Figure 6-5).

Engagement indicates that the pelvic inlet of the maternal bony pelvis is sufficiently large to allow descent of the fetal head.

Engagement is measured by palpation of the presenting part of the occiput.

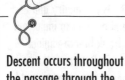

Descent occurs throughout the passage through the birth canal, as does flexion of the fetal head.

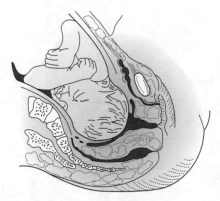

FIGURE 6-4. Engagement.
(Reproduced, with permission, from DeCherney AH, Pernoll ML. *Current Obstetric & Gynecologic Diagnosis & Treatment.* Norwalk, CT: Appleton & Lange, 1994: 211.)

Flexion

Flexion refers to the chin-to-chest position that the fetus takes. This passive motion facilitates the presentation of the smallest possible diameter of the fetal head to the birth canal.

Internal Rotation

Internal rotation refers to the fetal occiput gradually rotating toward the pubic symphysis (Figure 6-6).

Extension

Extension moves the occiput to the fetal back (Figure 6-7):
- Occurs after the fetus has descended to the level of the maternal vulva
- This descent brings the base of the occiput into contact with the inferior margin of the symphysis pubis, where the birth canal curves upward.
- The fetal head is delivered by extension from the flexed to the extended position, thus curving under and past the pubic symphysis.

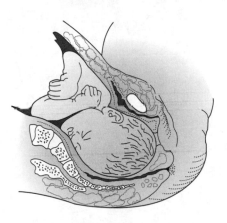

FIGURE 6-5. Descent.
(Reproduced, with permission, from DeCherney AH, Pernoll ML. *Current Obstetric & Gynecologic Diagnosis & Treatment.* Norwalk, CT: Appleton & Lange, 1994: 211.)

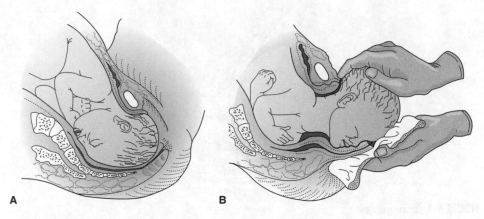

A   **B**

FIGURE 6-6. A. Anterior rotation of head. **B.** Modified Ritgen maneuver.
(Reproduced, with permission, from DeCherney AH, Pernoll ML. *Current Obstetric & Gynecologic Diagnosis & Treatment.*
Norwalk, CT: Appleton & Lange, 1994: 212.)

> The anterior shoulder is the one closest to the superior portions of the vagina, while the posterior shoulder is closest to the perineum and anus.

External Rotation ("Restitution")

External rotation occurs after delivery of the head, when the fetus resumes its normal "face-forward" position with the occiput and spine lying in the same plane (Figure 6-8).

External rotation is completed by rotation of the fetal body to the transverse position (i.e., one shoulder is anterior behind the pubic symphysis and the other is posterior).

Expulsion

After external rotation, further descent brings the anterior shoulder to the level of the pubic symphysis. The shoulder is delivered under the pubic symphysis and then the rest of the body is quickly delivered (Figures 6-9 and 6-10).

FIGURE 6-7. Extension.
(Reproduced, with permission, from DeCherney AH, Pernoll ML. *Current Obstetric & Gynecologic Diagnosis & Treatment.* Norwalk, CT: Appleton & Lange, 1994: 212.)

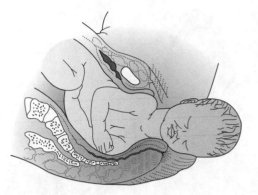

FIGURE 6-8. External rotation.

(Reproduced, with permission, from DeCherney AH, Pernoll ML. *Current Obstetric & Gynecologic Diagnosis & Treatment.* Norwalk, CT: Appleton & Lange, 1994: 212.)

STANDARD METHOD OF DELIVERY

Delivery of the Head: Modified Ritgen Maneuver

The modified Ritgen maneuver is a technique that allows for delivery of the fetal head with its smallest diameter passing through the introitus and over the perineum (see Figure 6-6B).

- A towel-draped, gloved hand is placed over the perineum and rectum and exerts upward pressure on the fetal chin.
- Simultaneously, a gloved hand is placed superiorly and exerts downward pressure over the fetal occiput.

It is done during a contraction when the head distends the vulva and perineum enough to open the vaginal introitus to ≥ 5 cm in diameter.

Checking for Nuchal Cord

A nuchal cord is when the umbilical cord wraps around the fetal neck. To check for this condition, following delivery of the head, a finger should be passed along the fetal neck to ascertain the presence of the cord.

- If so, a finger should be slipped under the cord and, if loose enough, it should be slipped over the infant's head.
- If the cord is wrapped tightly around the infant's neck, it should be cut between two clamps.
- The infant should then be delivered.

Typically, the rest of the body rapidly follows the delivery of the shoulders without effort.

Delivery of Shoulders

- Most frequently, the shoulders appear at the vulva just after external rotation and are born spontaneously (see Figures 6-9 and 6-10).

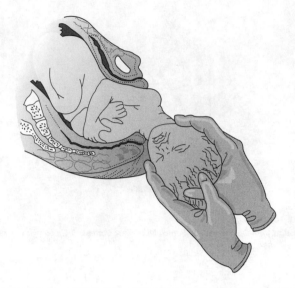

FIGURE 6-9. Delivery of anterior shoulder.
(Reproduced, with permission, from DeCherney AH, Pernoll ML. *Current Obstetric & Gynecologic Diagnosis & Treatment.* Norwalk, CT: Appleton & Lange, 1994: 212.)

- Occasionally, the shoulders must be extracted:
  - The sides of the head are grasped with both hands and *gentle* downward traction is applied until the anterior shoulder descends from under the pubic arch.
  - Next, *gentle* upward traction is applied to deliver the posterior shoulder.

Vaginal Lacerations

The perineum and anus become stretched and thin, which results in increased risk of spontaneous laceration and anterior tears involving the urethra and labia.

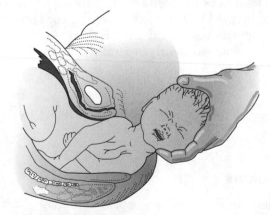

FIGURE 6-10. Delivery of posterior shoulder.
(Reproduced, with permission, from DeCherney AH, Pernoll ML. *Current Obstetric & Gynecologic Diagnosis & Treatment.* Norwalk, CT: Appleton & Lange, 1994: 212.)

FIRST DEGREE

Involve the fourchette, perineal skin, and vaginal mucosa, but *not* the underlying fascia and muscle

Repair: Absorbable sutures (e.g., 3-0 vicryl)

SECOND DEGREE

First degree plus the fascia and muscle of the perineal body but *not* the rectal sphincter

Repair: Done in layers, sometimes using a crown stitch to bring the perineal body together (e.g., with 3-0 vicryl)

THIRD DEGREE

Second degree plus involvement of the anal sphincter

Repair: Repair anal sphincter with interrupted sutures (e.g., 2-0 vicryl) and repair vagina as in second-degree laceration.

FOURTH DEGREE

Extend through the rectal mucosa to expose the lumen of the rectum

Repair: Same as third-degree repair plus careful repair of anal mucosa (e.g., with 4-0 vicryl)

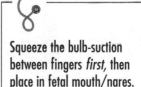

Proper repair of 4th-degree laceration is important to prevent future maternal problems (e.g., fecal incontinence).

Episiotomy

An episiotomy is the incision of the perineum and/or labia to aid delivery. There are two types:

1. *Midline:* The incision is made in the midline from the posterior fourchette. Most common.
2. *Mediolateral:* The incision is oblique starting from 5 o'clock or 7 o'clock position of the vagina. Causes more infection and pain.

Indications
- Risk of perineal rupture
- Shoulder dystocia
- Breech delivery
- Forceps/vacuum delivery

Postdelivery Tasks

1. Clear the nasopharynx:
   - To minimize infant aspiration of amniotic fluid debris and blood that may occur once the thorax is delivered and the baby can inspire
   - Use a bulb syringe to aspirate the mouth and nares.
2. Clamping and cutting the cord:
   - The umbilical cord is clamped by two instruments and cut in between.
   - The infant is handed to the pediatrician/nurse/assistant for examination.
   - A sample of cord blood is taken from the umbilical cord that remains attached to the placenta.

Squeeze the bulb-suction between fingers *first*, then place in fetal mouth/nares.

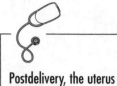

Postdelivery, the uterus should be firm and contracted, like a globular ball.

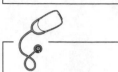

Signs of placental separation typically occur within 5 minutes of infant delivery.

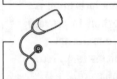

Placental delivery should *never* be forced before placental separation has occurred, otherwise inversion of the uterus may occur.

Postdelivery Uterine Exam

- The height and consistency of the uterine fundus are ascertained.
- A moderate amount of bleeding is normal.

Placental Separation

Signs
1. Uterus becomes globular and more firm.
2. There is often a sudden gush of blood.
3. The uterus rises in the abdomen due to the bulk of the placenta, which has (separated) passed down into the lower uterine segment and vagina.
4. The umbilical cord protrudes farther out of the vagina, indicating descent of the placenta.

Delivery of the Placenta

- Pressure is applied to the body of the uterus as the umbilical cord is held slightly taut.
- The uterus is lifted cephalad with the abdominal hand.
- This maneuver is repeated until the placenta reaches the introitus.
- As the placenta passes to the introitus, pressure on the uterus is stopped.
- The placenta is gently lifted away from the introitus.
- The maternal surface of the placenta should be examined to ensure that no placental fragments are left in the uterus.

Postdelivery Hemostasis

After the uterus has been emptied and the placenta delivered, hemostasis must be achieved:

- The primary mechanism is myometrial contraction → vasoconstriction.
- Oxytocin (Pitocin) is administered in the third stage of labor → myometrial contractions → reduces maternal blood loss.

Dystocia

Dystocia literally means difficult labor and is characterized by abnormally slow progress of labor.

Causes
1. Abnormalities of the expulsive forces:
   - Uterine dysfunction → uterine forces insufficiently strong or inappropriately coordinated to efface and dilate cervix
   - Inadequate voluntary muscle effort during second stage of labor
2. Abnormalities of presentation, position, or fetal development
3. Abnormalities of the maternal bony pelvis
4. Abnormalities of the birth canal

Monitoring Uterine Activity

UTERINE CONTRACTIONS

Uterine activity is monitored by internal or external uterine pressure monitors. Pressure is calculated in *Montevideo units*, calculated by increases in uterine pressure above baseline (8 to 12 mm Hg) multiplied by contraction frequency per 10 minutes.

UTERINE PRESSURE INCREASES AND STAGES OF LABOR

Uterine contractions in the first stage of labor increase progressively in intensity from 25 mm Hg to 50 mm Hg, and the frequency increases from three to five contractions per 10 minutes.

Contractions in the second stage increase further (aided by maternal bearing down) to 80 to 100 mm Hg, and the frequency increases to five to six per 10 minutes.

Vaginal Exams

Vaginal examinations should be kept to the minimum required for the evaluation of a normal labor pattern, for example, VE q 4 hours in latent phase and q 2 hours in active phase. Sterile glove and lubricant should be utilized.

Fetal Heart Rate Monitoring

The fetal heart rate (FHR) can be measured in two ways:

1. Intermittent auscultation with a fetal stethoscope or Doppler ultrasonic device
2. Continuous electronic monitoring of the FHR and uterine contractions

FIRST STAGE OF LABOR

Fetal heart rate should be recorded every 30 minutes (immediately after uterine contractions).

SECOND STAGE OF LABOR

Fetal heart rate should be recorded every 15 minutes (immediately after uterine contractions).

Maternal Vital Signs

Maternal blood pressure and pulse should be evaluated and recorded every 10 minutes.

Other Considerations

In most U.S. hospitals, oral intake is limited to small sips of water, ice chips, or hard candies.

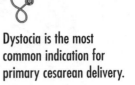

Dystocia is the most common indication for primary cesarean delivery.

Inhalation anesthesia may be needed for cesarean delivery or for management of complications in the third stage of labor. Thus, consumption of foods or liquids can cause aspiration.

HIGH-YIELD FACTS

Intrapartum

Same as above with addition of the following

Continuous Electronic Fetal Monitoring

Continuous electronic fetal monitoring should be done with evaluation of tracing every 15 minutes during first stage and every 5 minutes during second stage. It can be done in either of the following two ways:

1. *Internal electronic FHR monitoring:* Internal FHR monitoring is done with a bipolar spiral electrode attached to fetal scalp, which detects the peak R-wave voltage of the fetal electrocardiogram.
2. *External (indirect) electronic FHR monitoring:* FHR is detected through the maternal abdominal wall with a transducer that emits ultrasound. Uterine contractions are also detected.

Nonstress Test

If fetal compromise is suspected, the nonstress test (NST) is the first assessment of fetal well-being:
- The mother is placed in a left lateral, supine position.
- A continuous FHR tracing is obtained using external Doppler equipment.
- The heart rate changes that result from the fetal movements are determined:
  - A normal fetal response during each fetal movement is an acceleration in fetal heart rate of ≥ 15 bpm above the baseline for at least 15 seconds.
  - If at least two such accelerations occur in a 20-minute interval, the fetus is deemed healthy and the test is **reactive.**
- If an NST is **nonreactive,** it should be followed by a biophysical profile (BPP).

Biophysical Profile

A BPP uses ultrasonography and cardiotocography to ascertain fetal well-being by assessing the following five parameters:

1. Fetal breathing movements (chest wall movements)
2. Fetal activity (gross trunk or limb movements)
3. Amniotic fluid index
4. Fetal tone (flexion and extension of an extremity)
5. Reactivity (nonstress test)

A score of 0 or 2 is given for each parameter and a normal profile equals 8 to 10.

The physiologic basis for using the BPP lies in the fact that coordinated fetal activities (i.e., breathing and movement) require an intact, nonhypoxic central nervous system.

Amniotic Fluid Index

Amniotic fluid plays an important role in fetal lung development protection against trauma and infection.

Amniotic fluid index (AFI) is examined in the BPP and reflects the volume of amniotic fluid. The calculation of AFI is as follows: The maternal abdomen is divided into quadrants, and with ultrasound, the maximum vertical pocket of each quadrant is measured in centimeters and added.

Normal Amniotic Fluid Volumes
- Maximum amniotic fluid is at 28 weeks—800 mL
- After 28 weeks, amniotic fluid decreases.
- At 40 weeks, amniotic fluid is at 500 mL.

Abnormal Amniotic Fluid Volumes
- **Oligohydramnios** is < 5 amniotic fluid index.
  - Most common cause: Rupture of membranes.
  - Associated with intrauterine growth retardation (IUGR) in 60% of cases.
- **Polyhydramnios** is > 20 amniotic fluid index, or 2 L.

FETAL HEART RATE PATTERNS

Important definitions:
- **Hypoxemia:** Decreased oxygen content in blood
- **Hypoxia:** Decreased level of oxygen in tissue
- **Acidemia:** Increased concentration of hydrogen ions in the blood
- **Acidosis:** Increased concentration of hydrogen ions in tissue
- **Asphyxia:** Hypoxia with metabolic acidosis

See Table 6-2 for fetal heart rate patterns.

Reactivity and the Normal FHR

The normal fetal heart rate is 110 to 160 bpm. This baseline (a "baseline" rate refers to a heart rate lasting ≥ 10 minutes) normally has frequent periodic variations above and below termed **accelerations** (increases in HR) and **decelerations** (decreases in HR) (Figure 6-11).

TABLE 6-2. FHR Patterns

	Early Decel	Late Decel	Variable Decel
Significance	Benign	Abnormal	Mild
Shape	U shaped	U shaped	Variable (often V or W shaped)
Onset	Gradual	Gradual	Abrupt
Depth	Shallow	Shallow	Variable
When	End with the uterine contraction	End after the uterine contraction	Variable
Why	Head compression	Uteroplacental insufficiency	Cord compression and occasionally head compression
Initial treatment	None required	O$_2$, lateral decubitous position, Pitocin off	Amnioinfusion

71

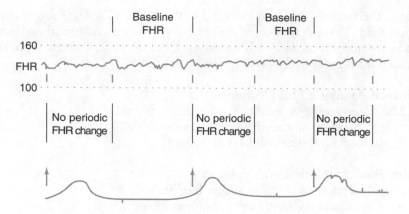

FIGURE 6-11. Fetal heart rate patterns.

(Reproduced, with permission, from Hon EH. *An Atlas of Fetal Heart Rate Patterns.* Harty Press, 1968.)

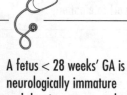

Reactive: 15-bpm increase of 15-second duration 2×/20 minutes.

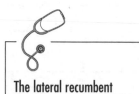

A fetus < 28 weeks' GA is neurologically immature and thus is not expected to have a "reactive" FHR.

A normally reactive fetal tracing has two accelerations of at least 15 bpm greater than the baseline, lasting for at least 15 seconds, in 20 minutes. It represents intact neurohumoral cardiovascular control mechanisms and indicates that the fetus is unstressed.

Periodic FHR Changes

Periodic FHR changes refers to accelerations and decelerations related to uterine contractions.

DECELERATIONS

Decelerations during labor have different meaning depending on when they occur in relation to contractions.

Early Decelerations

Early decelerations are *normal* and due to head compression during contractions. The timing of onset, peak, and end coincides with the timing of the contraction. The degree of deceleration is proportional to the contraction strength. The effect is regulated by vagal nerve activation.

NO intervention necessary!!

Late Decelerations

Late decelerations are *abnormal* and are due to **uteroplacental insufficiency** (not enough blood) during contractions. They begin at the peak of contraction and end slowly after the contraction has stopped.

The lateral recumbent position (either side) is best for maximizing cardiac output and uterine blood flow. (In the supine position, the vena cava and aortoiliac vessels may be compressed by the gravid uterus.)

> **Intervention**
> - **Change maternal position to the lateral recumbent position.**
> - **Give oxygen by face mask.**
> - **Stop oxytocin (Pitocin) infusion.**
> - Provide an IV fluid bolus.
> - Give an IV tocolytic drug (MgSO$_4$).
> - Monitor maternal blood pressure.
> - If persist longer than 30 minutes, fetal scalp blood pH should be obtained and C-section considered.

Variable Decelerations

Variable decelerations are *abnormal* and can be mild or severe. They are due to **cord compression** and sometimes **head compression.** They can occur at any time. If they are repetitive, suspicion is high for the cord to be wrapped around the neck or under the arm of the fetus.

> **Intervention**
> - **Amnioinfusion:** Infuse normal saline into the uterus through the intrauterine pressure catheter to alleviate cord compression.
> - Change maternal position to side/Trendelenburg position.
> - Deliver fetus with forceps or C-section.

FETAL TACHYCARDIA

Mild = 161 to 180 bpm
Severe = ≥ 181

Fetal tachycardia may indicate intrauterine infection, severe fetal hypoxia, congenital heart disease, or maternal fever.

BEAT-TO-BEAT VARIABILITY (BTBV)

> - **The single most important characteristic of the baseline FHR**
> - Variation of successive beats in the FHR BTBV is controlled primarily by the autonomic nervous system, thus an important index of fetal central nervous system (CNS) integrity
> - At < 28 weeks' GA, the fetus is neurologically immature; thus, decreased variability is expected.

> **Short-Term Variability (STV)**
> - Reflects instantaneous beat-to-beat (R wave to R wave) changes in FHR
> - The *roughness* (STV present) or *smoothness* (STV absent) of the FHR tracing
> - May be decreased/absent due to alterations in the CNS or inadequate fetal oxygenation

> **Long-Term Variability (LTV)**
> - Describes the oscillatory changes that occur in 1 minute
> - Results in waviness of baseline
> - Normal = 3 to 6 cycles/min

Decreases in BTBV

Beat-to-beat variability decreases with:
- Fetal acidemia
- Fetal asphyxia
- Maternal acidemia
- Drugs (narcotics, $MgSO_4$, barbiturates, etc.)

Increases in BTBV

Beat-to-beat variability increases with mild fetal hypoxemia.

Variable decelerations are abnormal.
They are classified as:
Mild
- Lasts < 30 sec and depth > 70 to 80 bpm

Moderate
- Lasts 30 to 60 sec and depth < 70 to 80 bpm
OR
- Lasts > 60 sec and depth = 70 to 80 bpm

Severe
- Lasts > 60 sec and depth < 70 bpm
May signify fetal **acidemia.**

If an FHR of 160 bpm lasts for ≥ 10 minutes, then tachycardia is present.

No BTBV (beat to beat variability) = fetal **acidosis, and the fetus must be delivered immediately.**

BTBV (beat to beat variability) can be reliably determined only with internal FHR monitoring (fetal scalp electrode).

Prolonged Decelerations

Isolated decelerations that last 2 to 10 minutes. Causes include:
- Cervical examinations
- Uterine hyperactivity
- Maternal hypotension → transient fetal hypoxia
- Umbilical cord compression

Management

- Stop Pitocin/prostaglandins.
- Change maternal position.
- Administer IV fluids.
- If mother is hypotensive, administer ephedrine/terbutaline.
- Administer maternal O_2.
- Rule out cord prolapse.

> **Short-term variability is thought to be the most important predictor of fetal outcome.**

ABNORMAL LABOR PATTERNS

- *Prolonged latent phase* (see Table 6-3)
- *Active phase abnormalities*—may be due to cephalopelvic disproportion (CPD), excessive sedation, conduction analgesia, and fetal malposition (i.e., persistent OP).
  - *Protraction disorders*—a slow rate of cervical dilation or descent
  - *Arrest disorders*—complete cessation of dilation or descent (see Table 6-3)

INDUCTION OF LABOR

> **If a deceleration has occurred without recovery after 2 minutes, an emergency C-section is required.**

Indications

Generally any condition that makes normal labor dangerous to mother or fetus is an indication.

Maternal
- Premature ROM
- Diabetes mellitus
- Heart disease
- Prolonged labor
- Prolonged pregnancy

Fetal
- IUGR
- Abnormal fetal testing
- Infection
- Rh incompatibility

Contraindications

Maternal
- Contracted pelvis
- Prior uterine surgery (controversial)

TABLE 6-3. Abnormal Labor Patterns

Labor Pattern	Diagnostic Criterion: Nulliparas	Diagnostic Criterion: Multiparas	Preferred Treatment	Exceptional Treatment
Prolongation disorder (prolonged latent phase)	> 20 hrs	> 14 hrs	Therapeutic rest (may be unrecognized false labor)	Oxytocin stimulation or cesarean delivery for urgent problems
Protraction disorder				
1. Protracted active phase dilatation	< 1.2 cm/hr	< 1.5 cm/hr		
2. Protracted descent	< 1 cm/hr	< 2 cm/hr	Expectant and support	Cesarean delivery for (cephalopelvic disproportion) CPD
Arrest disorders				
1. Prolonged deceleration phase	> 3 hrs	> 1 hr	Without CPD: Oxytocin	Rest if exhausted
2. Secondary arrest of dilatation	> 2 hrs	> 2 hrs		
3. Arrest of descent	> 1 hr	> 1 hr	With CPD: Cesarean delivery	Cesarean delivery
4. Failure of descent (no descent in deceleration phase or second stage of labor)	> 1 hr	> 1 hr		

- Classic cesarean section
- Myomectomy

Fetal
- Lung immaturity
- Acute distress
- Abnormal presentation

Induction Drugs

OXYTOCIN

A synthetic polypeptide hormone that stimulates uterine contraction:
- Acts promptly when given intravenously
- Should not be employed for more than a few hours

Complications
- Potent antidiuretic effects of oxytocin (oxytocin is related structurally and functionally to vasopressin or antidiuretic hormone) can cause water intoxication, which can lead to convulsions, coma, and death.
- Risk of uterine tetanic contractions (overstimulation)

PROSTAGLANDINS

Misoprostol, a synthetic PGE$_1$ analog:
- Can be administered intravaginally or orally
- Used for cervical ripening and induction

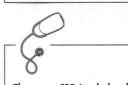

Scalp stimulation is done *between* decelerations to elicit a reactive acceleration and rule out metabolic acidosis.

The term *CPD* (cephalopelvic disproportion) has been used to describe a disparity between the size of the maternal pelvis and the fetal head that precludes vaginal delivery. This condition can rarely be diagnosed with certainty and is often due to malposition of the fetal head (i.e., asynclitism).

PGE$_2$ gel and vaginal insert:
- Both contain dinoprostone
- Used for cervical ripening in women at or near term

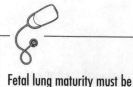
CESAREAN DELIVERY

The birth of a fetus through incisions in the abdominal wall (laparotomy) and the uterine wall (hysterotomy).

Basic Types

1. Low cervical (also called low-transverse cesarean section [LTCS]):
   - Incision made in lower uterine segment
   - Most common type performed
2. Classical:
   - Vertical incision made in uterine corpus
   - Done when:
     - Lower uterine segment not developed
     - Fetus is transverse lie with back down

Indications

- Repeat cesarean (elective; patient does not desire a trial of labor)
- Dystocia or failure to progress in labor
- Breech presentation
- Transverse lie
- Concern for fetal well-being (i.e., fetal distress)

VAGINAL BIRTH AFTER CESAREAN DELIVERY (VBAC)

- VBAC is associated with a small but significant risk of uterine rupture with poor outcome for mother and infant:
  - Classical uterine scar → 4 to 9% risk
  - Low-transverse incision → 0.2 to 1.5% risk
- Maternal and infant complications are also associated with an unsuccessful trial of labor.

The skin incision that you see on the maternal abdomen does not tell you the type of uterine incision that the patient received. For example, a woman may have a classical uterine incision, but a low transverse skin incision.

Candidates for VBAC

- **One or two prior LTCSs**
- Clinically adequate pelvis
- No other uterine scars or previous rupture
- Physician immediately available throughout active labor capable of monitoring labor and performing an emergency C-section
- Availability of anesthesia and personnel for emergency C-section

Contraindications for VBAC

- **Prior classical or T-shaped incision or other transfundal uterine surgery**
- Contracted pelvis
- Medical/obstetric complication that precludes vaginal delivery
- Inability to perform emergency C-section because of unavailable surgeon, anesthesia, sufficient staff, or facility

Forceps and Vacuum Delivery

INDICATIONS

Prolonged second stage, maternal heart disease, acute pulmonary edema, intrapartum infection, maternal aneurysm, prolapse of the cord, abnormal fetal heart rate, inadequate uterine contractions, abnormal positioning of fetal head, maternal exhaustion, or need to hasten delivery

PREREQUISITES FOR FORCEPS DELIVERY

A fully dilated cervix, ROM, engaged fetal head, > +2 station, no cephalopelvic disproportion, empty bladder, and vertex presentation

PAIN CONTROL DURING LABOR AND DELIVERY

Three essentials of obstetrical pain relief are simplicity, safety, and preservation of fetal homeostasis.

> Pain relief during labor is a benefit-versus-risk trade-off.

Uterine Innervation

Pain early in the first stage of labor is largely generated from uterine contractions. Visceral sensory fibers from the uterus, cervix, and upper vagina traverse through the Frankenhäuser ganglion (lies just lateral to the cervix) → pelvic plexus → middle and superior internal iliac plexus → lumbar and lower thoracic sympathetic chains → enter the spinal cord through the white rami communicantes associated with the 11th and 12th thoracic and first lumbar nerves.

Lower Genital Tract Innervation

During the second stage of labor, much of the pain arises from the lower genital tract:

- Painful stimuli from the lower genital tract are primarily transmitted by the pudendal nerve → passes beneath the posterior surface of the sacrospinous ligament (just as the ligament attaches to the ischial spine).
- The sensory nerve fibers of the pudendal nerve are derived from the ventral branches of the second, third, and fourth sacral nerves.

Nonpharmacological Methods of Pain Control

Women who are free from fear and who have confidence in their obstetrical staff require smaller amounts of pain medication:

> The peripheral branches of the pudendal nerve provide sensory innervation to the perineum, anus, and the medial and inferior parts of the vulva and clitoris.

- An understanding of pregnancy and the birth process
- Appropriate antepartum training in breathing
- Appropriate psychological support (e.g., by a friend or family member)
- Considerate obstetricians and labor assistants who instill confidence

Analgesia and Sedation

Pain relief with a narcotic (e.g., Stadol /Butorphanol) plus an antiemetic (e.g., promethazine) is typically sufficient, with **no significant risk** to the mother or infant:
- Bearable discomfort is still felt at the acme of an effective uterine contraction.
- Slightly increase uterine activity
- Does *not* prolong labor

INTRAMUSCULAR (IM)

Meperidine + Promethazine:
- Small doses given more frequently are preferable to large boluses less often.
- Analgesia is maximal 45 minutes post injection.

INTRAVENOUS (IV)

Meperidine + Phenergan:
- A more rapid effect is produced by this route—the maternal analgesic and fetal depressant effects are immediate post injection.

OTHER SAFE NARCOTICS

- Butorphanol (Stadol)
- Fentanyl
- Nalbuphine

NARCOTIC ANTAGONISTS

Naloxone hydrochloride:
- Displaces the narcotic from receptors in the CNS
- 0.1 mg/kg of body weight of the newborn injected into the umbilical vein
- Acts within 2 minutes

General Anesthesia

General anesthesia should not be induced until all steps preparatory to actual delivery have been completed, so as to minimize transfer of the agent to the fetus → avoids newborn respiratory depression.

CONCERNS OF GENERAL ANESTHESIA

- All anesthetic agents that depress the maternal CNS cross the placenta → depress the fetal CNS.
- General anesthetics can cause aspiration of gastric contents and particulate matter → airway obstruction → pneumonitis, pulmonary edema, and death.

HIGH-YIELD FACTS

Intrapartum

Uterine contractions and cervical dilation cause discomfort.

If delivery occurs within 1 hour of analgesia, neonatal depression may occur.

Nitrous oxide (N_2O) is the only anesthetic gas in current use in the intra-partum in the United States:

- Provides pain relief during labor and delivery
- Produces an altered consciousness
- Does *not* prolong labor or interfere with uterine contractions
- Self-administered N_2O in a 50% mixture with 50% O_2 (face mask) provides excellent pain relief in the second stage of labor.
- Also used for cesarean delivery and some forceps deliveries with IV administration of a short-acting barbituate (e.g., thiopental) and a muscle relaxant (e.g., succinylcholine)

> Prophylactic measures against aspiration include fasting for at least 6 hours prior to anesthesia and antacid administration before induction.

Regional Analgesia

Nerve blocks that provide pain relief for women in labor and delivery without loss of consciousness (anesthesia)

PUDENDAL BLOCK

- Local infiltration of the pudendal nerve with a local anesthetic agent (e.g., lidocaine)
- Allows pinching of the lower vagina and posterior vulva bilaterally without pain
- Effective, safe, and reliable method of providing analgesia for spontaneous delivery
- Can be used along with epidural analgesia

Complications

Inadvertant intravascular injection will cause systemic toxicity, hematoma, infection.

PARACERVICAL BLOCK

- Lidocaine or chloroprocaine is injected at the 3 o'clock and 9 o'clock positions around the cervix.
- Provides good relief of pain of uterine contractions during first stage of labor
- Requires additional analgesia for delivery because the pudendal nerves are not blocked

Complications

Fetal bradycardia (usually transient)

SPINAL (SUBARACHNOID) BLOCK

- Introduction of local anesthetic into the subarachnoid space
- Used for uncomplicated cesarean delivery and vaginal delivery of normal women of low parity
- Local anesthetics used include lidocaine and tetracaine.

Vaginal Delivery

- Low spinal block
- Level of analgesia extends to the tenth thoracic dermatome (corresponds to the level of the umbilicus)
- Popular for forceps or vacuum delivery

> Always pull back on the syringe prior to injection of anesthetic to look for blood flow into the syringe; if positive, you are in a vessel and must reposition your needle.

- Provides excellent relief of pain from uterine contractions
- Proceeded by infusion of 1 L of crystalloid solution → prevents hypotension

Cesarean Delivery

- A higher level of spinal blockade is necessary to at least the level of the eighth thoracic dermatome (just below the xiphoid process of the sternum).
- A larger dose of anesthetic agent is required to anesthetize the larger area → increased frequency and intensity of toxic reactions.

Complications with Spinal Analgesia

- Maternal hypotension
- Total spinal blockade
- Spinal (postpuncture) headache
- Convulsions
- Bladder dysfunction

Contraindications to Spinal Analgesia

- Severe preeclampsia
- Coagulation/hemostasis disorders
- Neurological disorders

EPIDURAL ANALGESIA

Injection of local anesthetic into the epidural or peridural space:
- *Lumbar epidural analgesia*—injection into a lumbar intervertebral space
- *Caudal epidural analgesia*—injection through the sacral hiatus and sacral canal

Relieves pain of uterine contractions, abdominal delivery (block begins at the eighth thoracic level and extends to first sacral dermatome) or vaginal delivery (block begins from the tenth thoracic to the fifth sacral dermatome)

The spread of the anesthetic agent depends on:

1. Location of the catheter tip
2. Dose, concentration, and volume of anesthetic agent used
3. Maternal position (e.g., head up, head down, horizontal)
4. Individual anatomy of epidural space (i.e., presence of synechiae may preclude a satisfactory block)

Complications

- Inadvertent spinal blockade (puncture of dura with subarachnoid injection)
- Ineffective analgesia
- Hypotension
- Convulsions

Effects on Labor

- Increased duration of labor
- Increased incidence of:
  - Chorioamnionitis

When vaginal delivery is anticipated in 10 to 15 minutes, a rapidly acting agent is given through the epidural catheter to effect perineal analgesia.

- Low-forceps procedures
- Cesarean deliveries
- Maternal pyrexia

Contraindications

- Actual/anticipated serious maternal hemorrhage
- Infection at or near sites for puncture
- Suspicion of neurological disease

LOCAL INFILTRATION

Employed for delivery:
- Before episiotomy and delivery
- After delivery in the site of lacerations to be repaired
- Around the episiotomy wound if there is inadequate analgesia

PELVIC TYPES

	Gynecoid	Android	Anthropoid	Platypelloid
Frequency	In 50% of all females	One third of white women; one sixth of nonwhite women	One fourth of white women; one half of nonwhite women	Rarest, < 3% of women
Inlet shape	Round	Heart shaped	Vertically oriented oval	Horizontally oriented oval
Sidewalls	Straight	Convergent	Convergent	Divergent, then convergent
Ischial spines	Not prominent (diameter ≥ 10 cm)	Prominent (diameter < 10 cm)	Prominent (diameter < 10 cm)	Not prominent (diameter > 10 cm)
Sacrum	Inclined neither anteriorly nor posteriorly	Forward and straight with little curvature	Straight = pelvis deeper than other three types	Well curved and rotated backward; short = shallow pelvis
Significance	Good prognosis for vaginal delivery	Limited posterior space for fetal head → poor prognosis for vaginal delivery	Good prognosis for vaginal delivery	Poor prognosis for vaginal delivery

HIGH-YIELD FACTS

Intrapartum

Postpartum

THE PUERPERIUM OF THE NORMAL LABOR AND DELIVERY

The period of confinement during birth and 6 weeks after. During this time, the reproductive tract returns anatomically to a normal nonpregnant state.

Uterine Changes

INVOLUTION OF THE UTERINE CORPUS

Immediately after delivery, the fundus of the contracted uterus is slightly below the umbilicus. After the first 2 days postpartum, the uterus begins to shrink in size. Within 2 weeks, the uterus has descended into the cavity of the true pelvis.

ENDOMETRIAL CHANGES: SLOUGHING AND REGENERATION

Within 2 to 3 days postpartum, the remaining decidua become differentiated into two layers:

1. Superficial layer → becomes necrotic → sloughs off as vaginal discharge = *lochia*
2. Basal layer (adjacent to the myometrium) → becomes new endometrium

Placental Site Involution

Within hours after delivery, the placental site consists of many thrombosed vessels. Immediately postpartum, the placental site is the size of the palm of the hand. The site rapidly decreases in size and by 2 weeks postpartum = 3 to 4 cm in diameter.

Changes in Uterine Vessels

Blood vessels are obliterated by hyaline changes and replaced by new, smaller vessels.

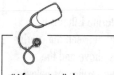

"Afterpains" due to uterine contraction are common and may require analgesia. They typically decrease in intensity by the third postpartum day.

Lochia is decidual tissue that contains erythrocytes, epithelial cells, and bacteria.
See Table 7-1.

TABLE 7-1. Lochia

Type	Description	When Observed
Lochia rubra	Red due to blood in the lochia	Days 1–3
Lochia serosa	More pale in color	Days 4–10
Lochia alba	White to yellow-white due to leukocytes and reduced fluid content	Day 11 →

When involution is defective, late puerperal hemorrhage may occur.

Changes in the Cervix and Lower Uterine Segment

The external os of the cervix contracts slowly and has narrowed by the end of the first week.

The thinned-out lower uterine segment (that contained most of the fetal head) contracts and retracts over a few weeks → uterine isthmus.

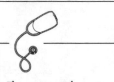

At the completion of involution, the cervix does *not* resume its pregravid appearance:
Before childbirth, the os is a small, regular, oval opening.
After childbirth, the orifice is a transverse slit.

Changes in the Vagina and Vaginal Outlet

Gradually diminishes in size, but rarely returns to nulliparous dimensions:
- Rugae reappear by the third week.
- The rugae become obliterated after repeated childbirth and menopause.

Peritoneum and Abdominal Wall

The broad ligaments and round ligaments slowly relax to the nonpregnant state.

The uterine isthmus is located between the uterine corpus above and the internal cervical os below.

The abdominal wall is soft and flabby due to the prolonged distention and rupture of the skin's elastic fibers → resumes prepregnancy appearance in several weeks, except for silver striae.

Urinary Tract Changes

The puerperal bladder:
- Has an increased capacity
- Is relatively insensitive to intravesical fluid pressure

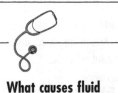

All postpartum women who cannot void should be promptly catheterized.

Hence, overdistention, incomplete bladder emptying, and excessive residual urine are common.

FLUID RETENTION AND THE RISK OF URINARY TRACT INFECTIONS

Residual urine + bacteriuria in a traumatized bladder + dilated ureters and pelves → increased risk of UTI. Between days 2 and 5 postpartum, "puerperal diuresis" typically occurs to reverse the increase in extracellular water associated with normal pregnancy.

Dilated ureters and renal pelves return to their prepregnant state from 2 to 8 weeks postpartum.

What causes fluid retention postpartum?
High estrogen levels in pregnancy → fluid retention
Increased venous pressure in the lower half of the body during pregnancy → fluid retention

Changes in the Breasts

DEVELOPMENT OF MILK-SECRETING MACHINERY

Progesterone, estrogen, placental lactogen, prolactin, cortisol, and insulin act together → growth and development of the milk-secreting machinery of the mammary gland:

- Midpregnancy—lobules of alveoli form lobes separated by stromal tissue, with secretion in some alveolar cells
- T3—alveolar lobules are almost fully developed, with cells full of proteinaceous secretory material
- Postpartum—rapid increase in cell size and in the number of secretory organelles. Alveoli distend with milk.

DEVELOPMENT OF THE MILK

At delivery, the abrupt, large decrease in progesterone and estrogen levels leads to increased production of alpha-lactalbumin → stimulates lactose synthase → increased milk lactose.

COLOSTRUM

Colostrum can be expressed from the nipple by the second postpartum day and is secreted by the breasts for 5 days postpartum.

MATURE MILK AND LACTATION

Colostrum is then gradually converted to mature milk by 4 weeks postpartum. Subsequent lactation is primarily controlled by the repetitive stimulus of nursing and the presence of prolactin.

Breast engorgement with milk is common on days 3 to 4 postpartum:

- Often painful
- Often accompanied by transient temperature elevation (puerperal fever)

Suckling stimulates the neurohypophysis to secrete oxytocin in a pulsatile fashion → contraction of myoepithelial cells and small milk ducts → milk expression

Changes in the Blood

- **Leukocytosis** occurs during and after labor up to 30,000/µL
- There is a relative **lymphopenia.**
- There is an absolute **eosinopenia.**
- During the first few postpartum days, the **hemoglobin** and **hematocrit** fluctuate moderately from levels just prior to labor.

By 1 week postpartum, the **blood volume** has returned to the patient's nonpregnant range.

CARDIAC OUTPUT

- The **cardiac output** remains elevated for ≥ 48 hours postpartum.
- By 2 weeks postpartum, these changes have returned to nonpregnant levels.

Colostrum is a deep yellow-colored liquid secreted by the breasts that contains minerals, protein, fat, antibodies, complement, macrophages, lymphocytes, lysozymes, lactoferrin, and lactoperoxidase.

Women with extensive pituitary necrosis (Sheehan syndrome) cannot lactate due to the absence of prolactin.

Puerperal fever seldom persists for > 4 to 16 hrs. Other causes of fever (e.g., mastitis, endometritis, UTI, thrombophlebitis) must be excluded.

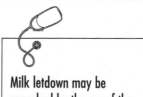

Milk letdown may be provoked by the cry of the infant or inhibited by stress or fright.

Elevation of **plasma fibrinogen** and the **erythrocyte sedimentation rate** remain for ≥ 1 week postpartum.

Changes in Body Weight

Most women approach their prepregnancy weight 6 months after delivery, but still retain approximately 1.4 kg of excess weight. Five to six kilograms are lost due to uterine evacuation and normal blood loss. Two to three kilograms are lost due to diuresis.

FACTORS THAT INCREASE PUERPERAL WEIGHT LOSS

- Weight gain during pregnancy
- Primiparity
- Early return to work outside the home
- Smoking

ROUTINE POSTPARTUM CARE

Immediately After Labor

FIRST HOUR

- Take BP and HR at least every 15 minutes.
- Monitor the amount of vaginal bleeding.
- Palpate the fundus to ensure adequate contraction:
  - If the uterus is relaxed, it should be massaged through the abdominal wall until it remains contracted.

First Several Hours

EARLY AMBULATION

Women are out of bed (OOB) within a few hours after delivery. Advantages include:
- Decreased bladder complications
- Less frequent constipation
- **Reduced frequency of puerperal venous thrombosis and pulmonary embolism**

CARE OF THE VULVA

The patient should be taught to cleanse and wipe the vulva from front to back toward the anus.

If Episiotomy/Laceration Repair

- An ice pack should be applied for the first several hours to reduce edema and pain.
- Periodic application of a local anesthetic spray can relieve pain as well.
- At 24 hours postpartum, moist heat (e.g., via warm sitz baths) can decrease local discomfort.
- The episiotomy incision is typically well healed and asymptomatic by week 3 of the puerperium.

BLADDER FUNCTION

Ensure that the postpartum woman has voided within 4 hours of delivery. If not:
- This typically indicates further trouble voiding to follow.
- An indwelling catheter may be necessary, with a prohylactic antibiotic after catheter removal.
- Consider a hematoma of the genital tract as a possible etiology.

The First Few Days

BOWEL FUNCTION

Lack of a bowel movement may be due to a cleansing enema administered prior to delivery. Encourage early ambulation and feeding to decrease the probability of constipation.

If Fourth-Degree Laceration

Fecal incontinence may result, even with correct surgical repair, due to injury to the innervation of the pelvic floor musculature.

DISCOMFORT/PAIN MANAGEMENT

During the first few days of the puerperium, pain may result due to:
- Afterpains
- Episiotomy/laceration repair
- Breast engorgement
- Postspinal puncture headache

Treat with any of the following:
- Codeine
- Aspirin
- Acetaminophen

ABDOMINAL WALL RELAXATION

Exercise may be initiated any time after vaginal delivery and after abdominal discomfort has diminished after cesarean delivery.

DIET

There are *no* dietary restrictions/requirements for women who have delivered vaginally. Two hours postpartum, the mother should be permitted to eat and drink.

Continue iron supplementation for a minimum of 3 months postpartum.

IMMUNIZATIONS

- The nonisoimmunized D-negative woman whose baby is D-positive is given 300 µg of anti-D immune globulin within 72 hours of delivery.
- Woman not previously immunized against/immune to rubella should be vaccinated prior to discharge.
- Unless contraindicated, woman may receive a diphtheria–tetanus toxoid booster prior to discharge.

1. Anticipated physiologic changes during the puerperium:
   - Lochia—the bloody discharge that follows delivery
   - Diuresis—the secretion and passage of large amounts of urine
   - Milk letdown—the influx of milk into the mammary ducts
2. She should go to hospital if she develops:
   - Fever
   - Excessive vaginal bleeding
   - Lower extremity pain and/or swelling
   - Shortness of breath
   - Chest pain
3. Family planning and contraception:
   - Do not wait until first menses to begin contraception; ovulation may come before first menses.
   - Contraception is essential after the first menses, unless a subsequent pregnancy is desired.

Lactational Amenorrhea Method of Contraception

The sole utilization of breast feeding to prevent ovulation and subsequent pregnancy:
   - The lactational amenorrhea method is 98% effective for up to 6 months if:
   - The mother is not menstruating
   - The mother is nursing > 2 to 3 times per night, and ≥ every 4 hours during the day without other supplementation.
   - The baby is < 6 months old.

Combined Oral Contraceptives Versus Progestin-Only Contraceptives in Postpartum

Combined oral contraceptive hormones reduce the amount of breast milk, although very small quantities of the hormones are excreted in the milk.

Progestin-only oral contraceptive pills are virtually 100% effective without substantially reducing the amount of breast milk.

Coitus in Postpartum

After 6 weeks, coitus may be resumed based on patient's desire and comfort. A vaginal lubricant prior to coitus may increase comfort.

Dangers of premature intercourse:
   - Pain due to continued uterine involution and healing of lacerations/episiotomy scars
   - Increased likelihood of hemorrhage and infection

Infant Care

Prior to discharge:
   - Follow-up care arrangements should be made

The likelihood of significant hemorrhage is greatest immediately postpartum.

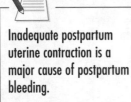

Inadequate postpartum uterine contraction is a major cause of postpartum bleeding.

Blood can accumulate within the uterus without visible vaginal bleeding: *Watch for:* Palpable uterine **enlargement** during the initial few hours postpartum.

- All laboratory results should be normal, including:
  - Coombs' test
  - Bilirubin
  - Hgb and Hct
  - Blood glucose
- Maternal serologic tests for syphilis and HbsAg should be nonreactive.
- Initial HBV vaccine should be administered.
- All screening tests required by law should be done (e.g., testing for phenylketonuria [PKU] and hypothyroidism).
- Patient education regarding infant immunizations and well-baby care

Discharge

VAGINAL DELIVERY

One to two days post hospitalization, if no complications

CESAREAN SECTION

Three to four days post hospitalization, if no complications

MATERNAL FOLLOW-UP CARE

Breast Feeding

Human milk is the ideal food for neonates for the first 6 months of life.

RECOMMENDED DIETARY ALLOWANCES

Lactating women need an extra 500 nutritious calories per day. Food choices should be guided by the Food Guide Pyramid, as recommended by the U.S. Department of Health and Human Services/U.S. Department of Agriculture.

BENEFITS

Uterine Involution

Nursing accelerates uterine involution.

Immunity

Colostrum and breast milk contain secretory IgA antibodies against *Escherichia coli* and other potential infections.

Milk contains memory T cells, which allows the fetus to benefit from maternal immunologic experience.

Colostrum contains interleukin-6, which stimulates an increase in breast milk mononuclear cells.

Nutrients

All proteins are absorbed by babies, and all essential and nonessential amino acids available.

GI Maturation

Milk contains epidermal growth factor, which may promote growth and maturation of the intestinal mucosa.

CONTRAINDICATIONS OF BREAST FEEDING

Infection

Mothers with:
- Cytomegalovirus (CMV)
- Chronic hepatitis B (HBV)
- HIV infection
- Breast lesions from active herpes simplex virus

Medications

Mothers ingesting the following contraindicated medications:
- Bromocriptine
- Cyclophosphamide
- Cyclosporine
- Doxorubicin
- Ergotamine
- Lithium
- Methotrexate

Mothers ingesting the following medications with unknown effects on the infant:
- Psychotropic drugs
- Antianxiety drugs
- Antidepressants
- Chloramphenicol
- Metoclopramide
- Metronidazole
- Tinidazole

Drug Abuse

Mothers who abuse the following drugs:
- Amphetamines
- Cocaine
- Heroin
- Marijuana
- Nicotine
- Phencyclidine

Radiotherapy

Mothers undergoing radiotherapy with:
- Gallium
- Indium
- Iodine
- Radioactive sodium
- Technetium

Nursing mothers rarely ovulate within the first 10 weeks after delivery. Non-nursing mothers typically ovulate 6 to 8 weeks after delivery.

Breast-fed infants are less prone to enteric infections than are bottle-fed babies.

CMV, HBV, and HIV are excreted in breast milk.

A common misperception: Mothers who have a common cold should not breast feed (FALSE).

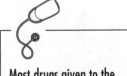

Most drugs given to the mother are secreted in breast milk. The amount of drug ingested by the infant is typically small.

Maternity/Postpartum Blues

A self-limited, mild mood disturbance due to biochemical factors and psychological stress:
- Affects 50% of childbearing women
- Begins within 3 to 6 days after parturition
- May persist for up to 10 days

SYMPTOMS

Similar to depression, but milder (see below)

TREATMENT

- Supportive—acknowledgement of the mother's feelings and reassurance
- Monitor for the development of more severe symptoms (i.e., of postpartum depression or psychosis).

Postpartum Depression

Similar to minor and major depression that can occur at any time:
- Classified as "postpartum depression" if it begins within 3 to 6 months after childbirth
- Eight to 15% of postpartum women develop postpartum depression within 2 to 3 months.

SYMPTOMS

Symptoms are the same as major depression.

NATURAL COURSE

- Gradual improvement over the 6 months postpartum
- The mother may remain symptomatic for months → years.

TREATMENT

- Pharmacologic intervention is typically required:
  - Antidepressants
  - Anxiolytic agents
  - Electroconvulsive therapy
- Mother should be co-managed with a psychiatrist (i.e., for psychotherapy to focus on any maternal fears or concerns).

Postpartum Psychosis

- Mothers have an inability to discern reality from that which is unreal (can have periods of lucidity).
- Occurs in 1 to 4/1,000 births
- Peak onset—10 to 14 days postpartum, but may occur months later

Thirty percent of adolescent women develop postpartum depression.

Criteria for major depression/post-partum depression: Two-week period of depressed mood or anhedonia nearly every day plus one of the following:
1. Significant weight loss or weight gain without effort (or ↑ or ↓ in appetite)
2. Insomnia or hypersomnia
3. Psychomotor agitation/retardation
4. Fatigue or loss of energy
5. Feelings of worthlessness/excessive or inappropriate guilt
6. Decreased ability to concentrate/think
7. Recurrent thoughts of suicide/death

HIGH-YIELD FACTS

Postpartum

If these drugs are prescribed to nursing mothers, infant blood concentrations of the drug should be monitored.

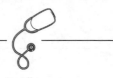

Usually remits after 2 to 3 days.

RISK FACTORS

- **History of psychiatric illness**
- **Family history of psych disorders**
- Younger age
- Primiparity

COURSE

Variable and depends on the type of underlying illness; often 6 months

TREATMENT

- Psychiatric care
- Pharmacologic therapy
- Hospitalization (in most cases)

Medical Conditions and Infections in Pregnancy

SOCIAL RISK FACTORS

Alcohol

- Alcohol is teratogenic.
- An occasional drink during pregnancy carries no known risk.
- Fetal alcohol syndrome (FAS) may occur with chronic exposure to alcohol in the later stages of pregnancy. Features may include:
  - Growth retardation
  - Facial anomalies:
    - Small palpebral fissures
    - Indistinct/absent philtrum
    - Epicanthic folds
    - Flattened nasal bridge
    - Short length of nose
    - Thin upper lip
    - Low-set, unparallel ears
    - Retarded midfacial development
  - Central nervous system (CNS) dysfunction:
    - Microcephaly
    - Mental retardation
    - Abnormal neurobehavior (e.g., attention deficit hyperactivity disorder)

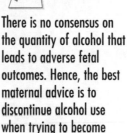

There is no consensus on the quantity of alcohol that leads to adverse fetal outcomes. Hence, the best maternal advice is to discontinue alcohol use when trying to become pregnant and during pregnancy.

Tobacco

- **The leading preventable cause of low birth weight in the United States**
- Smoking is associated with decreased birth weight and increased prematurity.
- There is a positive association between sudden infant death syndrome (SIDS) and smoking.
- Use of nicotine patch is controversial

Smoking by pregnant women and all household members should be stopped and not resumed postpartum.

Illicit Drugs

MARIJUANA

Derived from the plant *Cannabis sativa;* active ingredient, tetrahydrocannabinol:
- No evidence of significant teratogenesis in humans
- Metabolites detected in urine of users for days to weeks
- Commonly used by multiple substance abusers; thus, its presence in urine may identify patients at high risk for being current users of other substances as well

COCAINE

- Pregnancy does *not* increase one's susceptibility to cocaine's toxic effects
- **Complications of pregnancy:**
  - Spontaneous abortion and fetal death in utero
  - Preterm labor and delivery (25%)
  - Meconium-stained amniotic fluid (29%)

Teratogenic Effects of Cocaine
- Growth retardation
- Microcephaly
- Neurobehavioral abnormalities (e.g., impairment in orientation and motor function)
- SIDS

OPIATES

Heroin
- Three- to sevenfold increase in incidence of stillbirth, fetal growth retardation, prematurity, and neonatal mortality
- Signs of infant withdrawal occur 24 to 72 hours after birth.
- Treatment with methadone improves pregnancy outcome.

Newborn infants born to narcotic addicts are at risk for severe, potentially fatal narcotic withdrawal syndrome, characterized by:
- High-pitched cry
- Poor feeding
- Hypertonicity/tremors
- Irritability
- Sneezing
- Sweating
- Vomiting/diarrhea
- Seizures

HALLUCINOGENS

- No evidence that lysergic acid diethylamide (LSD) or other hallucinogens cause chromosomal damage or other deleterious effects on human pregnancy
- There have been no studies on the potential long-term effects on neonatal neurodevelopment.

AMPHETAMINES

Crystal methamphetamine ("ice," "blue ice"), a potent IV stimulant, has been associated with:

- Decreased fetal head circumference
- Placental abruption
- Intrauterine growth retardation (IUGR)
- Fetal death in utero

The anorectic properties of amphetamines may severely impair nutrition during pregnancy.

EXPOSURE TO VIOLENCE

- **Twenty percent of all pregnant women are battered during pregnancy.**
- **For some women, the violence is initiated at the time of pregnancy.**
- One half of women who are physically abused prior to pregnancy continue to be battered during pregnancy.
- *Ask:* "Are you in a relationship in which you are being hit, kicked, slapped, or threatened?"
- All abused patients should be given information regarding their immediate safety and referrals for counseling and support.

CONTRAINDICATIONS TO PREGNANCY

- Pulmonary hypertension:
  - Associated with a 50% maternal mortality rate and a > 40% fetal mortality rate
- Eisenmenger's syndrome:
  - Maternal mortality is 30 to 50%.

RISK INTERVENTIONS

Nutritional Recommendations
- Folic acid supplementation:
  - If previous pregnancies: 4 mg/day starting 4 weeks prior to conception, through T1
  - If nulligravida, 0.4 mg (400 µg) qd

Physical Activity Recommendations
- Women who exercise regularly before pregnancy are encouraged to continue.
- For the normal healthy woman, a low-impact exercise regimen may be continued throughout pregnancy.

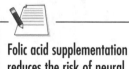

Folic acid supplementation reduces the risk of neural tube defects (NTDs).

Drug exposure is responsible for 2 to 3% of birth defects.

The placenta permits the passage of many drugs and dietary substances:
- Lipid-soluble substances readily cross the placenta.
- Water-soluble substances cross less well because of their larger molecular weight.
- The greater degree to which a drug is bound to plasma protein, the less likely it is free to cross.
- **The minimal effective dose should be employed.**

Embryological Age and Teratogenic Susceptibility

- 0–3 weeks—**predifferentiation phase of development:** The conceptus either does not survive exposure to teratogen or survives without anomalies.
- 3–8 weeks—**organogenesis phase:** Maximum susceptibility to teratogen-induced malformation.
- > 8 weeks—**organ growth phase:** A teratogen can interfere with growth but not organogenesis.

FDA (Food and Drug Administration) Pregnancy Drug Categories

CATEGORY A

Safety has been established using human studies.

CATEGORY B

Presumed safety based on animal studies

CATEGORY C

Uncertain safety—animal studies show an adverse effect, no human studies.

CATEGORY D

Unsafe—evidence of risk that may in certain clinical circumstances be justifiable

CATEGORY X

Highly unsafe—risk outweighs any possible benefit.

Vitamin A Derivatives

- Isotretinoin (Accutane):
  - For treatment of cystic acne
  - 25% risk of anomalies
  - Malformed infants have characteristic craniofacial, cardiac, thymic, and CNS anomalies.
- Etretinate (Tegison):
  - For treatment of psoriasis
  - Similar teratogenic effects to that of isotretinoin

- Vitamin A:
  - No evidence that normal doses are teratogenic
  - Large doses (≥ 25,000 IU/day) should be avoided because birth defects have been reported at these dosages.

Antineoplastics

Methotrexate and aminopterin are folic acid derivatives. They cause IUGR, mental retardation, and craniofacial malformations.

Anticoagulants

- Warfarin (Coumadin) crosses the placenta and is associated with chondrodysplasia punctata, presumably due to microhemorrhages during development.
  - Fetal and maternal hemorrhage has also been reported, but incidence can be reduced with careful control of the prothrombin time.
- Heparin, an alternative to Coumadin, has a large negative charge and does *not* cross the placenta.
  - Does *not* have any adverse fetal effects
  - Heparin-induced osteoporosis with fracture occurs in 1 to 2% of women in whom full anticoagulation has been achieved during pregnancy.
- Low-molecular-weight heparins (LMWH):
  - May have substantial benefit over standard unfractionated heparin
  - Molecules do *not* cross placenta

Heparin is the drug of choice in pregnant patients who require anticoagulation.

Low-molecular-weight heprain may be used in pregnancy.

Hypoglycemic Agents

Insulin is safe in pregnancy:
- Does *not* cross the placenta per large molecular weight (6,000)
- Dosage is unimportant as long as it is sufficient to maintain normal maternal glucose levels.

Oral hypoglycemic agents are currently under investigation for safety and efficacy during pregnancy.

Psychotropics

ANTICONVULSANTS

- Phenytoin decreases absorption of folate and decreases serum folate and causes craniofacial, limb, and mental defects.
- Valproic acid and carbamazepine use is associated with a 1% risk of neural tube defects.

ANTIDEPRESSANTS

- Imipramine (Tofranil):
  - Tricyclic antidepressant
  - Associated with fetal cardiac anomalies
- Fluoxetine (Paxil):
  - No increased risk of major malformations or developmental abnormalities has been observed.

- Chlordiazepoxide (Librium) is associated with congenital anomalies.
- Diazepam use perinatally has been associated with fetal hypothermia, hypotonia, and respiratory depression.

Analgesics

- Aspirin:
  - No teratogenic effects seen in T1
  - Significant perinatal effects seen, such as decreased uterine contractility, delayed onset of labor, prolonged duration of labor
  - Increases risk of antepartum bleeding and bleeding at delivery
- NSAIDs:
  - Ibuprofen (Motrin, Advil) and naproxen (Naprosyn) have not demonstrated any negative fetal effects with short-term use.
  - Chronic use may lead to oligohydramnios and constriction of the fetal ductus arteriosus.
- Acetaminophen (Tylenol, Datril) has shown no evidence of teratogenicity.

Antibiotics and Anti-infective Agents

- Penicillins, cephalosporins, and erythromycin are safe in pregnancy.
- Aminoglycosides (streptomycin)—risk of deafness
- Trimethoprim use in T1 is associated with increased risk of birth defects.
- Tetracyclines deposit in developing osseous sites and inhibit bone growth. They bind to developing enamel and discolor the teeth. Deciduous teeth are affected between 26 weeks' GA and infant age of 6 months.
- Doxycycline has no teratogenic risk in T1.
- Quinolones (Ciprofloxacin, Norfloxacin) have a high affinity for cartilage and bone tissue → may cause arthropathies in children.

Antiasthmatics

- Epinephrine (sympathomimetic amine) exposure after T1 has been associated with minor malformations.
- Terbutaline (Brethine) is not associated with birth defects.
  - Long-term use has been associated with increased risk of glucose intolerance.
- Isoproterenol (Isuprel) and Albuterol (Ventolin) are not teratogenic.
- Corticosteroids are inactivated by the placenta when maternally administered → < 10% of maternal dose is in the fetus.

Cardiovascular Drugs

- Angiotensin-converting enzyme inhibitors (Vasotec, Capoten) can cause fetal renal tubular dysplasia in T2 and T3 → oligohydramnios, fetal limb contractures, craniofacial deformities, hypoplastic lung development.
- Propranolol (Inderal) shows no evidence of teratogenicity:
  - Fetal bradycardia has been seen as a direct dose effect when given to mother 2 hours prior to delivery.
  - Increased risk of IUGR seen with maternal use

Androgens/Progestins

- Androgens may masculinize a developing female fetus
- Progestational agents (e.g., Danazol) (often synthetic testosterone derivatives) may cause clitoromegaly and labial fusion if given prior to 13 weeks' GA.

MEDICAL CONDITIONS AND PREGNANCY

> Pregnancy testing is recommended before prescribing hormonal medications in patients with anovulatory symptoms and menstrual irregularities.

Endocrine Disorders in Pregnancy

DIABETES MELLITUS

See Table 8-1.

- *Pregestational diabetes*—patient had DM before pregnancy
- *Gestational diabetes*—patient develops diabetes only during pregnancy. Gestational diabetes is classified as type A according to White classification.
  - White classification A1—controlled with diet
  - White classification A2—requires insulin

Screening

Screening is controversial, but tests often used are:

1. **Glucose challenge test**—at 26 to 28 weeks:
   - Give 50-mg glucose load (nonfasting state).
   - Draw glucose blood level 1 hour later.

TABLE 8-1. Diabetes Classifications

Class	Onset	Fasting Plasma Glucose	2-Hour Postprandial Glucose	Duration (yrs)	Vascular Disease	Therapy
A_1	Gestational	< 95 mg/dL	< 120 mg/dL	—	—	Diet and exercise
A_2	Gestational	< 95 mg/dL	> 120 mg/dL	—	—	Insulin

Class	Onset	Duration (yrs)	Vascular Disease	Therapy
B	> 20 yrs old	< 10	None	Insulin
C	10–19 yrs old	10–19	None	Insulin
D	Before age 10	> 20	Benign retinopathy	Insulin
F	Any	Any	Nephropathy (pronounced "neFropathy")	Insulin
R	Any	Any	Proliferative Retinopathy	Insulin
H	Any	Any	Heart	Insulin

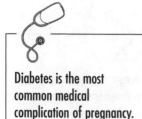

Diabetes is the most common medical complication of pregnancy.

Gestational diabetes probably results from **placental lactogen** secreted during pregnancy, which has large glucagon-like effects.

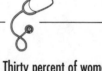

Thirty percent of women with gestational diabetes develop other diabetes later.

The CNS anomaly most specific to DM is **caudal regression.**

- > 140 is high (a 3-hour glucose tolerance test is then required to diagnose GDM).
- If ≥ 200, patient is diagnosed with GDM type A1 and a diabetic diet is initiated.
2. **3-Hour glucose tolerance test**—if glucose challenge test is > 140 and < 200
    - Draw fasting glucose level; normal(n) < 95
    - Give 100-g glucose load.
    - Draw glucose levels at 1 hour (n < 180), at 2 hours (n < 155), and at 3 hours (n < 140).
    - Positive for gestational diabetes if 2/4 high values

Risk Factors
- *Be extra careful to test:*
    - Previous or family history of gestational diabetes
    - Obesity
    - History of large babies
    - History of full-term stillbirth or child with cardiac defects

Effects of Gestational Diabetes

Maternal Effects
- Four times increased risk of preeclampsia
- Increased risk of bacterial infections
- Higher rate of C-section
- Increased risk of polyhydramnios
- Increased risk of birth injury

Fetal Effects
- Increased risk of perinatal death
- Three times increased risk of fetal anomalies (renal, cardiac, and CNS)
- Two to three times increased risk of preterm delivery
- Fetal macrosomia increases risk of birth injury.
- Metabolic derangements (hypoglycemia, hypocalcemia)

Management

The key factors involved in successful management of these high-risk pregnancies include:
- Good glucose control:
    - Prepregnancy glucose levels should be maintained during pregnancy with insulin.
    - Glucose control should be checked at each prenatal visit.

Starting at 32 to 34 weeks:
- *Fetal monitoring:*
    - Ultrasonography to evaluate fetal growth, estimated weight, amniotic fluid volume, and fetal anatomy at 16 to 20 weeks' GA
    - Nonstress test and amniotic fluid index testing weekly to biweekly depending on disease severity
    - Biophysical profile
    - Contraction stress test (oxytocin challenge test)
- *Early elective delivery:*
    - Fetal macrosomia must be ruled out with ultrasonography.

If fetal weight is > 4,500 g, elective cesarean section should be considered to avoid shoulder dystocia. Unless there is an obstetric complication, induction of labor and vaginal delivery are done.

HYPERTHYROIDISM/GRAVES' DISEASE

- Thyrotoxicosis complicates 1 in 2,000 pregnancies.
- Graves' disease is the most common cause of thyrotoxicosis in pregnancy.
- Treatment is propylthiouricil or methimazole or surgery. **Radioactive iodine is contraindicated in pregnancy.**

Thyroid Storm

Thyroid storm is a major risk. Precipitating factors are infection, labor, and C-section.

Treatment
- Beta blocker
- Sodium iodide
- Parathyroid hormone (PTH)
- Dexamethasone

25% mortality rate

Complications
- 1% risk of neonatal thyrotoxicosis
- Fetal goiter/hypothyroid, usually from PTU
- Preterm delivery
- Preeclampsia
- Preterm delivery

Hypothyroidism

Subclinical hypothyroidism is more common than overt hypothyroidism, and often goes unnoticed. Diagnosed by elevated TSH.

Postpartum Thyroiditis

Transient postpartum hypothyroidism or thyrotoxicosis associated with autoimmune thyroiditis is common:
- Between 1 and 4 months postpartum, 4% of all women develop transient thyrotoxicosis.
- Between 4 and 8 months postpartum, 2 to 5% of all women develop hypothyroidism.

Sheehan Syndrome

Pituitary ischemia and necrosis associated with obstetrical blood loss leading to hypopituitarism. Patients do not lactate postpartum due to low prolactin.

Epilepsy and Pregnancy

- Epileptic women taking anticonvulsants during pregnancy have double the general population risk of malformations and preeclampsia.
- Women with a convulsive disorder have an increased risk of birth defects even when they do not take anticonvulsant medications.

In normal pregnancy, total T_3 and T_4 are elevated but free thyroxine levels do not change.

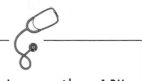

Propylthiouracil (PTU) is the drug of choice over methimazole for treating thyrotoxicosis in pregnancy.

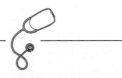

Overt hypothyroidism is often associated with infertility.

In women with type 1 DM, 25% develop postpartum thyroid dysfunction.

- Pregnant epileptics are more prone to seizures due to the associated stress and fatigue of pregnancy.
- The fetus is at risk for megaloblastic anemia.
- The pregnant female and her fetus are at risk for hemorrhage due to a deficiency of vitamin K–dependent clotting factors induced by anticonvulsant drugs.
- Management of the epileptic female should begin with prepregnancy counseling.
- Anticonvulsant therapy should be reduced to the minimum dose of the minimum number of anticonvulsant medications.
- Folic acid supplementation (5 mg/day) should be taken by those women taking anticonvulsants.
- Once pregnant, the patient should be screened for NTDs and congenital malformations.
- Blood levels of anticonvulsant medications should be checked at the beginning of pregnancy to determine the drug level that controls epileptic episodes successfully.

Folic acid supplementation is increased in the epileptic patient to 5 mg/day.

HIV and Pregnancy

- HIV infection is now among the 10 leading causes of death among children aged 1 to 4 years.
- The vast majority of cases of pediatric AIDS are secondary to vertical transmission from mother to fetus.

At the preconception visit, encourage maternal HIV screening.

The majority of new cases of AIDS in women are among those 20 to 29 years of age.

THE HIV+ PATIENT

- Reduce maternal viral load.
  - Zidovudine (ZDV) should be given in the antepartum period beginning at 14 weeks.
  - CD4+ counts and viral loads should be monitored at regular intervals.
  - Blood counts and liver functions should be monitored monthly while on ZDV.
- Reduce intrapartum transmission.
  - Give maternal intravenous ZDV.
- Reduce peripartum exposure.
  - Reduce duration of ruptured membranes.
  - Offer elective cesarean section to mother.
  - Avoid breast feeding.
- Administer newborn prophylaxis.
  - Give ZDV syrup to newborn for 6 weeks.

Anemia commonly occurs in mothers on ZDV.

Cardiovascular Disease

Pregnancy-induced hemodynamic changes have profound effects on underlying heart disease.

Cardiovascular disease (CVD) complicates 1% of all pregnancies and significantly contributes to maternal mortality.

MITRAL STENOSIS (MS)

Pathophysiology
- Increased preload due to normal increase in blood volume results in left atrial overload and backup into the lungs resulting in **pulmonary hypertension.**

Sequelae
- Tachycardia associated with labor and delivery is exacerbates the pulmonary HTN because of decreased filling time.
- *Postpartum period is the most hazardous time.*

Treatment
- Antibiotic prophylaxis

MITRAL VALVE PROLAPSE

These patients are normally asymptomatic and have a systolic click on physical exam. They will generally have a safe pregnancy. Antibiotics should be give for prophylaxis against endocarditis.

EISENMENGER SYNDROME AND OTHER CONDITIONS WITH PULMONARY HTN

These conditions are extremely dangerous to the mother and possibly justify the termination of pregnancies on medical grounds. Maternal mortality can be as high as 50%, with death usually occurring in the postpartum.

AORTIC STENOSIS

- Similar problems with mitral stenosis
- Avoid tachycardia and fluid overload.
- Give antibiotic prophylaxis.

Pulmonary Disease

The adaptations to the respiratory system during pregnancy must be able to satisfy the increased O_2 demands of the hyperdynamic circulation and the fetus. Advanced pregnancy may worsen the pathophysiological effects of many acute and chronic lung diseases.

ASTHMA

Epidemiology
One to four percent of pregnancies are complicated by asthma:
- 25% of asthmatics worsen in pregnancy.
- 25% improve.
- 50% have no change.

Management EXAM FACT
- Generally, asthma is exacerbated by respiratory tract infections, so killed influenza vaccine should be given.
- Pregnant asthmatics can be treated with theophylline, beta sympathomimetics, or steroids.

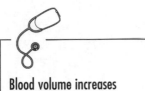

Cardiac output increases by 30 to 50% by midpregnancy.

Blood volume increases 50% by 30th week.

Twenty-five percent of women with mitral stenosis have cardiac failure for the first time during pregnancy.

Prolapse = okay to be Pregnant
Stenosis = Sick in pregnancy

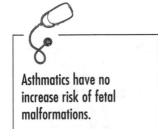

Asthmatics have no increase risk of fetal malformations.

Management of Status Asthmaticus
- Give oxygen.
- Give SQ terbutaline.
- Give IV corticosteroids.

PULMONARY EMBOLISM (PE)

The likelihood of venous thromboembolism in normal pregnancy and the puerperium is increased fivefold when compared to nonpregnant women of similar age:
- Occurs in 1/7,000 women
- Complications include maternal death.

Renal and Urinary Tract Disorders

Pregnancy causes hydronephrosis (dilatation of renal pelvis, calyces, and ureters) because the baby compresses the lower ureter and because the hormonal milieu decreases ureteral tone. This may lead to urinary stasis and increased vesicoureteral reflux.

Two to seven percent of pregnant women have UTIs; 25% are asymptomatic.

PYELONEPHRITIS

Acute pyelonephritis is the most common serious medical complication of pregnancy and occurs in 1 to 2% of pregnant women. Management includes:
- Hospitalization
- IV antibiotics (ampicillin or cefazolin)
- Monitor fluids

Acute Abdomen in Pregnancy

During advanced pregnancy, GI symptoms become difficult to assess and physical findings are often obscured by the enlarged uterus.

Differential
- Pylonephritis
- Appendicitis
- Pancreatitis
- Cholecystitis
- Ovarian torsion

APPENDICITIS

- Appendicitis is the most common surgical condition in pregnancy (occurs 1 in 2,000 births).
- Has usual symptoms
- Uterus displaces the appendix superiorly and laterally. Pain and tenderness may not be found at McBurney's point (RLQ).
- Incidence is same throughout pregnancy, but rupture is more frequent in T3 (40%) than T1 (10%).
- Management is appendectomy.

Pyelonephritis in pregnant women is on the right side 86% of the time.

Dangers of appendix rupture:
- Abortion
- Preterm labor
- Maternal–fetal sepsis → neonatal neurologic injury

Increased estrogens cause **increase in cholesterol** saturation, which, in addition to **biliary stasis**, leads to **more gallstones** in pregnant women.

CHOLELITHIASIS AND CHOLECYSTITIS

- Incidence of cholecystitis is 1 in 4,000 pregnancies (more common than nonpregnant).
- Same clinical picture as nonpregnant
- Medical management unless common bile duct obstruction or pancreatitis develops, in which case a cholescystectomy should be perfomed.
- High risk of preterm labor

Anemia

- *Physiologic anemia* is normal anemia in pregnancy because of hemodilution due to volume expansion.
- Anemia for a pregnant woman is a drop in Hgb by 10 g/dL or Hct by 30%.
- *Incidence:* 20 to 60% of pregnant women, 80% is iron-deficiency type
- *Risks:* Preterm delivery, IUGR, low birth weight
- Therapy is 325 mg tid of $FeSO_4$ (prophylaxis is q d)

INFECTION AND PREGNANCY

See Tables 8-2 through 8-4

Persistent nausea and vomiting in *late* pregnancy should prompt a search for underlying pathology (e.g., gastroenteritis, cholecystitis, pancreatitis, hepatitis, peptic ulcer, pyelonephritis, fatty liver of pregnancy, and psychological or social issues).

The two most common causes of anemia during pregnancy and the puerperium are iron deficiency and acute blood loss.

TABLE 8-2. Perinatal Infections

Intrauterine[a]	Viral	Bacterial	Protozoan
Transplacental	Varicella-zoster Coxsackie virus Parvovirus Rubella Cytomegalovirus Human immuno- deficiency virus (HIV)	*Listeria* Syphilis	Toxoplasmosis Malaria
Ascending infection	Herpes simplex (HSV)	Group B *Streptococcus* (GBS) Coliforms	
Intrapartum[b]			
Maternal exposure	HSV Papillomavirus HIV HBV	Gonorrhea *Chlamydia* GBS TB	
External contami- nation	HSV	*Staphylococcus* Coliforms	

TABLE 8-2. Perinatal Infections (continued)

Neonatal

Human trans-mission	HSV	*Staphylococcus*
Respirators and catheters		*Staphylococcus* Coliforms

[a] Bacteria, viruses, or parasites may gain access transplacentally or cross the intact membranes.
[b] Organisms may colonize and infect the fetus during L&D.

TABLE 8-3. Viral Infections and Their Potential Fetal Effects

Virus	Fetal Effects	Maternal Effects	Prophylaxis	Treatment
Varicella-zoster[a]	**Transmitted transplacentally** ■ Chorioretinitis ■ Cerebral cortical atrophy ■ Hydronephrosis ■ Cutaneous and bony leg defects (scars) ■ Microcephaly	Pneumonitis	Vaccine *not* recommended for pregnant women	Varicella-zoster immunoglobulin within 96 hrs of exposure C-section should be performed if there are active lesions.
Orthomyxoviridae	■ Infection ■ Neural tube defects	■ Pneumonia ■ Death	Vaccination is recommended for pregnant women who have chronic underlying disease or who are routinely exposed.	Amantadine within 48 hrs of onset of symptoms in non-immunized, high-risk patients
Parvovirus B19	■ Abortion ■ Death ■ Congenital anomalies ■ Hydrops	Viremia → slapped cheek appearance		If + serology → US; if + hydrops → consider fetal transfusion.
Rubella	**Congenital rubella syndrome** ■ Cataracts/glaucoma ■ Patent ductus arteriosus ■ Deafness ■ Mental retardation		Vaccination (attenuated live virus) of the non-pregnant female	Consider therapeutic abortion, depending on time of exposure during pregnancy.
Hepatitis B		Range from mild liver disfunction to death	Maternal screening early in pregnancy. Maternal HbsAg positive is high risk of transmitting to fetus. If mother is positive, give neonate HepB IgG at birth, 3 months, and 6 months.	

TABLE 8-3. Viral Infections and Their Potential Fetal Effects (continued)

Virus	Fetal Effects	Maternal Effects	Prophylaxis	Treatment
Cytomegalovirus	Causes in utero infection in 1% of all newborns but only 10% of infected show disease. ■ **Cytomegalic inclusion disease** ■ Hepatospleno-megaly ■ Thrombocytopenia ■ Microcephaly ■ Intracranial calcifications ■ Chorioretinitis ■ Mental retardation ■ Jaundice	Mononucleosis-like syndrome		None

a Infection may be especially severe in pregnant women.

TABLE 8-4. Bacterial Infections and Their Potential Fetal Effects

Bacteria	Fetal Effects	Maternal Effects	Prophylaxis	Treatment
Group B Streptococcus (*Streptococcus agalactiae*)	■ Preterm labor ■ Premature rupture of membranes ■ Ophthalmia neonatorum ■ Sepsis ■ Meningitis → neurologic sequelae in survivors	■ Chorioamnionitis ■ Puerperal sepsis ■ Mastitis ■ Osteomyelitis	Intrapartum maternal penicillin G in women with + cultures at 35–37 wks' GA	Neonatal penicillin G IM in the delivery room (there is no universal treatment)
Salmonella	■ Death	■ Enteritis ■ Bacteremia		IV fluid rehydration*a*
Borrelia burgdorferi (Lyme)	■ Congenital infection ■ Death ■ Preterm labor ■ Rash	■ Erythema migrans ■ Disseminated infection ■ Meningitis ■ Carditis ■ Arthritis		Oral amoxicillin or penicillin
Primary and secondary syphilis	■ Hepatosplenomegaly ■ Lymphadenopathy ■ Hemolysis			
Chlamydia trachomatis	■ Conjunctivitis ■ Pneumonia		■ Screen in early pregnancy	Erythromycin or azithromycin
Neisseria gonorrhoeae	■ Conjunctivitis ■ Otitis externa ■ Pharyngitis		Screen in early pregnancy	Penicillin or ceftriaxone

Bacteria	Fetal Effects	Maternal Effects	Prophylaxis	Treatment
Toxoplasma gondii	Transplacental infection occurs. ■ Congenital disease 　■ Hydrocephaly/ microcephaly 　■ Hepatospleno-megaly 　■ Seizures 　■ Intracranial calcifications 　■ Chorioretinitis 　■ Mental retardation			Spiramycin (macrolide antibiotic)

[a] Antimicrobials prolong the carrier state and are not given in uncomplicated infections.

Complications of Pregnancy

HYPERTENSION IN PREGNANCY

Hypertension-related problems in pregnancy are classified in four ways:
- Chronic hypertension (HTN)
- Pregnancy-induced HTN
- Preeclampsia
- Eclampsia

The hypertension in each of these diagnoses is classified as:
Mild: Systolic ≥ 140 mm Hg and/or diastolic ≥ 90 mm Hg
Severe: Systolic > 160 mm Hg and/or diastolic > 110 mm Hg

See Figure 9-1 for management algorithm.

The only cure for hypertension in pregnancy (except preexisting chronic HTN) is delivery.

Pathophysiology of Hypertension in Pregnancy

Normal
Arachadonic acid triggers two pathways:

1. Prostacycline: *Decreases blood pressure* via:
   - Decreased vasoconstriction
   - Increased uteroplacental blood flow
2. Thromboxane: *Increases blood pressure* via:
   - Increased vasoconstriction
   - Decreased uteroplacental blood flow

Hypertension-related deaths in pregnancy account for 15% (second after pulmonary embolism) of maternal deaths.

In Pregnancy-Hypertensive States
The balance is thought to be tipped toward the thromboxane pathway.

CHRONIC HYPERTENSION (HTN) AND PREGNANCY

Defined as hypertension that antecedes pregnancy:
Mild: Systolic ≥ 140 mm Hg and/or diastolic ≥ 90 mm Hg
Severe: Systolic > 160 mm Hg and/or diastolic > 110 mm Hg

If during pregnancy a chronic hypertensive patient's systolic blood pressure (BP) rises by 30 mm Hg or diastolic rises by 15 mm Hg, it is **pregnancy-induced hypertension superimposed on chronic hypertension.**

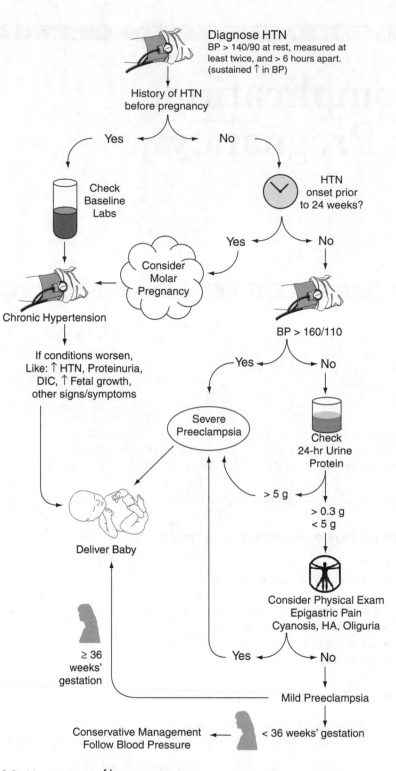

FIGURE 9-1. Management of hypertension in pregnancy.

(Redrawn, with permission, from Lindarkis NM, Lott S. *Digging Up the Bones: Obstetrics and Gynecology.* New York: McGraw-Hill, 1998: 60.)

Management

Mild: Early and serial ultrasounds, biophysicals
Severe:
- Serial ultrasounds and biophysicals
- Antihypertensives (methyldopa or nifedipine)

PREGNANCY-INDUCED HYPERTENSION (PIH)

Defined as hypertension during pregnancy in a previously normotensive woman (the patient had normal blood pressure prior to 20 weeks' gestation):
Mild: Systolic ≥ 140 mm Hg and/or diastolic ≥ 90 mm Hg
Severe: Systolic > 160 mm Hg and/or diastolic > 110 mm Hg (same as chronic HTN)

Subsets of PIH

1. **PIH** (simple)
2. **Preeclampsia:** Renal involvement leads to proteinuria.
3. **Eclampsia:** Central nervous system involvement leads to seizures.
4. **HELLP syndrome:** The clinical picture is dominated by hematologic and hepatic manifestations.

Complications

- Heart failure
- Cerebral hemorrhage
- Placental abruption
- Fetal growth restriction
- Fetal death

Management

Mild: Observe, bed rest
Severe: Always hospitalize + antihypertensive pharmacotherapy (hydralazine or labetalol short term, nifedipine or methyldopa long term)

Generally, for all pregnancy-hypertensive states:
Plus the following:
- If > 36 weeks/fetal lung maturity: Induce labor.
- If < 34 weeks/fetal lung immaturity: Steroids plus expectant management
- If fetal or maternal deterioration at any gestational age, induce labor

PREECLAMPSIA

Preeclampsia is pregnancy-induced hypertension with proteinuria +/− pathological edema. It is classified as mild or severe.

Preeclampsia rarely develops before 20 weeks and usually occurs in a first pregnancy.

Criteria for Mild Preeclampsia

- BP: ≥ 140 systolic or ≥ 90 diastolic
- Proteinuria: 300 mg to 5 g/24 hrs (norm: < 300 mg/24 hrs in pregnancy, < 150 mg/24 hrs in nonpregnant state)

Manifestations of Severe Disease

- BP: > 160 systolic or > 110 diastolic

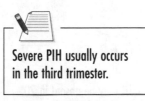

In PIH, you must monitor for intrauterine growth retardation (IUGR) and progression to superimposed preeclampsia (15 to 25% incidence).

Severe PIH usually occurs in the third trimester.

Symptoms of severe disease include:
- **Headache**
- **Visual disturbances**
- **Epigastric pain**

The only definitive treatment for PIH is delivery.

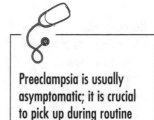

Preeclampsia is usually asymptomatic; it is crucial to pick up during routine prenatal visits.

- Proteinuria: > 5 g/24 hrs
- Elevated serum creatinine
- Oliguria (< 500 mL/24 hrs)
- Symptoms suggesting end organ involvement:
  - Headache
  - Visual disturbances
  - Epigastric/right upper quadrant pain
- Pulmonary edema
- Hepatocellular dysfunction (elevated aspartate transaminase [AST], alanine transaminase [ALT])
- Thrombocytopenia
- IUGR or oligohydramnios
- Microangiopathic hemolysis
- Grand mal seizures (eclampsia)

Predisposing Factors

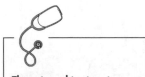

- Nulliparity
- Family history of preeclampsia–eclampsia
- Multiple fetuses
- Diabetes
- Chronic vascular disease
- Renal disease
- Hydatidiform mole
- Fetal hydrops

HELLP Syndrome

HELLP syndrome is a manifestation of preeclampsia with **h**emolysis, **e**levated **l**iver enzymes, and **l**ow **p**latelets. In contrast to typical presentations of preeclampsia, it is associated with:
- High morbidity
- Multiparous mothers
- Mothers older than 25
- Less than 36 weeks' gestation

Diagnosis of Preeclampsia

Once preeclampsia is suspected, the following tests should be done:

Blood: Electrolytes, blood urea nitrogen (BUN), creatinine, liver function tests (LFTs) (ALT, AST), complete blood count (CBC), uric acid, and platelet count

Urine: Sediment, 24-hour protein, 24-hour creatinine

Fetal: Ultrasound, nonstress test, biophysical profile

Management

Varies depending on severity of disease and gestational age of fetus:

Mild Preeclampsia
- Hospitalize, observe, bed rest, low-salt diet, monitor labs closely

Severe Preeclampsia
- **Hospitalize,** bed rest, low salt, low calories
- **Antihypertensive pharmacotherapy:** Hydralazine or labetalol short term, nifedipine or methyldopa long term
- **Anticonvulsive therapy:** Magnesium sulfate

Plus the following:

- If > 36 weeks/fetal lung maturity: Induce labor.
- If < 34 weeks/fetal lung immaturity: Steroids plus expectant management
- If fetal or maternal deterioration at any gestational age: Induce labor.

The only cure is delivery.

ECLAMPSIA

Criteria

- Mild or severe preeclampsia
- Generalized seizures

Management

1. Control of the convulsions (magnesium sulfate IV and IM)
2. Correction of hypoxia and acidosis
3. BP control (hydralazine or labetalol)
4. Delivery after control of convulsions

ANTIHYPERTENSIVE AGENTS USED IN PREGNANCY

Short-Term Control
- *Hydralazine:* IV or PO, direct vasodilator
  Side effects: Systemic lupus erythematosus (SLE)-like syndrome, headache, palpitations
- *Labetalol:* IV or PO, nonselective beta-1 and alpha-1 blocker
  Side effects: Headache and tremor

Long-Term Control
- *Methyldopa:* PO, false neurotransmitter
  Side effects: Postural hypotension, drowsiness, fluid retention
- *Nifedipine:* PO, calcium channel blocker
  Side effects: Edema, dizziness
- *Atenolol:* PO, selective beta-1 blocker
  Side effect: breathlessness

PRETERM LABOR

Criteria

Gestational age (GA) < 37 weeks with regular uterine contractions and:
- Progressive cervical change

or

- A cervix that is 2 cm dilated

or

- A cervix 80% effaced

or

- Ruptured membranes

- 25% of seizures are before labor.
- 50% of seizures are during labor.
- 25% of seizures are post-labor (may be encountered up to 10 days postpartum).

Magnesium toxicity (7 to 10 mEq/L) is associated with loss of patellar reflexes. Treat with calcium gluconate 10% solution 1 g IV.

Braxton Hicks contractions (irregular, nonrhythmical, usually painless contractions that begin at early gestation and increase as term approaches) may make it difficult to distinguish between true and false labor.

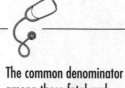

The common denominator among these fetal and maternal conditions that may induce preterm labor has not been determined.

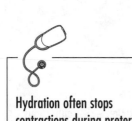

Most infants born after 34 weeks' GA will survive (the survival rate is within 1% of the survival rate beyond 37 weeks).

Hydration often stops contractions during preterm labor.

Epidemiology

Preterm labor has been associated with the following findings:

1. **Infection:**
   - Systemic
   - Pyelonephritis urinary tract infection (UTI)/sexually transmitted disease (STD)
   - Chorioamnionitis
2. **Maternal factors:**
   - Low socioeconomic status
   - Coitus
   - Long work hours
   - Youth
   - Grand multiparity
   - ETOH/smoking/narcotics
   - Previous preterm labor
   - Previous abortion
   - Preeclampsia/eclampsia/HTN
3. **Anomalies:**
   - Uterine (septated uterus, fibroids)
   - Cervical incompetence
   - Multifetal pregnancy
   - Polyhydramnios
   - Fetal anomalies
   - Placenta previa/abruptio

Assessment

- Frequency of uterine contractions
- Possible causes such as infection
- Confirm GA of fetus (i.e., by ultrasound).
- Assess fetal well-being with a biophysical profile.

Management of Preterm Labor

HYDRATION

Always hydrate first in preterm labor. It often stops contractions. Dehydration causes antidiuretic hormone (ADH) secretion, and ADH mimics oxytocin (both made in posterior pituitary).

TOCOLYTIC THERAPY

Tocolysis is used if < 34 weeks.

Tocolytic Agents
- IV magnesium sulfate—suppresses uterine contractions
- Oral calcium channel blocker (nifedipine)
- Beta mimetics (ritodrine, terbutaline)—stimulate beta-2 receptors on myometrial cells → increase cyclic adenosine monophosphate (cAMP) → decrease intracellular Ca → decrease contractions
  Side effects: Pulmonary edema, tachycardia, headaches

- Prostaglandin inhibitors (indomethacin)
  Side effects: Premature constriction of ductus arteriosus, pulmonary HTN, and interventricular hemorrhage

Contraindications to Tocolysis
- Severe **B**leeding from any cause
- Severe **A**bruptio placentae
- Fetal **D**eath/life-incompatible anomaly
- **C**horioamnionitis
- Severe pregnancy-induced **H**ypertension
- **U**nstable maternal hemodynamics

Action
- Acts as Ca^{2+} antagonist and reduces actin–myosin interaction (at 7 mg/100 mL)

Side Effects
- Decreases deep tendon reflexes (at 8 to 10 mg/100 mL)
- Respiratory/cardiac depression (at > 12 mg/100 mL)
- Flushing, warmth, headaches, nystagmus, dizziness, dry mouth, hypocalcemia

About Magnesium Sulfate

- Magnesium sulfate antagonizes Ca and decreases intracellular Ca, thus decreasing contractions. It is 70 to 90% effective in achieving 2 to 3 days of tocolysis.
  Side effects: Depressed reflexes, pulmonary edema, fatigue. Toxicity is treated with calcium gluconate.

Mg Level	Side Effect
4–7 mg	Uterine contractions decreased
8–12 mg	Depressed deep tendon reflexes
> 12 mg	Respiratory/cardiac depression

Corticosteroids

- Given to patients in preterm labor from 24 to 35 weeks unless they have chorioamnionitis
- Reduce fetal mortality: Accelerate fetal lung maturity (decreases respiratory distress syndrome [RDS]), reduce intraventricular hemorrhage, and reduce necrotizing enterocolitis

Lecithin–Sphingomyelin Ratio

An amniocentesis may be performed to assess fetal lungs for risk of RDS. Fetal lungs are mature if:
- Phosphatidylglycerol is present in amniotic fluid

or
- Lecithin–sphingomyelin ratio is > 2

Mnemonic for contraindications to tocolysis: **BAD CHU**
- Severe **B**leeding from any cause
- Severe **A**bruptio placentae
- Fetal **D**eath/life-incompatible anomaly
- **C**horioamnionitis
- Severe pregnancy-induced **H**ypertension
- **U**nstable maternal hemodynamics

Complications of Pregnancy

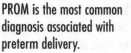

PROM is the most common diagnosis associated with preterm delivery.

Prolonged rupture of membranes can be caused by premature rupture (PROM) *or* an abnormally long labor (not PROM).

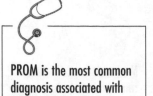

The patient's history alone is correct in 90% of patients. Urinary leakage or excess vaginal discharge can be mistaken for PROM.

Nitrazine may be false positive with contamination from blood, semen, or vaginitis.

Premature rupture denotes spontaneous rupture of fetal membranes *before the onset of labor*. This can occur at term (PROM) or preterm (PPROM).

Etiology

Unknown but hypothesized: Vaginal and cervical infections, incompetent cervix, abnormal membranes, nutritional deficiencies

Risks

- *Prolonged rupture of membranes:* The rupture of membranes > 18 to 24 hours before labor. Patients who do not go into labor immediately will have prolonged rupture of membranes and are at increasing risk of infection as the duration of rupture increases:
  - **Chorioamnionitis** and other infections
  - Neonatal infection
  - Umbilical cord prolapse

Only if preterm PROM:
- *Prematurity:* If PROM occurs at < 37 weeks, the fetus is at risk of being born prematurely.
- *Oligohydramnios:* If PROM occurs at < 24 weeks, there is a risk of oligohydramnios (depleted amniotic fluid), which may cause **pulmonary hypoplasia.** *Survival at this age is low.*

Diagnosis of Rupture of Membranes (ROM)

A digital exam should *not* be performed, as it increases the risk of infection:
- **Sterile speculum examination:**
  - Visualize extent of cervical effacement and dilation, and exclude prolapsed cord or protruding fetal extremity.
  - **Pool test:** Identify fluid coming from the cervix or pooled in the posterior fornix of the vagina → supports diagnosis of PROM.
- **Nitrazine test:** Put fluid on nitrazine paper, which turns blue if fluid is alkaline. Alkaline pH indicates fluid is amniotic.
- **Ferning test:** A swab from the posterior fornix is smeared on a slide, allowed to dry, and examined under a microscope for "ferning" → + for amniotic fluid.

Management of All PROM Patients

- Evaluate patient for chorioamnionitis (common etiology of PROM):
  - Fever > 38°C, leukocytosis, maternal/fetal tachycardia, uterine tenderness, malodorous vaginal discharge
  - Gram stain and culture of amniotic fluid to assess for chorioamnionitis
- If positive for chorioamnionitis, delivery is performed despite GA, and antibiotics are initiated (ampicillin, gentamicin).

Specific Management for PROM at Term

Ninety percent of term patients go into spontaneous labor within 24 hours after rupture:
- Patients in active labor should be allowed to progress.
- If labor is not spontaneous, it should be induced or cesarean delivery should be performed.

Specific Management of PPROM

Fifty percent of preterm patients go into labor within 24 hours after rupture.

Generally, one needs to balance the risks of premature birth against the risk of infection (which increases with the time that membranes are ruptured before birth). Management is aimed at assessing these risks and acting accordingly:
- Gram stain and culture of amniotic fluid to assess for chorioamnionitis
- If chorioamnionitis is suspected, begin ampicillin and/or erythromycin prophylaxis.
- Amniotic fluid assessment of lecithin–sphingomyelin ratio for lung maturity
- Perform ultrasound to assess gestational age, position of baby, and level of fluid.
- If < 34 weeks, give steroids to decrease incidence of RDS.
- Expectant management
- **ROM:** Rupture of membranes
- **PROM:** Premature rupture of membranes (ROM before the onset of labor)
- **PPROM:** Preterm (< 37 weeks) premature rupture of membranes
- **Prolonged rupture of membranes:** Rupture of membranes that lasts > 18 hours

If nitrazine and pooling are nonconfirmatory, ferning test is useful.

Don't get the ROMs mixed up!

THIRD-TRIMESTER BLEEDING

INCIDENCE

Occurs in 2 to 5% of pregnancies

WORKUP

- History and physical
- Vitals
- Labs: CBC, coagulation profile, type and cross, urine analysis

See Figure 9-2 for management algorithm.

Determine whether blood is maternal or fetal or both:
- **Apt test:** Put blood from vagina in tube with KOH:
  - Turns brown for maternal
  - Turns pink for fetus
- **Kleihauer–Betke test:** Take blood from mother's arm and determine percentage of fetal RBCs in maternal circulation: > 1% = fetal bleeding.
- **Wright's stain:** Vaginal blood; nucleated RBCs indicate fetal bleed.

Golden rule:
Never initially do a pelvic exam in a third-trimester bleed.

Apt, Kleihauer–Betke, and Wright's stain tests determine if blood is fetal, maternal, or both.

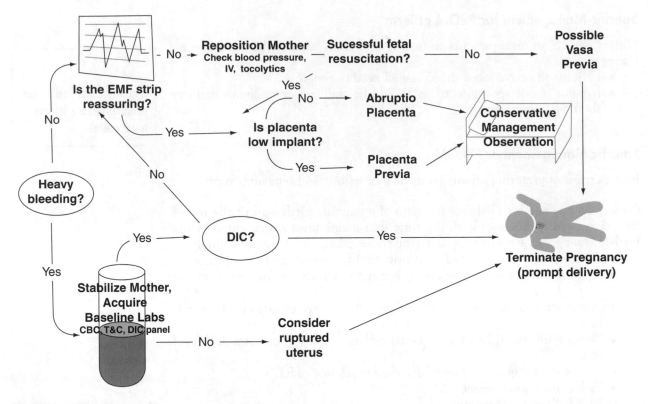

FIGURE 9-2. Management of third-trimester bleeding.

(Redrawn, with permission, from Lindarkis NM, Lott S. *Digging Up the Bones: Obstetrics and Gynecology.* New York: McGraw-Hill, 1998: 50.)

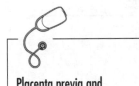

Placenta previa and abruption are most common.

Most nonobstetric causes result in relatively little blood loss and minimal threat to the mother and fetus.

DIFFERENTIAL

Obstetric Causes
- Placental abruption
- Placenta previa
- Vasa previa/velamentous insertion
- Uterine rupture
- Circumvillate placenta
- Extrusion of cervical mucus ("bloody show")

Nonobstetric Causes
- Cervicitis
- Polyp
- Neoplasm

Placental Abruption (Abruptio Placentae)

Premature separation of placenta from uterine wall before the delivery of baby (see Figure 9-3)

INCIDENCE

0.5 to 4%

MORTALITY

- Maternal: 1 to 5%
- Fetal: 50 to 80%

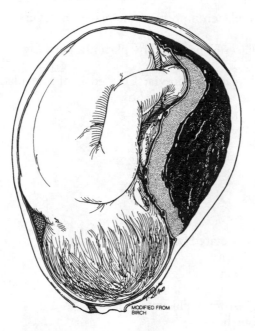

FIGURE 9-3. Placental abruption.

(Reproduced, with permission, from Cunningham FG, MacDonald PC, Gant NF, et al. *Williams Obstetrics,* 20th ed. Stamford, CT: Appleton & Lange, 1997: 747.)

RISK FACTORS

Trauma (usually shearing, such as a car accident), preeclampsia (and maternal HTN), smoking, cocaine abuse, high parity, previous history of abruption

CLINICAL PRESENTATION

- Vaginal bleeding (maternal and fetal blood present)
- **Constant and severe back pain** or uterine tenderness
- Irritable, tender, and typically hypertonic uterus
- Evidence of fetal distress
- Maternal shock

DIAGNOSIS

- Ultrasound will show retroplacental hematoma only part of the time.
- Clinical and pathological findings

MANAGEMENT

- Correct shock (packed RBCs, fresh frozen plasma, cryoprecipitate, platelets).
- Expectant management: Close observation of mother and fetus with ability to intervene immediately
- If there is fetal distress, perform C-section.

Placenta Previa

A condition in which the placenta is implanted in the immediate vicinity of the cervical canal. It can be classified into three types:

> Pregnant woman + car accident + back pain = abruption.

> Bleeding is present in 50 to 80% of cases.

- **Complete placenta previa:** The placenta covers the entire internal cervical os.
- **Partial placenta previa:** The placenta partially covers the internal cervical os.
- **Marginal placenta previa:** One edge of the placenta extends to the edge of the internal cervical os.

See Figure 9-4.

INCIDENCE

0.5 to 1%

ETIOLOGY

Unknown, but associated with:
- Increased parity
- Older mothers
- Previous abortions
- Previous history of placenta previa
- Fetal anomalies

CLINICAL PRESENTATION

- **Painless,** profuse bleeding in T3
- Postcoital bleeding
- Spotting during T1 and T2
- Cramping (10% of cases)

**Painless bleeding =
Placenta Previa**

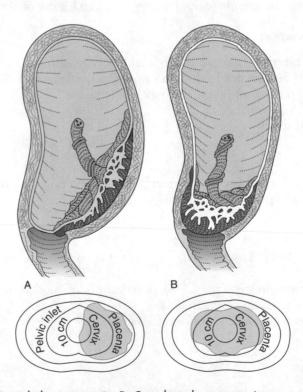

FIGURE 9-4. A. Partial placenta previa. **B.** Complete placenta previa.

(Reproduced, with permission, from DeCherney AH, Pernoll ML. *Current Obstetric & Gynecologic Diagnosis & Treatment.* Norwalk, CT: Appleton & Lange, 1994: 404.)

- **Transabdominal ultrasound** (95% accurate)
- **Double set-up exam:** Take the patient to the operating room and prep for a C-section. Do speculum exam: If there is local bleeding, do a C-section; if not, palpate fornices to determine if placenta is covering the os. The double set-up exam is performed only on the rare occasion that the ultrasound is inconclusive.

MANAGEMENT

Cesarean section is always the delivery method of choice for placenta previa. The specific management is geared toward different situations.

For Preterm
- If there is no pressing need for delivery, monitor in hospital or send home after bleeding has ceased.
- Transfusions to replace blood loss, and tocolytics to prolong labor to 36 weeks if necessary

Even after the bleeding has stopped, repeated small hemorrhages may cause IUGR.

For Mature Fetus
- C-section

For a Patient in Labor
- C-section

If Severe Hemorrhage
- C-section regardless of fetal maturity

Fetal Vessel Rupture

Two conditions cause third-trimester bleeding resulting from fetal vessel rupture: (1) Vasa previa and (2) velamentous cord insertion. These two conditions often occur together.

VASA PREVIA

A condition in which the fetal cord vessels unprotectedly pass over the internal os, making them susceptible to rupture and bleeding

Incidence

0.03 to 0.05%

Presentation

Rapid vaginal bleeding and fetal distress (sinusoidal variation of fetal heart rate)

Management

Correction of shock and immediate C-section

> Vaginal bleeding + sinusoidal variation of fetal heart rate = fetal vessel rupture.

HIGH-YIELD FACTS

Complications of Pregnancy

VELAMENTOUS CORD INSERTION

The velamentous insertion of the umbilical cord into the fetal membranes: In other words, the fetal vessels insert between amnion and chorion. This leaves them susceptible to ripping when the amniotic sac ruptures.

Epidemiology

- 1% of single pregnancies
- 10% of twins
- 50% of triplets

Clinical Presentation

Vaginal bleeding with fetal distress

Management

Correction of shock and immediate C-section

Uterine Rupture

The ripping of the uterine musculature through all of its layers, usually with part of the fetus protruding through the opening

Incidence

0.5%

Risk Factors

Prior uterine scar is associated with 40% of cases:
- Vertical scar: 5% risk
- Transverse scar: 0.5% risk

Presentation and Diagnosis

- **Sudden cessation of uterine contractions with a "tearing" sensation**
- **Recession of the fetal presenting part**
- Increased suprapubic pain and tenderness with labor (may not be readily apparent if analgesia/narcotics are administered)
- Vaginal bleeding (or bloody urine)
- Sudden, severe fetal heart rate decelerations
- Sudden disappearance of fetal heart tones
- Maternal hypovolemia from concealed hemorrhage

Management

- Total abdominal hysterectomy is treatment of choice (after delivery).
- If childbearing is important to the patient, rupture repair is possible but risky.

Other Obstetric Causes of Third-Trimester Bleeding

Circumvillate placenta: The chorionic plate (on fetal side of the placenta) is smaller than the basal plate (located on the maternal side), causing amnion and chorion to fold back onto themselves. This forms a ridge around the placenta with a central depression on the fetal surface.

> All pregnant patients with a previous cesarean section must be consented for an elective "trial of labor" (vaginal delivery) with knowledge of the risk of uterine rupture:
> < 1% if previous low transverse C-section × 1
> < 2% if previous low transverse C-section × 2
> 10% if previous classical C-section × 1

Extrusion of cervical mucus ("bloody show"): A consequence of efface-ment and dilation of the cervix, with tearing of the small veins → slight shedding of blood. Treatment is rarely necessary.

ABNORMALITIES OF THE THIRD STAGE OF LABOR

Immediate Postpartum Hemorrhage

- Postpartum hemorrhage denotes excessive bleeding (> 500 mL in vagi-nal delivery; > 1,000 for C-section) following delivery.
- Blood loss during first 24 hours: "Early" postpartum hemorrhage
- Blood loss between 24 hours and 6 weeks after delivery: "Late" postpar-tum hemorrhage

Causes

- Coagulation defects
- Uterine atony (myometrium cannot contract postpartum)
- Ruptured uterus
- Degrees of retained placental tissue
- Bleeding from the placental implantation site
- Trauma to the genital tract and adjacent structures

Most common cause is uterine atony. Normally the uterus contracts, com-pressing blood vessels and preventing bleeding.

Risk Factors

- Blood transfusion/hemorrhage during a previous pregnancy
- Coagulopathy
- Vaginal birth after cesarean (VBAC)
- High parity
- Large infant
- Midforceps delivery

Management

1. Manually compress and massage the uterus—controls virtually all cases of hemorrhage due to atony.
2. Obtain assistance.
3. Give oxytocin (20 units in 1 L of lactated Ringer's) or mether-gonovine or prostaglandins if oxytocin is ineffective.
4. If not previously done, obtain blood for typing and crossmatching/be-gin fluid or blood replacement.
5. Carefully explore the uterine cavity to ensure that all placental parts have been delivered and that the uterus is intact.
6. Inspect the cervix and vagina.
7. Place Foley and monitor urine output.

If all this fails:
- Hysterectomy

or

- Radiographic embolization of pelvic vessels

or

- Uterine artery ligation or hypogastric artery ligation

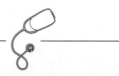

One unit of blood contains 500 mL.

Incidence of excessive blood loss following vaginal delivery is 5 to 8%.

CARPIT (pronounced "carpet")
Coagulation defect
Atony
Rupture
Placenta retained
Implantation site
Trauma

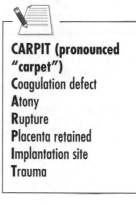

The cause of the postpartum bleeding should be sought out and treated immediately.

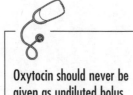

Oxytocin should never be given as undiluted bolus because serious hypotension can result.

Increta = Invades
Percreta = Penetrates

Abnormal Placentation

The abnormal implantation of the placenta in the uterus: These conditions can cause retention of the placenta after birth.

Types of Abnormal Placentation

Placenta accreta: An abnormally adherent implantation of the placenta in which the placental villi attach directly to the myometrium rather than to the decidua basalis

Placenta increta: An abnormally adherent implantation in which the placental villi invade the myometrium

Placenta percreta: An abnormally adherent implantation in which the placental villi penetrate through the myometrium

ETIOLOGY

These conditions are associated with:
- Placenta previa
- Previous C-section
- Previous dilation and curettage (D&C)
- Grand multiparity

MANAGEMENT

All of these conditions often result in postpartum hemorrhage (third stage of labor hemorrhage) and require hysterectomy.

Uterine Inversion

This medical emergency results from an inexperienced person's pulling too hard when delivering the placenta. It can be a result of abnormal placental implantation. Morbidity results from shock and sepsis.

INCIDENCE

1 in 2,200 deliveries

MANAGEMENT

- Call for assistance.
- An anesthesiologist should anesthetize.
- Separate placenta from uterus and replace inverted uterus by pushing on the fundus toward the vagina.
- Oxytocin is given after uterus is restored to normal configuration and anesthesia is stopped.

Macrosomia

Defined as birth weight > 4,500 g:

Risk factors for macrosomia: Diabetes, obesity, previous history, post-term pregnancy, multiparity, and advanced maternal age

Macrosomic infants are at risk for: Birth trauma, jaundice, hypoglycemia, low Apgar scores, childhood tumors

In the majority of instances, bacteria responsible for pelvic infections are those that normally reside in the bowel and colonize the perineum, vagina, and cervix.

Causes

Gram-positive cocci: Group A, B, and D streptococci
Gram-positive bacilli: *Clostridium* species, *Listeria monocytogenes*
Aerobic gram-negative bacilli: *Escherichia coli, Klebsiella, Proteus* species
Anaerobic gram-negative bacilli: *Bacteroides bivius, B. fragilis, B. disiens*
Other: *Mycoplasma hominis, Chlamydia trachomatis*

Risk Factors

- Prolonged rupture of membranes
- C-section
- Colonization of the lower genital tract with certain microorganisms (i.e., group B streptococci, *C. trachomatis, M. hominis,* and *Gardnerella vaginalis*
- Premature labor
- Frequent vaginal exams

Diagnosis

- Fever > 100.4°F (38°C)
- Soft, tender uterus
- Lochia has a foul odor.
- Leukocytosis (WBC > 10,000/μL)
- Malaise

Management

- Identify source of infection (i.e., perform urinalysis).
- Identify the cause of infection (i.e., culture the lochia).
- Assess the severity of the infection.
- Treat (i.e., with antibiotics).

Types of Postpartum Infections

ENDOMETRITIS

- A postpartum uterine infection involving the decidua, myometrium, and parametrial tissue
- Also called *metritis with pelvic cellulitis, endomyometritis,* and *endopara-metritis*
- Typically develops postpartum day 2 to 3
- Treat with IV antibiotics (gentamicin and clindamycin) until patient is afebrile for 24 to 48 hours.

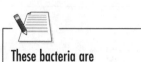

The uterine cavity is sterile before rupture of the amniotic sac.

These bacteria are commonly responsible for female genital infections.

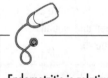

Endometritis is relatively uncommon following vaginal delivery, but a major problem after C-section.

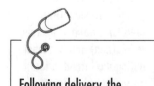

Following delivery, the bladder and lower urinary tract remain somewhat hypotonic → residual urine and reflux.

HIGH-YIELD FACTS

Complications of Pregnancy

URINARY TRACT INFECTION

- Caused by catheterization, birth trauma, conduction anesthesia, and frequent pelvic examinations
- Presents with dysuria, frequency, urgency, and low-grade fever
- Rule out pyelonephritis (costovertebral angle tenderness, pyuria, hematuria).
- Obtain a urinalysis and urinary culture (*E. coli* is isolated in 75% of postpartum women).
- Treat with appropriate antibiotics.

CESAREAN SECTION WOUND INFECTION

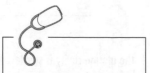

Wound infection occurs in 4 to 12% of patients following C-section.

- Fever that persists to the fourth or fifth postoperative day suggests wound infection.
- Wound erythema and tenderness several days after surgery
- Obtain Gram stain and cultures from wound material.
- Wound should be drained, irrigated, and debrided.
- Antibiotics should be given if extensive infection is suspected.

EPISIOTOMY INFECTION

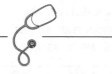

Antibiotic prophylaxis with IV cefazolin is commonly employed.

- Look for pain at the episiotomy site, disruption of the wound, and a necrotic membrane over the wound.
- Rule out the presence of a rectovaginal fistula with a careful rectovaginal exam.
- Open, clean, and debride the wound to promote granulation tissue formation.
- Sitz baths are recommended.
- Reassess for possible closure after granulation tissue has appeared.

MASTITIS

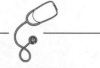

The more extensive the laceration/incision, the greater the chance of infection and wound breakdown.

- Affects 1 to 2% of postpartum women
- Two types: Epidemic (nosocomial) and nonepidemic:
  - **Epidemic mastitis** is caused by infant acquiring *Staphylococcus aureus* in his nasopharynx from the hospital. Mother presents on day 2 to 4 with fever and breast tenderness. Treat with penicillin and isolate from other patients.
  - **Endemic (nonepidemic) mastitis** presents weeks or months after delivery, usually during period of weaning. Mother presents with fever, systemic illness, and breast tenderness. Treat with penicillin or dicloxacillin. Continue breast feeding.

Breast engorgement (painful, swollen, firm breasts) is *not* mastitis (due to infection) and is normal during the second to fourth postpartum day. Treat with supportive bra, 24-hour demand feedings, and ice packs if not breast feeding.

Spontaneous Abortion, Ectopic Pregnancy, and Fetal Death

FIRST-TRIMESTER BLEEDING

DIFFERENTIAL DIAGNOSIS

- Spontaneous abortion
- Ectopic pregnancy
- Hydatidiform mole
- Benign and malignant lesions (i.e., choriocarcinoma, cervical cancer)

WORKUP

- Vital signs (rule out shock/sepsis/illness)
- Pelvic exam (look at cervix, source of bleed)
- Beta-human chorionic gonadotropin (hCG) level, complete blood count (CBC), antibody screen
- Ultrasound (US) (assess fetal viability; *abdominal US detects fetal heart motion by ≥ 7 weeks' gestational age [GA]*)

See Figure 10-1 for management algorithm.

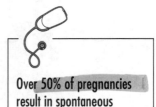

Over 50% of pregnancies result in spontaneous abortion.

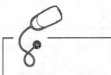

A fetus of < 20 weeks' gestational age (GA) or weighing < 500 g that is aborted = an "abortus."

SPONTANEOUS ABORTION

Spontaneous abortion is the termination of pregnancy resulting in expulsion of an immature, nonviable fetus:

- Occurs in 50 to 75% of all pregnancies
- Most are unrecognized because they occur before or at the time of the next expected menses.
- Fifteen to 20% of clinically diagnosed pregnancies are lost in T1 or early T2.

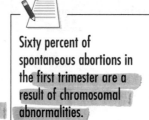

Sixty percent of spontaneous abortions in the first trimester are a result of chromosomal abnormalities.

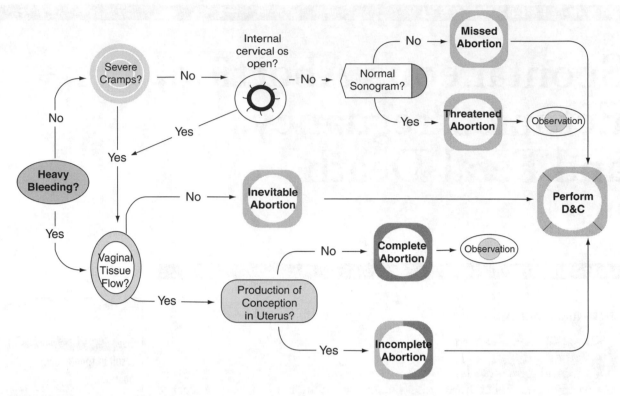

FIGURE 10-1. Management of first-trimester bleeding.

(Redrawn, with permission, from Lindarkis NM, Lott S. *Digging Up the Bones: Obstetrics and Gynecology.* New York: McGraw-Hill, 1998: 43.)

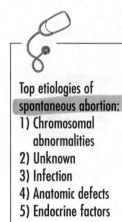

Top etiologies of spontaneous abortion:
1) Chromosomal abnormalities
2) Unknown
3) Infection
4) Anatomic defects
5) Endocrine factors

ETIOLOGIES

Chromosomal Abnormalities

- Majority of abnormal karyotypes are numeric abnormalities as a result of errors during gametogenesis, fertilization, or the first division of the fertilized ovum.
- Frequency:
  - Trisomy—50 to 60%
  - Monosomy (45,X)—7 to 15%
  - Triploidy—15%
  - Tetraploidy—10%

Infectious Agents

Infectious agents in cervix, uterine cavity, or seminal fluid can cause abortions. These infections may be asymptomatic:
- *Toxoplasma gondii*
- Herpes simplex
- *Ureaplasma urealyticum*
- *Mycoplasma hominis*

Uterine Abnormalities

- Septate/bicornuate uterus—25 to 30%
- Cervical incompetence
- Leiomyomas (especially submucosal)
- Intrauterine adhesions (i.e., from curettage)

Endocrine Abnormalities

- Progesterone deficiency
- Polycystic ovarian syndrome (POS)—hypersecretion of luteinizing hormone (LH)
- Diabetes—uncontrolled

Immunologic Factors

- Lupus anticoagulant
- Anticardiolipin antibody (antiphospholipid syndrome)

Environmental Factors

- Tobacco—≥ 14 cigarettes/day increases abortion rates
- Alcohol
- Irradiation
- Environmental toxin exposure

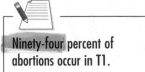

Ninety-four percent of abortions occur in T1.

THREATENED ABORTION

Threatened abortion is vaginal bleeding that occurs in the first 20 weeks of pregnancy, without the passage of products of conception (POC) or rupture of membranes. Pregnancy continues, although up to 50% result in loss of pregnancy.

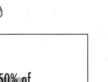

Twenty to 50% of threatened abortions lead to loss of pregnancy.

DIAGNOSIS

Speculum exam reveals blood coming from a **closed cervical os, without amniotic fluid or POC in the endocervical canal.**

MANAGEMENT

Bed rest with sedation and without intercourse

Threatened abortion: Vaginal bleeding in first 20 weeks of pregnancy without passage of POC and without rupture of membranes

INEVITABLE ABORTION

Inevitable abortion is vaginal bleeding, cramps, and **cervical dilation.** Expulsion of the POC is imminent.

DIAGNOSIS

Speculum exam reveals blood coming from an **open** cervical os. Menstrual-like cramps typically occur.

MANAGEMENT

- Surgical evacuation of the uterus
- Rh typing—D immunoglobulin (RhoGAM) is administered to Rh-negative, unsensitized patients to prevent isoimmunization.

Inevitable abortion is different from threatened abortion because it has cervical dilation.

INCOMPLETE ABORTION

Incomplete abortion is the passage of some, but not all, POC from the cervical os.

DIAGNOSIS

- Cramping and heavy bleeding
- Enlarged, boggy uterus
- Dilated internal os with POC present in the endocervical canal or vagina

MANAGEMENT

- Stabilization (i.e., IV fluids and oxytocin if heavy bleeding is present)
- Blood typing and crossmatching for possible transfusion if bleeding is brisk or low Hgb/patient symptomatic
- Rh typing
- POC are removed from the endocervical canal and uterus with ring forceps. Suction dilation and curettage (D&C) is performed after vital signs have stabilized.
- Karyotyping of POC if loss is recurrent

COMPLETE ABORTION

Complete abortion is the complete passage of POC.

DIAGNOSIS

- Uterus is well contracted.
- Cervical os may be closed.
- Pain has ceased.

MANAGEMENT

- Examine all POC for completeness and characteristics.
- Between 8 and 14 weeks, curettage is necessary because of the large possibility that the abortion was incomplete.
- Observe patient for further bleeding and fever.

MISSED ABORTION

Missed abortion is when the POC are retained after the fetus has expired.

DIAGNOSIS

- The pregnant uterus fails to grow, and symptoms of pregnancy have disappeared.
- Intermittent vaginal bleeding/spotting/brown discharge and a firm, closed cervix
- Decline in quantitative beta-hCG
- US confirms lack of fetal heartbeat.

MANAGEMENT

Although most women will spontaneously deliver a dead fetus within 2 weeks, the psychological stress imposed by carrying a dead fetus and the dangers of coagulation defects favor the practice of labor induction and early delivery:

- Check fibrinogen level, partial thromboplastin time (PTT), antibody screen, and ABO blood type.
- Evacuate the uterus (suction D&C in first trimester) or induce labor with IV oxytocin and cervical dilators or prostaglandin E_2 suppositories.
- Administer RhoGAM to Rh-negative, unsensitized patients.

SEPTIC ABORTION

Septic abortion results from a maternal infection leading to sepsis, fetal infection, and fetal death. The infection is usually polymicrobial, often with *E. coli* and other gram-negative organisms.

DIAGNOSIS

- Generalized pelvic discomfort, pain, and tenderness
- Signs of peritonitis
- Fever of 37.8 to 40.6°C (100 to 105°F)
- Malodorous vaginal and cervical discharge
- Leukocytosis

MANAGEMENT

- Cultures of uterine discharge and blood
- Check CBC, urinalysis (UA), serum electrolytes, liver function tests (LFTs), blood urea nitrogen (BUN), creatinine, and coagulation panel.
- Abdominal and chest films to exclude free air in the peritoneal cavity → helps determine the presence of gas-forming bacteria or foreign body
- Prompt uterine evacuation (D&C), IV antibiotics, IV fluids

RECURRENT ABORTION

Three or more successive clinically recognized pregnancy losses prior to 20 weeks' GA constitutes recurrent abortion.

Women with two successive spontaneous abortions have a recurrence risk of 25 to 45%.

ETIOLOGY

- Parental chromosomal abnormalities (balanced translocation is the most common)
- Anatomic abnormalities (congenital and acquired)
- Endocrinologic abnormalities
- Infections (e.g., *Chlamydia, Ureaplasma*)
- Autoimmunity
- Unexplained (majority of cases)

MANAGEMENT

- Investigate possible etiologies.
- Potentially useful investigative measures include:

1. Parental peripheral blood karyotypes
2. Sonohysterogram (intrauterine structural study)
3. Luteal-phase endometrial biopsy
4. Anticardiolipin and antiphosphatidyl serine antibodies
5. Lupus anticoagulant
6. Cervical cultures for *Mycoplasma, Ureaplasma, Chlamydia*

See Table 10-1.

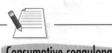

If **POC** are retained in septic abortion, a severe coagulopathy with bleeding often occurs; otherwise, prognosis is good.

Consumptive coagulopathy is an uncommon, but serious, complication of septic abortion.

Recurrent abortion is three or more successive abortions.

Women with a history of recurrent abortion have a 23% chance of abortion in subsequent pregnancies that are detectable by ultrasound.

A clinical investigation of pregnancy loss should be initiated after two successive spontaneous abortions in the first trimester, or one in the second trimester.

TABLE 10-1. Types of Abortions

Complete abortion	Complete expulsion of POC before 20 weeks' gestation; cervix dilated
Incomplete abortion	Partial expulsion of some POC before 20 weeks' gestation; partially dilated cervix
Threatened abortion	No cervical dilatation or expulsion of POC; intrauterine bleeding before 20 weeks' gestation occurs
Inevitable abortion	Threatened abortion with a dilated cervical os
Missed abortion	Retention of nonviable POC for 4–8 weeks or more; often proceeds to complete abortion
Recurrent spontaneous abortion	Three or more consecutive spontaneous abortions
Septic abortion	Abortion associated with severe hemorrhage, sepsis, bacterial shock, and/or acute renal failure
Therapeutic abortion (induced)	Termination of pregnancy before the period of fetal viability in order to protect the life or health of the mother
Elective abortion (induced)	Termination of pregnancy before fetal viability at the request of the patient; not due to maternal or fetal health risks

> Ectopic pregnancy is the leading cause of pregnancy-related death during T1. Diagnose and treat *before* tubal rupture occurs to decrease the risk of death!

ECTOPIC PREGNANCY (EXTRAUTERINE PREGNANCY)

Ectopic pregnancy is the implantation of the blastocyst anywhere other than the endometrial lining of the uterine cavity. It is a **medical emergency** (see Figure 10-2).

Epidemiology

- > 1/50 pregnancies in the United States is ectopic.
- Carries a 7- to 13-fold increase in recurrence risk

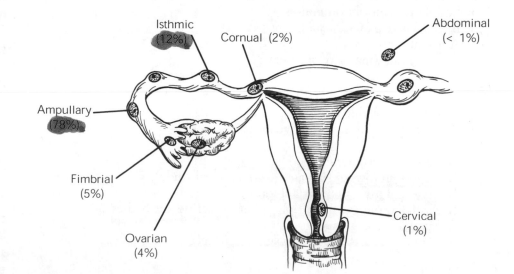

FIGURE 10-2. Sites of ectopic pregnancy.

(Reproduced, with permission, from Pearlman MD, Tintinalli JE, eds. *Emergency Care of the Woman.* New York: McGraw-Hill, 1998: 22.)

Etiology/Risk Factors

- **Fallopian tube transport malfunction** due to:
  - Infection such as *Chlamydia* and gonorrhea (50%)
  - Previous ectopic pregnancy
  - Previous tubal surgery
  - Abdominal surgery resulting in adhesions
  - Endometriosis
  - Congenital abnormalities (often from diethylstilbestrol [DES] exposure)
  - Pregnancy with intrauterine device in place
- **Assisted reproduction:**
  - Ovulation-inducing drugs
  - In vitro fertilization

Symptoms and Diagnosis

- Amenorrhea followed by irregular vaginal bleeding
- Adnexal tenderness or mass
- US evidence of an adnexal mass without intrauterine gestation or an adnexal gestational sac with a fetal pole and cardiac activity
- Less-than-normal increase in hCG
- A serum progesterone level lower than normal for patients with an intrauterine pregnancy (i.e., < 25 ng/mL)
- Laparoscopy shows an adnexal mass or abdominal gestation.

Signs of Rupture

- Shock
- Bleeding
- Increased abdominal pain

Management

There are two options of treatment:

Operative

- Laparoscopy or laparotomy with salpingostomy or segmental resection if the tube is to be retained and salpingectomy if the tube requires removal

Medical

- Intramuscular methotrexate (prevents DNA synthesis via its antifolate actions)
- Patient is monitored as an outpatient.
- 67 to 100% effective

The primary causes of ectopic pregnancy include conditions that either prevent or impede passage of a fertilized ovum through the fallopian tube.

Classic triad of ectopic pregnancy:
- Amenorrhea
- Vaginal bleeding
- Abdominal pain

These usually indicate rupture.

Always do a β-hCG level on a premenopausal woman with abdominal pain.

If ruptured, always stabilize with IV fluids, blood replacement, and pressors if necessary. Operative repair is used.

FETAL DEATH

- Fetal death is defined as death prior to complete expulsion or extraction from the mother, regardless of the duration of pregnancy.
- Fetal death can result in a spontaneous abortion and a missed abortion.

Causes

A carefully performed autopsy is the single most useful step in identifying the cause of fetal death.

T1 (1 to 14 Weeks)

- **Chromosomal abnormalities**
- Environmental factors (e.g., medications, smoking, toxins)
- Infection (e.g., herpes simplex virus, human papillomavirus, mumps, *Mycoplasma*)
- Antiphospholipid antibodies (after 10 weeks)
- Maternal anatomic defects (e.g., maternal müllerian defects)
- Endocrine factors (e.g., progesterone insufficiency, thyroid dysfunction)
- Maternal systemic disease (e.g., diabetes)
- Unknown

T2 (14 to 28 Weeks)

- Anticardiolipin antibodies
- Antiphospholipid antibodies
- Chromosomal abnormalities
- Anatomic defects of uterus and cervix
- Infection (e.g., BV, syphilis)
- Erythroblastosis
- Placental pathological conditions (e.g., circumvallate placentation, placenta previa)

T3 (28 Weeks to Term)

- Anticardiolipin antibodies
- Placental pathological conditions (e.g., circumvallate placentation, placenta previa, abruptio placentae)
- Infection

Time Nonspecific

- Trauma
- Cord entanglement
- Electric shock
- Maternal systemic disease
- Maternal infection

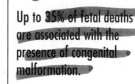

The frequency of chromosomal abnormalities in stillbirths is 10 times higher than that in live births.

Up to 35% of fetal deaths are associated with the presence of congenital malformation.

HIGH-YIELD FACTS

Spontaneous Abortion

134

DIC, or consumptive coagulopathy is a pathological condition associated with inappropriate activation of the coagulation and fibrinolytic system. Most commonly, it is associated with one of the following disease states:

- Fetal demise
- Amniotic fluid embolism
- Preeclampsia–eclampsia
- Placental abruption

Pathophysiology

In pathologic states (i.e., via thromboplastin production from dead POC), the coagulation cascade is activated, which results in consumption of platelets and coagulation factors. Fibrin deposition in small vessels results in bleeding and circulatory obstruction.

Diagnosis

- Physical exam may reveal multiple bleeding points associated with purpura and petechiae.
- Lab evaluation reveals thrombocytopenia, hypofibrinogenemia, an elevated prothrombin time, and increased fibrin split products.

Management

Supportive therapy to correct/prevent shock, acidosis, and tissue ischemia and, if applicable, prompt termination of pregnancy. Ultimately, the only care is to correct the underlying cause.

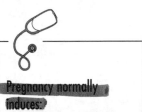

Pregnancy normally induces:
- Increases in coagulation factors I (fibrinogen), VII, VIII, IX, and X
- Increased activation of platelet clotting

In any obstetric complication, obtain a coagulation panel and fibrin split-product levels to monitor for DIC.

HIGH-YIELD FACTS

Spontaneous Abortion

Induced Abortion

DEFINITION

The termination of a pregnancy medically or operatively before fetal viability; definition of viability varies from state to state

Abortion may not be denied in first 3 months of pregnancy in any state.

ASSESSMENT OF THE PATIENT

Physical assessment is crucial before an elective abortion:
- **Ultrasound** should be performed if there is a discrepancy between dates and uterine size.
- Patient's **blood type and Rh type** must be evaluated; if Rh negative, RhoGAM should be administered prophylactically.
- Careful patient counseling should be performed.

TYPES OF INDUCED ABORTION

Elective voluntary: Interruption of pregnancy at the request of the mother
Therapeutic: Interruption of pregnancy for the purpose of safeguarding the health of the mother

INDICATIONS FOR THERAPEUTIC ABORTION

Maternal Indications
- Cardiovascular disease
- Genetic syndrome (e.g., Marfan's)
- Hematologic disease (e.g., TTP)
- Metabolic (e.g., proliferative diabetic retinopathy)
- Neoplastic (e.g., cervical cancer; mother needs prompt chemotherapy)
- Neurologic (e.g., Berry aneurysm; cerebrovascular malformation)
- Renal disease
- Intrauterine infection
- Severe preeclampsia/eclampsia

Fetal Indications
- Major malformation (e.g., anencephaly)
- Genetic (e.g., Tay–Sachs disease)

METHODS OF ABORTION

First Trimester

MEDICAL

- Antiprogesterones such as mifepristone (RU 486) or epostane; used only before 9 weeks' gestation. Without progesterone, the uterine lining sloughs off.
- Methotrexate IM + intrauterine misoprostol 1 week later; used only before 9 weeks' gestation. Methotrexate is a folic acid antagonist that interferes with cell division.

SURGICAL

Cervical dilation followed by aspiration curettage (D&C): Risks include cervical/uterine injury and Asherman's syndrome.

Second Trimester

MEDICAL

Intravaginal prostaglandin E_2 (PGE_2) or $PGF_{2\alpha}$ with urea

SURGICAL

Dilation and evacuation

Complications of Surgical Abortions

- Infection
- Incomplete removal of products of conception (POC)
- Disseminated intravascular coagulation (DIC)
- Bleeding
- Cervical laceration
- Uterine perforation/rupture
- Psychological sequelae
- Death

> Medical methods of abortions can only be used in first 9 weeks.

> What abortion method has the lowest complication rate? Dilation and evacuation. Risks include: Hemorrhage/perforation.

Medical

- Intra-amnionic infusion of hyperosmolar fluid (saline + urea)
- High-dose IV oxytocin (induces uterine contractions)

Surgical

- Hysterotomy is used only if other methods have been unsuccessful. A hysterotomy is a C-section of a preterm fetus.
- Hysterectomy

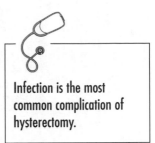

Infection is the most common complication of hysterectomy.

Death is a risk of abortion, but it is **10 times less** than the risk of death from giving birth.

HIGH-YIELD FACTS

Induced Abortion

HIGH-YIELD FACTS

Induced Abortion

High-Yield Facts in Gynecology

Contraception

GENERAL METHODS OF PREVENTING PREGNANCY

- Barrier
- Hormonal
- Intrauterine device (IUD)
- Sterilization

BARRIER METHODS

FEMALE CONDOM

Rarely used because of expense and inconvenience (it must not be removed for 6 to 8 hours after intercourse). It offers labial protection, unlike the male condom.

MALE CONDOM

Types
- Latex (cheapest and most common)
- Polyurethane (newest, sensitive, expensive)
- Animal skins (sensitive, least protection against sexually transmitted diseases [STDs])

Efficacy
- 88 to 98%, depending on if used properly

The only contraception effective in protecting against STDs

Drawbacks
- Interruption of coitus
- Decreased sensation

DIAPHRAGM

A flexible ring with a rubber dome that must be fitted by a gynecologist: It forms a barrier from the cervix to the anterior vaginal wall. It must be inserted with spermicide and left in place after intercourse for 6 to 8 hours.

Types
- Flat or coil spring type (for women with good vaginal tone)
- Arcing type (for poorer tone or vaginal/uteral irregularities such as cystoceles or long cervices)
- Wide seal rim

Efficacy
- 82 to 94%

Complications
- If left in for too long, may result in *Staphylococcus aureus* infection (which may lead to **toxic shock syndrome**)

CERVICAL CAP

A smaller version of a diaphragm that fits directly over the cervix; more likely to cause irritation or toxic shock syndrome. It is more popular in Europe.

Efficacy
- 82 to 94%

SPERMICIDE

Foams, gels, creams placed in vagina up to 30 minutes before intercourse

Types
- Nonoxynol-9 and octoxynol-3; effective for only about 1 hour

Efficacy
- 80 to 97%

SPONGE

A polyurethane sponge containing nonoxynol-9 that is placed over the cervix: It can be inserted up to 24 hours before intercourse.

Efficacy
- 84%

Risk
- Toxic shock syndrome

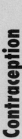

Efficacy rates for spermicides are much higher when combined with other barriers (e.g., condoms, diaphragms).

HORMONAL AGENTS

ORAL CONTRACEPTIVES

Efficacy
- 97 to 99.9%

The following are the various types of oral contraceptives.

Combination Pills
Contain estrogen and progestin; come as fixed dosing and phasic dosing:
- **Fixed dosing**—requires the same dose every day of cycle
- **Phasic dosing**—gradual increase in amount of progestin as well as some changes in the level of estrogen

Mechanism (there are several)

- **Estrogen** suppresses follicle-stimulating hormone (FSH) and therefore prevents follicular emergence.
- **Progesterone** suppresses the midcycle gonadotropin-releasing hormone (GnRH) surge, which suppresses luteinizing hormone (LH) and therefore prevents ovulation.
- Causes thicker cervical mucus
- Causes decreased motility of fallopian tube
- Causes endometrial atrophy

Progestin-Only Pills

Contain only progestin: There is LH suppression and therefore no ovulation. *The main differences from combination pills are:*

- A mature follicle *is* formed (but not released).
- No "sugar-pill" is used.

Progestin-only pills are used in the following circumstances:

- Lactating women (progestin, unlike estrogen, does *not* suppress breast milk)
- Women > 40 years old
- Women who cannot take estrogens for other medical reasons (e.g., estrogen-sensitive tumors)

Benefits of Oral Contraceptives

- Decreases risk of ovarian cancer by 75%
- Decreases risk of endometrial cancer by 50%
- Decreases bleeding and dysmenorrhea
- Regulates menses
- Protects against pelvic inflammatory disease (PID) (thicker mucus)
- Protects against fibrocystic change, ovarian cysts, ectopic pregnancy, osteoporosis, acne, and hirsutism

Risks of Oral Contraceptives

- Increases risk of venous thromboembolism/stroke (3/10,000)
- Increases risk of myocardial infarction (in smokers over 35 years old)
- Depression

Contraindications of Oral Contraceptives

- Thromboembolism
- Cerebrovascular accident (CVA) or coronary artery disease (CAD)
- Breast/endometrial cancer
- Cholestatic jaundice
- Undiagnosed vaginal bleeding
- Hepatic disease
- Known/suspected pregnancy
- Concomitant anticonvulsant therapy
- Some antibiotics
- Relative contraindications: Migraines, hypertension (HTN), lactation

In combination oral contraceptives, at the time of desired/expected menstruation, a placebo, or "sugar-pill," is given to simulate the natural progesterone withdrawal.

Mechanism in a nutshell:
Estrogen inhibits FSH.
Progestin inhibits LH.

Estrogen suppresses breast milk, so combination pills are not used for nursing mothers. Progestin-only pills are preferred.

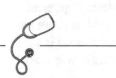

Oral contraceptives' link to an increase in breast cancer is not proven.

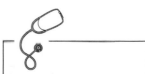

Why is estrogen a procoagulant? Estrogen increases factors VII and X and decreases antithrombin III.

Side Effects of Oral Contraceptives

- Breakthrough bleeding
- Breast tenderness
- Nausea (10 to 30% of women)

INJECTABLE HORMONAL AGENT

Medroxyprogesterone acetate (Depo-Provera) IM injection given every 3 months

Efficacy
- 99.7%

Mechanism of Action

Sustained high progesterone level to block LH surge (and hence ovulation). Thicker mucus and endometrial atrophy also contribute. There is no FSH suppression.

Indications

- Systemic lupus erythematosus (SLE)
- Migraines
- Headaches
- Heavy bleeding

Side Effects of Injectable Hormonal Agents

- Bleeding irregularity/spotting
- 5 lb/yr weight gain
- Unknown when period will resume after treatment cessation
- Alopecia
- Mood changes
- Decreased high-density lipoprotein (HDL)
- Decreased libido

Contraindications

- Known/suspected pregnancy
- Undiagnosed vaginal bleeding
- Breast cancer
- Liver disease

> **Women with SLE who want birth control should use injectable progesterone. Also good for people with poor compliance (e.g., retarded or drug addicts)**

IMPLANTABLE HORMONAL AGENT

Subcutaneous implantation of six rods containing levonorgestrel (a progesterol), which lasts about 5 years

Efficacy
- 99.8%

Mechanism of Action

- Suppression of LH surge
- Thickened mucus
- Endometrial atrophy

Side Effects

- Irregular bleeding
- Acne
- Decreased libido
- Adnexal enlargement
- Possible difficult removal

Indications

- Oral contraceptives contraindicated/intolerated
- Smokers over 35 years old
- Women with diabetes mellitus, HTN, CAD

Contraindications

- Thrombophlebitis/embolism
- Known/suspected pregnancy
- Liver disease/cancer
- Breast cancer
- Concomitant anticonvulsant therapy

INTRAUTERINE DEVICE

Insertion of a T-shaped device (Paragard or Progestasert) into the endometrial cavity with a nylon filament extending through the cervix to facilitate removal

Efficacy
- 97%

Types

- *Paragard*—made with copper and lasts 10 years
- *Progestasert*—releases progesterone and lasts 1 year

Mechanism of Action

- Prevents fertilization by creating a hostile environment (a sterile inflammatory reaction) for sperm and for a fertilized ovum
- Prevents ovulation and causes endometrial atrophy (Progestasert only)

Indications

- Oral contraceptives contraindicated/intolerated
- Smokers over 35 years old

Contraindications

- Multiple sexual partners
- History of PID
- Immunocompromised (e.g., HIV, sickle cell disease)
- Known/suspected pregnancy

Complications

- PID
- Uterine perforation

The IUD filament provides an access for bacteria, so it is a high risk for infection.

- Ectopic pregnancy
- Menorrhagia and metrorrhagia
- IUD expulsion

POSTCOITAL/EMERGENCY CONTRACEPTION

Indicated after rape, barrier contraception failure, or any other unprotected intercourse

Efficacy
- > 95%

Most Common Regimen
- Two tablets of a combination estradiol (50 µg) and norgestrel (0.5 µg) at time of examination
- Two more tablets 12 hours later

Nausea occurs in about one half of cases following regimen.

Sterilization

With about 1 million procedures/yr in the United States, sterilization is the most popular form of birth control. There are 1 to 4 pregnancies per 1,000 sterilizations.

Male type: Vasectomy

Female type: Tubal ligation

Tubal ligation is twice as common as vasectomy.

VASECTOMY

Excision of a small section of both vas deferens, followed by sealing of the proximal and distal cut ends: Ejaculation still occurs.

Sperm can still be found proximal to the surgical site, so to ensure sterility one must:

- Have two consecutive negative sperm counts

or

- Use contraception for 6 weeks or 15 ejaculations

TUBAL LIGATION

Procedures can be performed either postpartum (immediately after delivery) or during an interval (between pregnancies).

Laparoscopic Tubal Ligation

Eighty to 90% of tubal ligations are done laparoscopically. All methods occlude the fallopian tubes bilaterally.

ELECTROCAUTERY

This involves the cauterization of a 3-cm zone of the isthmus. It is the most popular method (very effective but most difficult to reverse).

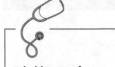

CLIPPING

The Hulka clip, similar to a staple, is applied at a 90° angle on the isthmus. It is the most easily reversed method but also has the highest failure rate.

BANDING

A length of isthmus is drawn up into the end of the trocar, and a silicone band, or Falope ring, is placed around the base of the drawn-up portion of fallopian tube.

Laparotomy Methods of Tubal Ligation

POMEROY METHOD

A segment of isthmus is lifted and a suture is tied around the approximated base. The resulting loop is excised, leaving a gap between the proximal and distal ends. This is the most popular laparoscopic method.

PARKLAND METHOD

Similar to the Pomeroy but without the lifting, a segment of isthmus is tied proximally and distally and then excised.

MADLENER METHOD

Similar to the Pomeroy but without the excision, a segment of isthmus is lifted and crushed and tied at the base.

IRVING METHOD

The isthmus is cut, with the proximal end buried in the myometrium and the distal end buried in the mesosalpinx.

KROENER METHOD

Resection of the distal ampulla and fimbrae following ligation around the proximal ampulla

UCHIDA METHOD

Epinephrine is injected beneath the serosa of the isthmus. The mesosalpinx is pulled back off the tube, and the proximal end of the tube is ligated and excised. The distal end is not excised. The mesosalpinx is reattached to the excised proximal stump, while the long distal end is left to "dangle" outside of the mesosalpinx.

PARTIAL OR TOTAL SALPINGECTOMY

Removal of part or all of the fallopian tube

LUTEAL-PHASE PREGNANCY

A luteal-phase pregnancy is a *pregnancy diagnosed after tubal sterilization but conceived before*. Occurs around 2 to 3/1,000 sterilizations. It is prevented by either performing sensitive pregnancy tests prior to the procedure or performing the procedure during the follicular phase.

REVERSIBILITY OF TUBAL LIGATION

Around one third of tubal ligations can be reversed such that pregnancy can result. Some types of sterilization (i.e., banding, clipping) are more reversible.

Even pregnancies after reversal are ectopic until proven otherwise, and therefore reversal does not preclude a full ectopic workup.

COMPLICATIONS OF TUBAL LIGATION

- **Poststerility syndrome:** Pelvic pain/dysmenorrhea, menorrhagia, ovarian cyst
- **Fistula formation:** Uteroperitoneal fistulas can occur, especially if the procedure is performed on the fallopian tubes < 2 to 3 cm from the uterus.

OTHER METHODS OF STERILIZATION

Colpotomy

Utilizes entry through the vaginal wall near the posterior cul-de-sac and occludes the fallopian tubes by employing methods similar to those performed in laparoscopy and laparotomy

Hysterectomy

Removal of the uterus, either vaginally or abdominally; rarely performed for sterilization purposes

Failure rate is below 1%. **Pregnancy after hysterectomy = ectopic pregnancy = emergency.**

HIGH-YIELD FACTS

Sterilization

Infertility

DEFINITION

- The inability to conceive **after 12 months** of unprotected sexual intercourse
- Affects 15% of couples

There are two types:
Primary infertility: Infertility in the absence of previous pregnancy
Secondary infertility: Infertility after previous pregnancy

> - Female factors account for 40 to 50% of infertile couples.
> - 40% of infertile couples have multiple causes.

FEMALE FACTORS AFFECTING INFERTILITY

- Tubal disease—20%
- Anovulation—15%
- Unexplained—10%
- Multifactorial—40%

INFERTILITY WORKUP

Semen Analysis

Performed after at least 48 hours of abstinence, with examination maximum 2 hours from time of ejaculation (for those who prefer to donate at home)

CHARACTERISTICS OF SEMEN ANALYSIS

- *Volume*—normal, > 2 mL
- *Semen count*—normal, ≥ 20 million/mL
- *Motility*—normal, > 50% with forward movement
- *Morphology*—normal, > 40% normal

TREATMENT FOR ABNORMAL SPERM FINDINGS

- Urology referral
- Quitting smoking, ETOH
- Avoidance of lubricants

> Calcium channel blockers and furantoins can impair sperm function and quantity.

- Intrauterine insemination (sperm injected through cervix)
- Intracytoplasmic sperm injection
- Artificial insemination

If semen analysis is normal, continue workup with analysis of ovulation.

Methods of Analyzing Ovulation

- **History of monthly menses** is a strong indicator of normal ovulation.
- **Basal body temperature (BBT)**—body temperature rises about 0.5 to 1°F during the luteal phase due to the increased level of progesterone. Presence of BBT increase is a good indicator that ovulation is occurring.
- Measurement of **luteal-phase progesterone** level (normal, 4 ng/mL)
- **Sonogram**—determines normal or abnormal endometrial anatomy
- **Endometrial biopsy**—determines histologically the presence/absence of ovulation

POSSIBLE CAUSES AND TREATMENTS OF ANOVULATION

- **Pituitary insufficiency:** Treat with intramuscular luteinizing hormone/follicle-stimulating hormone (LH/FSH).
- **Hypothalamic dysfunction:** Treat with bromocriptine (a dopamine agonist)
- **Polycystic ovary syndrome:** Treat with clomiphene or human menopausal gonadotropin (hMG).
- **Other causes:** Hyper/hypothyroid, androgen excess, obesity/starvation, galactorrhea

If ovulation analysis and semen analysis are normal, analysis of the internal architecture is performed to determine if there is an anatomical impediment to pregnancy.

Internal Architecture Study

Hysterosalpingogram
- Performed during follicular phase
- Radio-opaque dye is injected into cervix and uterus and should fill both fallopian tubes and spill into peritoneal cavity.
- Allows visualization of uterus and fallopian tubes
- There is risk of salpingitis.

TREATMENT FOR STRUCTURAL ABNORMALITIES

- Microsurgical tuboplasty
- Neosalpingostomy
- Tubal reimplantation for intramural obstruction

If findings of the semen analysis, ovulation analysis, and hysterosalpingogram are normal, an exploratory laparoscopy can be done.

Exploratory Laparoscopy

A laparoscope is inserted transabdominally to visualize the pelvis:
- Check for adhesions.
- Check for endometriosis.

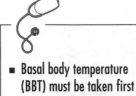

- Basal body temperature (BBT) must be taken first thing in the morning. A monthly rise in BBT indicates ovulation is occurring.
- Ovulation = highest temperature of month

Clomiphene: An antiestrogen that inhibits negative feedback on the central nervous system

Hysterosalpingogram is neither sensitive nor specific (smooth muscle spasm occludes tubes) for determining the presence of anatomical problems.

Endometriosis is found in about one third of infertile women.

TREATMENT

- Laparoscopic lysis of adesions
- Laparoscopic endometriosis ablation
- Medical treatment of endometriosis

ASSISTED REPRODUCTIVE TECHNOLOGIES

Definition

Directly retrieving eggs from ovary followed by manipulation and replacement: **Generally employed for inadequate spermatogenesis.** The following are examples.

In Vitro Fertilization (IVF) and Embryo Transfer

Fertilization of eggs in a lab followed by uterine placement: Intracytoplasmic sperm injection is a subtype of IVF to aid severe male factors. Success rate of IVF is about 20%.

Gamete Intrafallopian Transfer (GIFT)

Egg and sperm placement in an intact fallopian tube for fertilization: Success rate of GIFT is about 25%.

Zygote Intrafallopian Transfer (ZIFT)

Zygote (fertilized in vitro) is created and placed in fallopian tube, where it proceeds to uterus for natural implantation: Success rate of ZIFT is about 30%.

Menstruation

DEVELOPMENT

Puberty

Puberty is the transition from childhood to reproductive potential. More commonly, it refers to the final stage of maturation known as adolescence.

Puberty is believed to begin with *disinhibition* of the pulsatile gonadotropin-releasing hormone (GnRH) secretion from the hypothalamus (mechanism is unknown).

SECONDARY SEX CHARACTERISTICS

Development of the secondary sexual characteristics proceeds in the following order:

1. Breast budding (thelarche)
2. Axillary and pubic hair growth (pubarche)
3. First menses (menarche)

TANNER STAGES

The Tanner stages of development refer to the sequence of events of breast and pubic hair development.

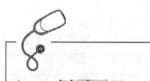

Average thelarche — 10 years old due to ↑ estradiol
Average pubarche — 11 years old due to ↑ adrenal hormones
Average menarche — 12 years old due to ↑ estradiol

Precocious Puberty

Appearance of the secondary sexual characteristics before 8 years of age is referred to as precocious puberty.

Causes	Manifestation
Idiopathic (most common)	Thelarche/pubarche/menarche
Tumors (of the hypothalamic–pituitary stalk; prevent negative feedback)	Thelarche/pubarche/menarche
Inflammation of the hypothalamus (leads to ↑ GnRH)	Thelarche/pubarche/menarche
21-Hydroxylase deficiency (cortisol pathway is blocked, leading to excess androgens)	Pubarche

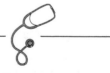

Tanner stages:
Stage 1: Prepubertal child
Stages 2–4: Developmental stages
Stage 5: Adult

Causes	Manifestation
Excess estrogens from: ■ Exogenous sources (e.g., oral contraceptives) ■ Estrogen-secreting tumors	Thelarche and menarche

THE MENSTRUAL CYCLE

The menstrual cycle is the cyclical changes that occur in the female reproductive system (see Figure 15-1): The hypothalamus, pituitary, ovaries, and uterus interact to cause ovulation approximately once per month (average 28 days [+/− 7 days]).

Menstruation—Days 1 Through 4 (First Part of the Follicular Phase)

- In the absence of fertilization, **progesterone withdrawal results in endometrial sloughing** (menses).
- Prostaglandins contained in those endometrial cells are released, often resulting in cramps from uterine contractions.

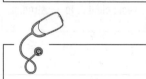

Many follicles are stimulated by FSH, but *the follicle that secretes more estrogen than androgen will be released.* This dominant follicle releases more and more estradiol so that its positive feedback causes an LH surge.

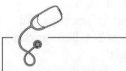

Average menses = 3 to 6 days

Blood loss in menstruation averages 30 to 50 mL, should not form clots. > 80 mL is an abnormal amount of blood loss.

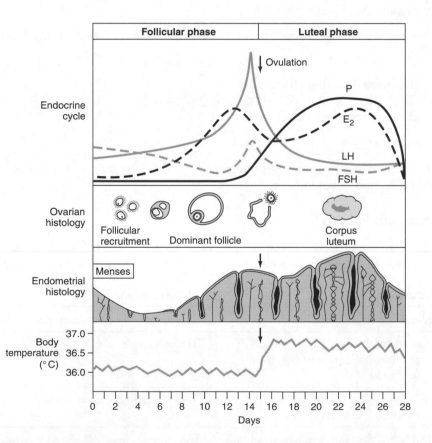

FIGURE 15-1. The menstrual cycle.

(Reproduced, with permission, from Fauci AS, Braunwald E, Isselbacher KJ, et al. *Harrison's Principles of Internal Medicine,* 14th ed. New York: McGraw-Hill, 1998: 2101.)

Follicular Phase (Proliferative Phase)—Days 1 Through 14

The follicular phase begins on the first day of menses. Now that progesterone levels have fallen with the death of the corpus luteum, all hormone levels are low. Without any negative feedback, **GnRH** from the hypothalamus causes follicle-stimulating hormone **(FSH)** levels to rise.

FSH released from the pituitary stimulates maturation of granulosa cells in the ovary. The granulosa cells secrete **estradiol** in response.

Estradiol causes luteinizing hormone **(LH)** to be released from the pituitary while at the same time inhibiting **FSH** release. In the meantime, the **estradiol** secretion also causes the endometrium to proliferate.

LH acts on the theca cells to increase secretion of **androgens** (which are converted to estradiol), prepare the cells for progesterone secretion, and cause further granulosa maturation.

Ovulation—Day 14

The **LH surge** causes the oocyte to be released from the follicle. What remains is the corpus luteum, which secretes **progesterone.**

Luteal Phase—Days 14 Through 28

The effect of **LH** on the follicle was to change its secretion from **estradiol** to **progesterone.** This happens before ovulation.

The corpus luteum survives only about 11 days in the absence of hCG, during which time it continues **progesterone** secretion.

Progesterone causes the endometrium to mature in preparation for possible implantation. It becomes highly vascularized with increased gland secretion.

Progesterone also causes inhibition of **FSH** and **LH** release.

If fertilization does not occur, the corpus luteum dies, **progesterone** levels fall, and the cycle begins again.

Main event of menstruation: Absence of progesterone causes endometrial sloughing.

Two main events in follicular phase:
- FSH causes follicle maturation and estrogen secretion.
- Estrogen causes endometrial proliferation.

Main event of ovulation: LH surge causes oocyte to be released.

Main events of luteal phase: Corpus luteum secretes progesterone, which causes:
- Endometrial maturation
- ↓ FSH, ↓ LH

The corpus luteum would be maintained after fertilization by human chorionic gonadotropin (hCG) released by the embryo.

AMENORRHEA

Primary amenorrhea: Absence of menses by age 16
Secondary amenorrhea: Absence of menses for ≥ 6 months in a woman who previously had normal menses

Etiologies

Etiologies of amenorrhea are categorized by where in the hormone cascade the lesion is.

HYPOTHALAMIC CAUSES OF AMENORRHEA

All hypothalamic causes result in ↓ FSH/LH levels:
- **Kallman's syndrome:** Congenital lack of GnRH
- **Pituitary stalk compression:** Tumors, granulomas, irradiation
- **↓ GnRH release:** Stress, anorexia, hyperprolactinemia, severe weight loss, extreme exercise

PITUITARY CAUSES OF AMENORRHEA

All pituitary causes result in ↓ FSH/LH levels:
- **Sheehan's syndrome:** Pituitary infarction resulting from hypotension during delivery, usually resulting from hemorrhage
- **Tumors:** Either compress stalk (as above) or are prolactin-secreting tumors
- **Hemosiderosis:** Iron deposition in pituitary that impairs its function

OVARIAN CAUSES OF AMENORRHEA

All ovarian causes result in ↑ FSH/LH levels:
- **Premature ovarian failure:** Menopause before age 35
- **Savage's syndrome:** Ovarian resistance to FSH/LH
- **Enzyme defects:** Most commonly 17α-hydroxylase deficiency
- **Turner's syndrome** (XO karyotype): Ovarian dysgenesis
- **Polycystic ovary disease (PCOD):** ↑ Estrogen levels cause ↑ LH levels, which cause abnormal follicular growth and androgen secretion.

UTERINE CAUSES OF AMENORRHEA

- Imperforate hymen
- Uterine causes have *normal* levels of FSH/LH
- Congenital absence of uterus
- **Asherman's syndrome:** Uterine scarring and adhesions following dilation and curettage (D&C)

Evaluation of Amenorrhea

I. Is it primary or secondary?
First step to evaluating amenorrhea is to determine if it is primary or secondary (see Figure 15-2).

Workup	Positive Findings Indicate
1. Examine hymen	Imperforate hymen
2. Determine presence of uterus	No uterus: Do karyotyping and consider testicular feminization, müllerian agenesis, 46,XY steroid enzyme defects
3. Determine if there is breast development	Yes: Work up as secondary amenorrhea. No: Work up as progestin-negative secondary amenorrhea (below).

II. Secondary amenorrhea workup
Once you have determined that the amenorrhea is not primary, do a secondary amenorrhea workup (see Figure 15-3). The secondary amenorrhea workup is divided into two groups: Without galactorrhea and with galactorrhea:

Absence of menses for 3 to 6 months is defined as **oligomenorrhea.**

When diagnosing amenorrhea, always rule out pregnancy first.

Progestin challenge test: Give progestin for 5 days and then stop. This stimulates progesterone withdrawal. If ovaries are secreting estrogen, sloughing will occur and menses results. No menses indicates no ovaries, no estrogen, or blood flow obstruction.

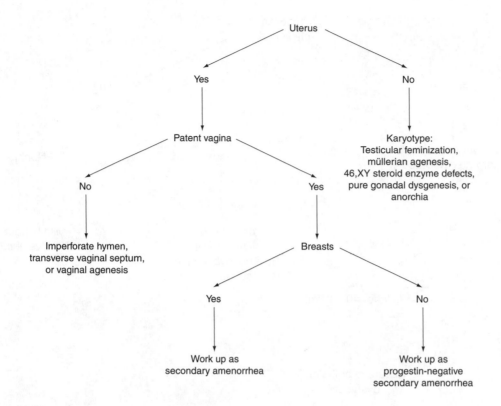

FIGURE 15-2. Workup for primary amenorrhea.

(Redrawn, with permission, from DeCherney AH, Pernoll, ML. *Current Obstetric & Gynecologic Diagnosis & Treatment.* Norwalk, CT: Appleton & Lange, 1994: 1010.)

1. Without galactorrhea, administer **Progestin Challenge:** Give progestin and if menses results, ovaries are secreting estrogen.
   - If the progestin challenge results in menses, then the diagnosis is one of the following
     - PCOD
     - Ovarian or adrenal tumor
     - Hypothalamic dysfunction
   - If progestin challenge is **negative:**
   a) **Heteroscopy** to determine if Asherman's syndrome is the cause
   b) **Check FSH level:**
     - If ↑, suspect **ovarian** causes.
     - If ↓, suspect **hypothalamic–pituitary** failure.
2. Amenorrhea + galactorrhea:
   - Check TSH levels. If low, hypothyroidism is the cause.
   - If TSH is normal, check prolactin levels. Prolactin levels are high, perform a CT/MRI of the brain to confirm a prolactinoma.

See Figure 15-4.

> Prolactin inhibits GnRH pulsations, and therefore inhibits ovulation.

Menstruation

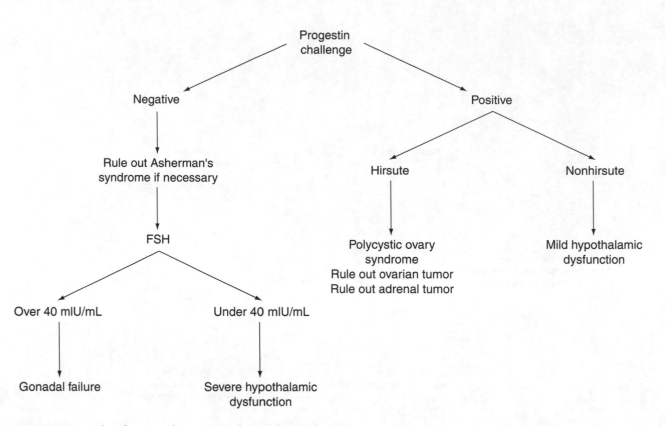

FIGURE 15-3. Workup for secondary amenorrhea without galactorrhea.
(Redrawn, with permission, from DeCherney AH, Pernoll ML. *Current Obstetric & Gynecologic Diagnosis & Treatment.* Norwalk, CT: Appleton & Lange, 1994: 1012.)

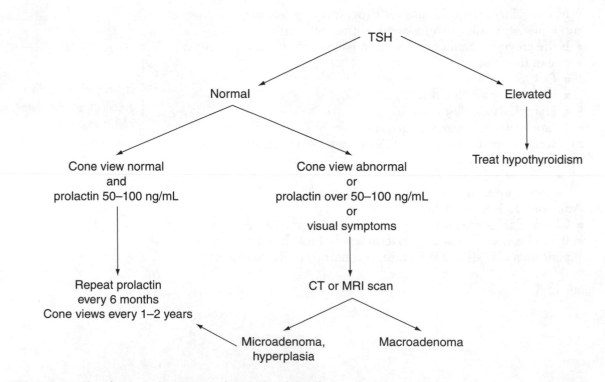

FIGURE 15-4. Workup for secondary amenorrhea with galactorrhea.
(Redrawn, with permission, from DeCherney AH, Pernoll ML. *Current Obstetric & Gynecologic Diagnosis & Treatment.* Norwalk, CT: Appleton & Lange, 1994: 1011.)

Treatment of Amenorrhea

Hypothalamic Causes
- Tumor removal
- Weight gain
- Stress relief
- Exogenous pulsatile GnRH

Pituitary Causes
- Tumor removal
- Bromocriptine (dopamine agonist inhibits prolactin release)
- Exogenous FSH/LH

Ovarian Causes
- Ovarian failure—in vitro fertilization, oral contraceptives
- PCOD—clomiphene (an antiestrogen)

Uterine Causes
- Obstruction—surgery

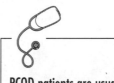

Early menopause is idiopathic.

PCOD patients are usually obese and have hirsutism and insulin resistance. It is the most common cause of hirsutism.

HYPERPROLACTINEMIA

Elevated prolactin levels could be due to:
- Hypothyroidism—check TSH level (hypothyroidism causes a rise in prolactin).
- Central nervous system (CNS) tumors—perform head CT/MRI.
- Drugs:
  - Dopamine antagonists
  - Methyldopa
  - Serotonin agonists
- Spinal cord lesions—perform spinal CT/MRI.

PREMENSTRUAL SYNDROME (PMS)

PMS refers to a group of symptoms experienced during the luteal phase of the menstrual cycle. Symptoms are cyclic in nature with resolutions and exacerbations.

Symptoms may manifest as:
- *Somatic complaints:* Headaches, bloating, breast tenderness
- *Emotional changes:* Anxiety, depression, irritability
- *Behavior symptoms:* Problems concentrating, food cravings, sleep changes

Management of PMS

- Diet—luteal-phase reductions in alcohol, caffeine, fats, tobacco, refined sugars: Decreases irritability by decreasing fluctuation in blood sugar levels
- Sodium restriction—decreases edema
- Oral contraceptive pills—cause anovulation, and this improves symptoms

- Nonsteroidal anti-inflammatory drugs (NSAIDs)—decrease inflammation found in PMS
- Selective serotonin reuptake inhibitors (SSRIs)
- GnRH agonists

SOME MOST COMMONS

- **Most common method of family planning:** Tubal sterilization
- **Most common reason for neonatal sepsis:** Chorioamnionitis (GBS, *E. coli*)
- **Most common reason for hospitalization in women of reproductive age:** Endometriosis
- **Most common postoperative complication:** Pulmonary atelectasis
- **Most common cause of primary amenorrhea:** Gonadal dysgenesis
- **Most common cause of fetal morbidity and mortality:** Preterm labor

ANDROGEN EXCESS, HIRSUTISM, AND VIRILISM

Androgens

Androgens are steroid hormones produced in the gonads (ovaries in women, the testes in males) and in the adrenal glands.

EFFECTS OF ANDROGEN EXCESS: HIRSUTISM AND VIRILIZATION

Androgens promote hair growth at puberty, although to different extents in each sex. Females, with low levels of androgens, develop visible pubic and axillary hair. Males, with greater concentrations of androgen, get additional hair growth on the face and chest, as well as masculinization (i.e., increased muscle mass, broadening of shoulders, and deepening of the voice).

Excess androgen in women will also result in these changes as well. In this context, these effects are termed hirsutism and virilism.

Hirsutism—the development of increased terminal hairs on the chest, abdomen, and face in a woman.

Virilization—the development of masculine characteristics in a woman, such as deepening of the voice, clitoromegaly, loss of female body contour, decreased breast tissue, and male pattern balding.

Hair Types

Vellus hairs are fine hairs found on most parts of the body. They are barely visible. **Terminal hairs** are the coarse, darker hairs found, for example, in the axilla and pubic region. Androgens facilitate the conversion of vellus to terminal hairs.

PRODUCTION OF ANDROGENS

In women, androgens are produced in two locations: The adrenals and the ovaries (in males, they are produced in the adrenals and testes).

ADRENAL PRODUCTION OF ANDROGENS

The **zona fasciculata** and the **zona reticularis** of the adrenal cortex produce androgens, as well as cortisol. ACTH regulates production.

A third layer of the adrenal cortex, the **zona glomerulosa,** produces aldosterone and is regulated by the renin–angiotensin system.

All three hormones—cortisol, androgens, and aldosterone—are derived from cholesterol. Androgen products from the andrenal are found mostly in the form of dehydroepiandrosterone (DHEA) and dehydroepiandrosterone-sulfate (DHEAS). Elevation in these products represents increased adrenal androgen production.

OVARIAN PRODUCTION OF ANDROGENS

In the ovaries, first, LH stimulates the theca cells to produce androgens (androstenedione and testosterone). Then, FSH stimulates granulosa cells to convert these androgens to estrone and estradiol. When LH levels become disproportionately greater than FSH levels, androgens become elevated.

PATHOLOGIES

Excess androgen can be either ovarian etiology or adrenal, neoplastic, or benign.

ADRENAL ETIOLOGIES

Cushing's Syndrome and Cushing's Disease

Cushing's syndrome is a general term meaning hypercortisolism along with the clinical picture that goes with it—moon face, buffalo hump, weakness, etc. Exogenous or endogenous cortisol can be the cause.

Cushing's disease is a subset of Cushing's syndrome, in which the increased cortisol level is due to ACTH hypersecretion by the pituitary, usually secondary to a benign pituitary adenoma. It accounts for 70% of Cushing's syndromes. Virilism and hirsutism are associated with this condition because the ACTH stimulates androgen production as well.

Paraneoplastic syndromes in which tumors (usually small cell lung cancer) produce ectopic ACTH are another cause of increased cortisol. These account for 15% of Cushing's syndromes.

Adrenal tumors (adenoma or carcinoma) account for the remaining 15% of Cushing's syndromes. In general, adenomas produce only cortisol, so no hirsutism or virilization is present. Carcinomas, by contrast, often produce androgens as well as cortisol, so they may present with signs of hirsutism and virilization.

Congenital Adrenal Hyperplasias

Congenital adrenal hyperplasia is a general term for disease entities involving defects in steroid, androgen, and mineral corticoid synthesis. Two such common entities that result in virilism and hirsutism due to increased androgens are 21-hydroxylase deficiency and 11β-hydroxylase deficiency.

Cortisol production in the adrenals:
Where? zonas fasciculata and reticularis
Regulated by? ACTH
Derived from? Cholesterol

DHEA and DHEAS are androgen products from the adrenals. Increased levels of these indicate that the source is adrenal.

High LH:FSH ratio in the context of androgen excess indicates that ovary is the source.

HIGH-YIELD FACTS

Menstruation

21-Hydroxylase deficiency—this is the most common congenital adrenal hyperplasia. The condition has various levels of severity. Affected individuals lack an enzyme crucial to cortisol and mineral corticoid production. Therefore, hormone synthesis is shunted to excessive production of androgens. Elevated serum 17-hydroxyprogesterone levels are found as well. In the severe form, affected females have ambiguous genitalia at birth, along with severe salt wasting and cortisol insufficiency. A milder form presents simply with virilization and hirsutism of females after puberty.

11β-Hydroxylase deficiency—this condition is associated with decreased cortisol, but increased mineral corticoids and androgens. The resultant picture is a severe hypertension with virilization/hirsutism (which results in pseudohermaphroditism of female babies). 11-Deoxycortisol levels are high.

OVARIAN ETIOLOGIES

Polycystic Ovarian Syndrome (PCOS)

PCOS is a common condition (affecting 5% of reproductive age women) and is characterized by hirsutism, virilization, amenorrhea, obesity, and diabetes (sometimes). Ovaries are found to have multiple inactive cysts with hyperplastic ovarian stroma. The LH:FSH ratio is often greater than 3:1. The cause is unknown, and the treatment is oral contraceptives.

Hyperthecosis

Hyperthecosis is when an area of luteinization occurs in the ovary, along with stromal hyperplasia. The luteinized cells produce androgens and hirsutism and virilization may result.

Theca Lutein Cysts

As described above, theca cells produce androgens and granulose cells transform the androgens to estrogens. Theca lutein cysts produce abnormally high levels of androgens, in excess of the amount that can be converted to estrogens. Diagnosis is made by ovarian biopsy.

Luteoma of Pregnancy

Luteoma of pregnancy is a benign tumor that grows in response to human chorionic gonadotropin. Virilization may occur in both the mother and the female fetus, although it may occur in the fetus alone. The tumor usually disappears postpartum, as do the clinical features.

Androgen-Secreting Ovarian Neoplasms

Sertoli–Leydig cell tumors and **hilar (Leydig) cell tumors** are rare conditions in which the neoplasms secrete androgens. They can often be distinguished from each other in that Sertoli–Leydig tumors usually present in young women with palpable masses and hilar cell tumors are found in postmenopausal women with nonpalpable masses.

Granulosa–theca cell tumors and **gonadoblastomas** are other examples of androgen-secreting ovarian tumors.

Abnormal Uterine Bleeding

DEFINITIONS

Menstrual abnormalities include:

- **Polymenorrhea**—menses with regular intervals that are too short (under 21 days)
- **Menorrhagia**—menses that are too long in duration (over 7 days) and/or menses associated with excessive blood loss (> 80 mL) occurring at *normal* intervals
- **Hypermenorrhea**—menses that are too long in duration (over 7 days) and/or menses associated with excessive blood loss (> 80 mL) occurring at *regular but not necessarily normal* intervals
- **Oligomenorrhea**—menses with intervals that are too long (cycle lasts more than 35 days)
- **Metrorrhagia**—bleeding occurring at irregular intervals; intermenstrual bleeding
- **Menometrorrhagia**—combination of both menorrhagia and metrorrhagia; menses too long in duration or excessive blood loss + irregular bleeding intervals
- **Kleine regnung**—bleeding for 1 to 2 days during ovulation (scant)

For an overview of bleeding, see Figure 16-1.

Menorrhagia—bleeding too long or too much. Menorrhagia is clinically signified by clots, anemia, increase in number of pads, and soiled clothing.

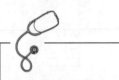

Metrorrhagia—the metro never comes according to schedule (bleeding at irregular intervals).

DIFFERENTIAL DIAGNOSES FOR MENORRHAGIA

Leiomyoma
Adenomyosis
Cervical cancer
Coagulopathy
Endometrial
  Hyperplasia
  Polyps
  Cancer

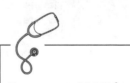

Use mnemonic **LACCE** for differential diagnoses of menorrhagia:
Leiomyoma
Adenomyosis
Cervical cancer
Coagulopathy
Endometrial
Hyperplasia
Polyps
Cancer

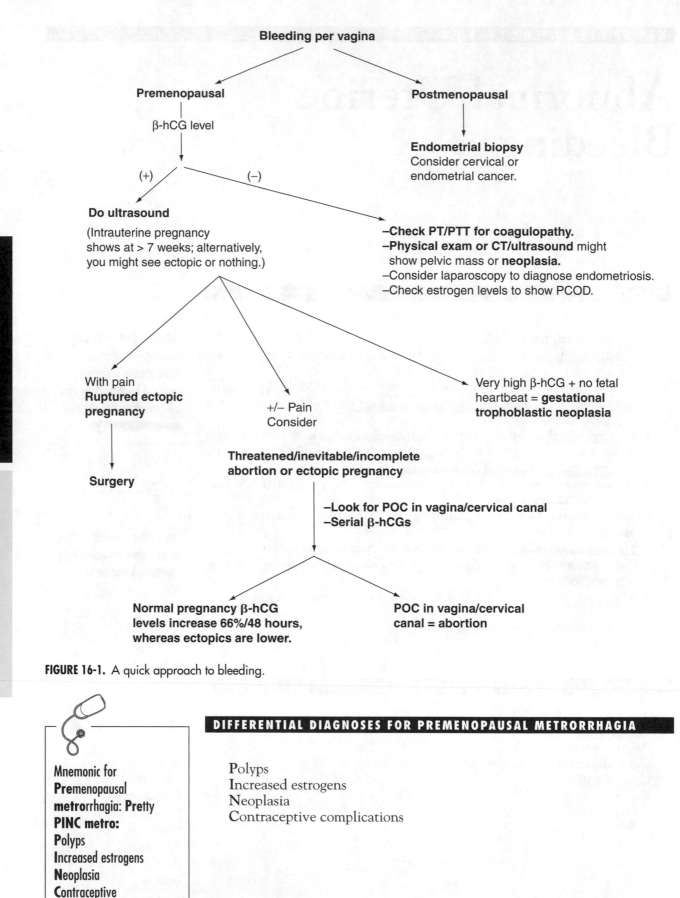

Bleeding per vagina

Premenopausal

β-hCG level

(+)   (−)

Postmenopausal

Endometrial biopsy
Consider cervical or
endometrial cancer.

Do ultrasound

(Intrauterine pregnancy
shows at > 7 weeks; alternatively,
you might see ectopic or nothing.)

–Check PT/PTT for coagulopathy.
–Physical exam or CT/ultrasound might
  show pelvic mass or **neoplasia.**
–Consider laparoscopy to diagnose endometriosis.
–Check estrogen levels to show PCOD.

With pain
**Ruptured ectopic
pregnancy**

+/− Pain
Consider

Very high β-hCG + no fetal
heartbeat = **gestational
trophoblastic neoplasia**

Surgery

**Threatened/inevitable/incomplete
abortion or ectopic pregnancy**

–Look for POC in vagina/cervical canal
–Serial β-hCGs

**Normal pregnancy β-hCG
levels increase 66%/48 hours,
whereas ectopics are lower.**

**POC in vagina/cervical
canal = abortion**

FIGURE 16-1. A quick approach to bleeding.

Mnemonic for
**Premenopausal
metro**rrhagia: **Pretty
PINC metro:**
Polyps
Increased estrogens
Neoplasia
Contraceptive

DIFFERENTIAL DIAGNOSES FOR PREMENOPAUSAL METRORRHAGIA

Polyps
Increased estrogens
Neoplasia
Contraceptive complications

Dysfunctional uterine bleeding (DUB) is abnormal uterine bleeding unrelated to anatomic lesions; usually caused by hormonal dysfunction.

DUB is a diagnosis *made by exclusion* after workup for other causes of abnormal uterine bleeding (caused by anatomical lesions) is negative.

CLASSIFICATION OF DUB

DUB is classified as either anovulatory or ovulatory, though it is *most often caused by anovulation*:

Anovulatory DUB: Anovulation results in constant endometrial proliferation without progesterone-mediated maturation and shedding. The "overgrown" endometrium continually and irregularly sheds. Causes of anovulatory DUB include:
- Polycystic ovaries (polycystic ovarian disease [PCOD])
- Obesity
- Unopposed exogenous estrogen

Ovulatory DUB: Inadequate progesterone secretion by corpus luteum causes a luteal-phase defect and results in DUB; it often presents with polymenorrhea or metrorrhagia.

EVALUATION OF DUB

History

- Thorough menstrual and reproductive history
- Signs of systemic disease (thyroid, liver, kidney)
- Social (extreme exercise, weight changes)
- Presence or absence of ovulation (regularity, premenstrual body changes)

TREATMENT OF DUB

- High-dose oral contraceptive pills

or

- Medroxyprogesterone acetate ≥ 10 days

Because DUB is usually caused by anovulation (PCOD, exogenous estrogens, obesity), oral contraceptives prevent DUB by mimicking the normal menstrual cycle changes to allow for endometrial maturation and sloughing. If DUB is ovulatory, nonsteroidal anti-inflammatory drugs are useful.

Only if medical treatment fails should endometrial ablation or hysterectomy be performed.

TREATMENT OF ACUTE BLEEDING EPISODES

- High-dose oral or IV estrogen
- High-dose oral contraceptives
- D&C

Tumors (benign and malignant) often present with menorrhagia or metrorrhagia.

Postcoital bleeds suggest trauma, infections, or cervical cancer.

HIGH-YIELD FACTS

Abnormal Uterine Bleeding

POSTMENOPAUSAL BLEEDING

Postmenopausal bleeding is vaginal bleeding more than 1 year after menopause.

Differential Diagnoses for Postmenopausal Bleeding

Endometrial
  Hyperplasia
  Cancer
Cervical cancer
Vulvar cancer
Estrogen-secreting tumor
Vaginal atrophy (most common)

Studies to Get

- **Endometrial biopsy and endocervical curettage** (because of the prevalence and danger of endometrial lesions)
- Pap smear for cervical dysplasia, neoplasia
- Ultrasound
- Hysteroscopy
- +/− Computed tomography (CT)

> Always do an endometrial biopsy when encountering postmenopausal bleeding because of the strong possiblity of endometrial cancer.

OTHER BLEEDING TIPS

- **Postcoital bleeding in pregnant woman: Consider placenta previa.**
- **Postcoital bleeding in nonpregnant woman: Consider cervical cancer.**
- **Postmenopausal bleeding: Consider endometrial cancer.**
- **Premenopausal bleeding: Consider PCOD.**

HIGH-YIELD FACTS

Abnormal Uterine Bleeding

Pelvic Pain

CHRONIC PELVIC PAIN

Definition and Criteria

- ≥ 6 months of pain
- Incomplete relief by medical measures
- Altered activities due to pain (e.g., missed work, homebound, depression, sexual dysfunction)

Etiologies

Leiomyoma
Endometriosis
Adhesions, adenomyosis
Pelvic inflammatory disease (PID)
Infections other than PID
Neoplasia

Workup

1. Detailed history (focusing on above etiologies):
   - Temporal pattern
   - Radiation
   - Associated symptoms
   - Past surgeries
   - Last menstrual period (LMP)
2. Physical exam:
   Look for:
   - Masses
   - Cervical motion tenderness
   - Gastrointestinal (GI) complaints
   - Neurological testing
3. Relation of pain to basal body temperature elevation (to rule out mittelschmerz pain associated with ovulation)
4. Blood work:
   - Complete blood count (CBC)
   - Pregnancy test

Pelvic pain accounts for 12% of hysterectomies, 40% of diagnostic laparoscopies, and 40% of 2° and 3° office visits.

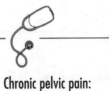

Chronic pelvic pain:
Think of "leapin' " pain.
Leiomyoma
Endometriosis
Adhesions, adenomyosis
Pelvic inflammatory disease (PID)
Infections other than PID
Neoplasia

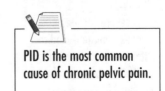

PID is the most common cause of chronic pelvic pain.

Mittelschmerz is pelvic pain associated with ovulation.

Laparoscopy is the final, conclusive step in diagnosing pelvic pain, but it should only be done once psychogenic causes are considered carefully.

Differential of acute pelvic pain:
"A ROPE"
- **A**ppendicitis
- **R**uptured ovarian cyst
- **O**varian torsion/abscess
- **P**ID
- **E**ctopic pregnancy

You always want to immediately rule out *life-threatening* and emergent conditions:
- Appendicitis
- Ectopic pregnancy
- Ovarian abscess
- Ruptured ovarian cyst

Pain severe for the patient to seek emergent medical attention must be quickly worked up because of the various life-threatening etiologies.

- STS (serotest for syphilis)
- Urinalysis (UA)
- Occult blood
- Blood culture
5. Radiographic studies:
    - Abdominal and vaginal sonogram
    - Computed tomography (CT)
    - Magnetic resonance imaging (MRI)
    - Barium enema
    - Bone scan
    - Renal sonogram/intravenous pyelogram (IVP)
6. Colonoscopy and/or cystoscopy (should be perfomed if all above are inconclusive)
7. Rule out psychosomatic pain.
8. Diagnostic laparoscopy

ACUTE PELVIC PAIN

Differential of Acute Pelvic Pain

- Appendicitis
- Ruptured ovarian cyst (most common)
- Ovarian torsion/abscess
- PID
- Ectopic pregnancy
(spells **"A rope"**)

See Table 17-1.

Etiologies

Same etiologies as above plus the following:
- GYN—all require surgery:
    - Ruptured ovarian cyst (*life threatening*)
    - Adnexal torsion
    - Tubo-ovarian abscess (*life threatening*)
- OB:
    - Ectopic pregnany (*life threatening*)—requires surgery
    - Abortion (spontaneous, threatened, incomplete)
- GI/GU:
    - Diverticulitis
    - Appendicitis (*life threatening*)—requires surgery
    - Urinary tract infection (UTI)
    - Inflammatory bowel disease (IBD), irritable bowel syndrome (IBS)

Workup

1. History
2. Physical exam (cervical motion tenderness, adnexal tenderness, and abdominal tenderness are all signs of PID)
3. Labs:
    - Pregnancy test (positive might indicate ectopic pregnancy or abortion)

- CBC (PID or appendicitis might give elevated WBCs)
- UA (leukocytes indicate possible UTI)
4. Pelvic sonogram (will show cysts and possibly torsion)
5. Diagnostic laparoscopy

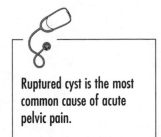

Ruptured cyst is the most common cause of acute pelvic pain.

TABLE 17-1. Differential Diagnosis of Acute GYN Pelvic Pain

	Clinical and Laboratory Findings					
Disease	**CBC**	**UA**	**Pregnancy Test**	**Culdocentesis**	**Fever**	**Nausea and Vomiting**
Ruptured ectopic pregnancy	Hematocrit low after treatment of hypovolemia	Red blood cells rare	Positive. Beta-hCG low for gestational age	High hematocrit Defibrinated, nonclotting sample with no platelets Crenated red blood cells	No	Unusual
Salpingitis/PID	Rising white blood cell count	White blood cells occasionally present	Generally negative	Yellow, turbid fluid with many white blood cells and some bacteria	Progressively worsening; spiking	Gradual onset with ileus
Hemorrhagic ovarian cyst	Hematocrit may be low after treatment of hypovolemia	Normal	Usually negative	Hematocrit generally < 10%	No	Rare
Torsion of adnexa	Normal	Normal	Generally negative	Minimal clear fluid if obtained early	No	Rare
Degenerating leiomyoma	Normal or elevated white blood cell count	Normal	Generally negative	Normal clear fluid	Possibly	Rare

Reproduced, with permission, from Pearlman MD, Tintinalli JE, eds. *Emergency Care of the Woman*. New York: McGraw-Hill, 1998: 508.

Endometriosis

DEFINITION

Endometriosis is the condition in which endometrial tissue is found outside of the uterus, often causing pain and/or infertility.

PREVALANCE

Five to 10% of women in reproductive age

PATHOPHYSIOLOGY

The ectopic endometrial tissue is *functional*. It responds to hormones and goes through *cyclic changes*, such as menstrual bleeding.

The result of this ectopic tissue is "ectopic menses," which causes peritoneal inflammation, pain, fibrosis, and, eventually, adhesions.

Tissue in endometriosis is viable and behaves normally.

SITES OF ENDOMETRIOSIS

Common
- Ovary (bilaterally)
- Cul-de-sac
- Fallopian tubes
- Uterosacral ligaments
- Bowel

Less Common
- Cervix
- Vagina
- Bladder

Rare
- Nasopharynx
- Lungs

Exam scenario: 37-year-old female complains of hemoptysis with each period. Diagnosis: Endometriosis of nasopharynx or lung

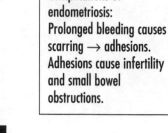

Complications of endometriosis: Prolonged bleeding causes scarring → adhesions. Adhesions cause infertility and small bowel obstructions.

ADHESIONS

Adhesions from prolonged endometriosis can cause:
- **Infertility** from fallopian tube or outer uterine adhesions
- **Small bowel obstruction** from intestinal adhesions

THEORIES OF ETIOLOGY

Though the etiology is unknown, there are three theories:

1. **Retrograde menstruation:** Endometrial tissue fragments are transported through the fallopian tubes and implant there or intra-abdominally.
2. **Mesothelial (peritoneal) metaplasia:** Peritoneal tissue becomes endometrial-like and responds to hormones.
3. **Vascular/lymphatic transport:** Endometrial tissue is transported via blood vessels and lymphatics.

CLINICAL PRESENTATION

Dyspareunia (painful intercourse) presents most commonly as pain with deep penetration.

Most commonly in women in their late 20s and early 30s:
- Pelvic pain:
  - Dysmenorrhea
  - Dyspareunia—implants on pouch of Douglas
  - Dyschezia (pain with defecation)—implants on rectosigmoid
- Infertility
- Vaginal staining (from vaginal implants)

SIGNS

- Retroflexed, tender uterus
- Nodular uterosacral ligaments
- Ovarian mass (endometrioma)
- Blue/brown vaginal implants (rare):
  - "Chocolate cyst"—an implant that occurs *within the ovarian capsule* and bleeds, creating a small blood-filled cavity in the ovary

DIAGNOSIS

1. **Laparoscopy or laparotomy:** Ectopic tissue *must be seen for diagnosis:*
   - Blue implants—new
   - Brown implants—older
   - White implants—oldest
2. **Biopsy:** Positive findings contain glands, stroma, hemosiderin.

- 30% asymptomatic
- If left untreated, most lead to increasing pain and possible bowel complications.
- Often, there is improvement with pregnancy secondary to temporary cessation of menses.

Maximum time on estrogen suppression should be 6 months due to adverse effects.

TREATMENT

Medical

All of these treatments suppress estrogen:
- Gonadotropin-releasing hormone (GnRH) agonists—suppress follicle-stimulating hormone (FSH); creates a pseudomenopause
- Progesterone (with or without estrogen)—creates a pseudopregnancy
- Danazol—an androgen derivative that suppresses FSH/LH, thus also causing pseudomenopause

The pulsatile fashion of endogenous GnRH stimulates FSH secretion. GnRH agonists are not pulsatile and therefore end up suppressing FSH.

Surgical

- Conservative (if reproductivity is to be preserved): **Laparoscopic lysis** of adhesions and implants

or

- Definitive: Total abdominal hysterectomy and bilateral salpingo-oophorectomy (TAH/BSO)

ADENOMYOSIS

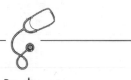

Pseudomenopause—↓ FSH/LH rather than ↑ FSH/LH as seen in "real" menopause.

Definition

Adenomyosis is endometrial tissue found *within the myometrium*. Adenomyosis and endometriosis rarely coexist.

Signs and Symptoms

Common
- Uterine enlargement
- Dysmenorrhea
- Menorrhagia

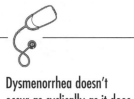

Dysmenorrhea doesn't occur as cyclically as it does in endometriosis.

Treatment

- GnRH agonist
- Mifepristone (RU 486)—a progesterone antagonist
- TAH/BSO if severe

HIGH-YIELD FACTS

Endometriosis

Adenomyosis

- Found in older women
- Doesn't respond to hormonal stimulation
- Noncyclical

Endometriosis

- Found in young women
- Tissue is responsive to estrogen.

- Cyclical

Pelvic Masses

DIFFERENTIAL DIAGNOSES

- Leiomyoma
- Pregnancy
- Endometriosis/adenomyosis
- Ovarian neoplasm
- Tubo-ovarian abscess (TOA)
- Ovarian cyst
- Adhesions (to uterus)
- Also, congenital anomalies, other carcinomas/sarcomas

Leiomyomas are the most common causes of undiagnosed pelvic masses.

HISTORIES SUGGESTIVE OF DIAGNOSES

In different contexts, pelvic masses are more likely to carry different diagnoses. The following are contexts and the likely diagnosis:

Context in Which Pelvic Mass Is Found	Likely Diagnosis
Painless abnormal uterine bleeding	Leiomyoma
Amenorrhea	Pregnancy, ovarian cysts
Dysmenorrhea	Endometriosis
Reproductive age	Pregnancy, ovarian cysts, leiomyoma, TOA, ovarian neoplasm
Postmenopausal	Neoplasm
History of pelvic inflammatory disease (PID)	Signs/symptoms of systemic illness—TOA, adhesions
History of surgery/endometriosis	Adhesions

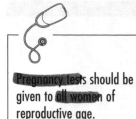
DIAGNOSTIC TESTS FOR VARIOUS CAUSES OF PELVIC MASSES

Pregnancy: Pregnancy test

Ovarian cysts: Physical exam (+ ultrasound (US) if needed for confirmation)

Leiomyoma: Physical exam (+ US, hysteroscopy if needed for confirmation)

Ovarian neoplasm: US, computed tomography (CT) scan, CA-125 level, surgical exploration, high level of suspicion due to age, family history

Endometrial neoplasm: ECC, D&C

Endometriosis/adenomyosis: Laparotomy/scopy

Tubo-ovarian abscess: History of PID, tender mass, KUB x-ray (showing ileus)

BENIGN OVARIAN MASSES

FUNCTIONAL OVARIAN CYSTS

Follicular Cysts

Follicular cysts are the most common functional ovarian cysts.

PHYSIOLOGY

Failure of rupture or incomplete resorption of the ovarian follicle results in a cyst. Just like the original follicle, the ovarian cyst is granulosa cell lined and contains a clear to yellow estrogen-rich fluid.

SIGNS AND SYMPTOMS

- Asymptomatic
- Oligomenorrhea
- Polymenorrhea
- Unilateral abdominal pain
- Acute pelvic pain (usually signifies rupture)

DIAGNOSIS

- Physical exam—pelvic and abdominal exam
- Sonography if necessary to confirm diagnosis

TREATMENT

- No treatment may be necessary, since most cysts resolve spontaneously within 2 months.
- Oral contraceptives may aid in the symptomatic patient.
- If the cyst is unresolved after 2 months, laparotomy/scopy is indicated to evaluate/rule out neoplasia.

Lutein Cysts

There are two types of lutein cysts: **Corpus luteum cysts** and **theca lutein cysts.**

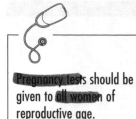
Pregnancy tests should be given to all women of reproductive age.

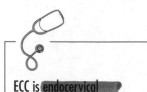
ECC is endocervical curettage—scraping of the endocervical canal with subsequent cytological examination.

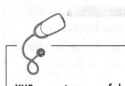
KUB x-ray is x-ray of the **k**idneys, **u**reters, and **b**ladder (portions of the intestines are also visualized).

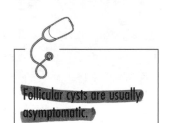
Follicular cysts are usually asymptomatic.

CORPUS LUTEUM CYST

The corpus luteum cyst is an enlarged and longer living, but *otherwise normal*, corpus luteum. It can produce progesterone for weeks longer than normal.

Signs/symptoms: Unilateral tenderness + amenorrhea
Diagnosis: History and physical/pelvic exam (once ectopic pregnancy has been ruled out), sonogram
Treatment (only if symptomatic): Analgesics, oral contraceptives, laparotomy/scopy if ruptured

Corpus hemorragicum is formed when there is hemorrhage into a corpus luteum cyst. If this ruptures, the patient will present with acute pain +/- bleeding symptoms (i.e., syncope, orthostatic changes).

THECA LUTEIN CYST

Increased levels of human chorionic gonadotropin (hCG) can cause *follicular overstimulation* and lead to theca lutein cysts, which are often *multiple and bilateral*.

Conditions that cause elevated hCG levels:
- Gestational trophoblastic disease (molar pregnancy)
- Polycystic ovarian disease
- Ovulation-inducing agents (clomiphene or hCG)
- Multiple gestation:

Signs/symptoms: Signs and symptoms are usually due to the accompanying condition that causes the elevated hCG.
Diagnostic finding: Elevated hCG levels
Treatment: One must treat the underlying condition; theca lutein cyst will resolve once hCG levels come down.

Pregnancy test must be performed to rule out ectopic pregnancy!

Amenorrhea is due to prolonged progesterone production.

LEIOMYOMAS (FIBROIDS)

Leiomyomas are localized, benign, *smooth muscle tumors of the uterus*. They are *hormonally responsive* and therefore become bigger and smaller corresponding to the menstrual cycle.

EPIDEMIOLOGY

Leiomyomas are found in 25 to 33% of reproductive-age women and in up to 50% of black women.

They are almost always multiple.

They are the most common indication for hysterectomy.

Extremely rarely do leiomyomas progress to malignancy (leiomyosarcoma).

SEQUELAE

Changes in uterine fibroids over time (i.e., postmenopausal) include:
- *Hyaline degeneration*
- *Calcification*
- *Red degeneration* (painful interstitial hemorrhage, often with pregnancy)
- *Cystic degeneration*—may rupture into adjacent cavities

UTERINE LOCATIONS OF LEIOMYOMAS

Submucous—just below endometrium; tend to bleed
Intramural—within the uterine wall
Subserous—just below the serosa/peritoneum

Leiomyomas are most commonly of the subserous type.

SYMPTOMS

- **Asymptomatic** in > 50% of cases
- **Bleeding** +/− anemia—one third of cases present with bleeding. Bleeding is usually menorrhagia, caused by:
  - Abnormal blood supply
  - Pressure ulceration
  - Abnormal endometrial covering
- **Pain**—secondary dysmenorrhea
- **Pelvic pressure**
- **Infertility**

DIAGNOSIS

- **Physical exam** (bimanual pelvic and abdominal exams): Fibroids are smooth, firm, and usually midline.
- **Sonography** (may also be visualized by x-ray, magnetic resonance imaging (MRI), CT, hysterosalpingogram (HSG), hysteroscopy, or intravenous urogram)
- Pap, ECC, and D&C can be done to rule out malignancy.

TREATMENT

No treatment is indicated for most women, as this hormonally sensitive tumor will likely shrink with menopause.

Pregnancy is usually *uncomplicated*. Bed rest and narcotics are indicated for pain with red degeneration. Tocolytics can be given to control/prevent premature contractions.

Treatment is usually initiated when:

- Tumor is > 12 to 14 weeks' gestation size.
- Hematocrit falls.
- Tumor is compressed (ureter, vessel).

Gonadotropin-releasing hormone (GnRH) agonists can be given for up to 6 months to shrink tumors (i.e., before surgery) and control bleeding:

Myomectomy—surgical removal of the fibroid in infertile patients with no other reason for infertility

Hysterectomy—indicated for women without future reproductive plans and with unremitting disability

---

Submucosal and intramural types of fibroids usually present as menorrhagia. Subserous type often presents with torsion.

Pregnancy with fibroids does carry increased risk for **preterm labor** and **fetal malpresentation.**

About one third of fibroids recur following myomectomy.

Cervical Dysplasia

OVERVIEW

Cervical dysplasia and cervical cancer lie on a continuum of conditions. Cervical dysplasia can take one of three paths:

1. Progress to cancer
2. Remain the same and not progress
3. Regress to normal

Preinvasive lesions
(confined to epithelium)
→ Normal epithelium
↓ Invasive cancer

RISK FACTORS FOR CERVICAL DYSPLASIA AND CERVICAL CANCER

- Human papillomavirus (HPV) infection
  80% of cases
  Risk highest if infected > 6 months
  Types 16, 18, 31, 33, high oncogenic potential
- High sexual activity (increase risk of viral/bacterial infections)
  Multiple sexual partners
  Intercourse at early age (± 17 years)
- Low socioeconomic status
- Genetic predisposition
- Cigarette smoking (smokers are deficient in folic acid and deficiency plays role in dysplasia)
- Alcohol, 2 to 4 drinks/wk, can increase risk of HPV infection.
- Oral contraceptives, particularly with use > 5 years (condoms decrease risk in these women) *post-coital contraception*
- Young women whose mothers took DES during pregnancy

Risk factors for cervical dysplasia:
OSHA Ends Dirt, Garbage, and Chemicals:
Oral contraceptives
Sex
HPV
Alcohol
Education/poverty
Diethylstilbestrol (DES)
Genetics
Cigarettes

LOCATION OF CERVICAL DYSPLASIA: TRANSFORMATION ZONE

The transformation zone is the area between the old and the new squamo-columnar junctions.

The squamo-columnar junction exists between the squamous epithelium of the vagina and ectocervix and the columnar epithelium of the endocervix. With age, metaplasia occurs, transforming columnar cells to squamous cells and thereby advancing the squamo-columnar junction proximally toward the

The adolescent cervix is more susceptible to carcinogenic stimuli.

endocervix. The area between the original junction and the new junction is the transformation zone.

Cervical dysplasia almost always forms at transformation zone.

PAP SMEAR

A cytologic screening test for cervical neoplasia

Technique

- A speculum is placed in the vagina to expose the uterine cervix (no digital exams or lubricants in the vagina prior to the Pap).
- Cells are scraped from the ectocervix with a spatula, then from the endocervix using an endocervical brush.
- The cells are smeared on a glass slide, fixative spray is applied, and the cells are examined.

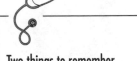

Two things to remember about Pap smear:
1. It is a screening tool.
2. It provides cytologic information, not histologic.

Success Rate of Pap

- Decreases incidence and mortality rate of invasive cervical cancer by 90%
- 80% sensitivity
- 99% specificity

Indications for Pap Smear

According to the American College of Obstetricians and Gynecologists (ACOG) (1989) recommendations:

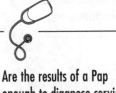

Are the results of a Pap enough to diagnose cervical cancer? No—Pap smear only gives cytology. Colposcopy and biopsy are needed for histology, which is necessary for diagnosis, staging, and treatment.

- Every woman should have a Pap smear (and pelvic exam) annually after age 18 or after onset of sexual activity.
- If three consecutive Pap smears and pelvic exams 1 year apart are normal, the screening interval can be lengthened.
- Lengthening is not recommended if the patient or her sexual partner has more than one other sexual partner.

Microscopic Analysis of Pap Smear

Cytologic analysis of cells taken from a Pap smear will indicate cervical dysplasia if there is:

- Clumping of chromatin
- Decreased cytoplasm resulting in a higher nucleus/cytoplasm ratio

Classification of Pap Smear Abnormalities

Remember, Pap smear gives information about cervical cytology. Two different systems exist that describe the possible findings of a Pap smear:

1. Modern Classification System A.K.A. CIN (cervical intraepithelial neoplasia): Describes the degree of abnormality of the cells
2. Bethesda system (SIL, squamous intraepithelial lesion): Describes three things: (1) the adequacy of the Pap test performed, (2) the degree of abnormality, and (3) a description of the cells

Modern Classification vs. Bethesda System

The following chart correlates the Bethesda staging with the CIN staging. All the terms are possible results of a Pap smear.

	Modern Classification System (CIN)	Bethesda Staging
Squamous lesions	Normal	Normal Benign cellular changes
	Atypical cells, possible inflammatory	Reactive cellular changes Atypical squamous cells of undetermined significance (ASCUS)
	CIN I—mild dysplasia: Neoplastic cells confined to lower one third of epithelium (60% spontaneously regress)	Low-grade squamous intraepithelial lesion (LGSIL)
	CIN II—moderate dysplasia: Involvement of two thirds of epithelium (43% regress)	High-grade squamous intraepithelial lesion (HGSIL)
	CIN III—severe dysplasia (carcinoma in situ): Involvement up to the basement membrane of the epithelium (33% regress, 12% advance to invasive cancer)	
	Squamous cell carcinoma	Squamous cell carcinoma
Glandular lesions	Atypical glandular cells	Atypical glandular cells of undetermined significance (AGCUS) AGCUS divides into endocervical or endometrial

Pap Smear Findings and Workup

- ASCUS—repeat Pap every 4 to 6 months until three consecutive negative smears.
- AGCUS—repeat Pap or perform biopsy.
- LGSIL—the majority regress or persist without regression, so either repeat Pap every 4 to 6 months or perform colposcopy with endocervical curettage (ECC).
- HGSIL—colposcopy with ECC

Definition

Low-magnification microscopic viewing with green filter light of cervix, vagina, and vulva

Indications

Abnormal finding on Pap smear:
- HGSIL and sometimes LGSIL
- Any other suspicious lesions

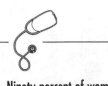

Ninety percent of women with abnormal cytologic findings can be adequately evaluated with colposcopy.

What must be completely visualized for adequate colposcopic evaluation? The transformation zone

Procedure

1. Speculum is inserted for visualization of the cervix.
2. Acetic acid is applied. Acetic acid dehydrates cells and causes precipitation of nucleic proteins in the superficial layers. The neoplastic cells appear whiter because of higher nucleus/cytoplasm ratio.
3. Colposcopy: Then a low-power microscope (colposcope) is used with green light to look for dysplasia. Signs of dysplasia include whiteness and abnormal vessels.
4. Cervical biopsy: Neoplastic and dysplastic areas are then biopsied under colposcopic guidance. Contraindications include acute PID or cervicitis. Pregnancy is NOT a contraindication.
5. ECC: A curette is then placed in the cervical canal to obtain endocervical cells for cytologic examination.

Information Provided by Colposcopy and ECC

If biopsy results or ECC is positive, cone biopsy or loop electrodiathermy excision procedure (LEEP)

CONE BIOPSY AND LEEP

Cone biopsy: A procedure performed in the operating room in which a cone-shaped biopsy is removed, including part of the endocervical canal
LEEP: A procedure performed in an office setting in which a small wire loop can be electrified to cauterize and remove a biopsy sample: Part of the endocervical canal is removed.

Indications for Cone Biopsy/LEEP

1. Inadequate view of transformation zone on colposcopy
2. Positive ECC
3. ± 2 grade discrepancy between colposcopic biopsy and Pap
4. Treatment for HGSIL
5. Treatment for adenocarcinoma-in-situ

LEEP as Treatment

LEEP can also be used to diagnose and treat CIN and VIN (vulvar intraepithelial neoplasia).

Guidelines for LEEP Treatment
- Never treat during pregnancy.
- Never treat without excluding invasive carcinoma.
- When treating, ablate entire transformation zone.
- Always excise keratinizing lesions.

CRYOTHERAPY

Cryotherapy is an outpatient procedure that uses a probe cooled with N_2O to $-70°F$ to ablate lesions.

Cryotherapy Indications and Complications

Indications: Treatment of LGSIL or HGSIL only if it is a lesion completely visualized on colposcopic exam

Complications: Include discharge, failure of therapy for HGSIL

LASER THERAPY

Light Amplification by Stimulated Emission of Radiation (LASER): A high-energy photon beam generates heat at impact and vaporizes tissue.

Indications for Laser Therapy

1. Excision or ablation of CIN
2. Ablation during laparoscopic surgery (e.g., endometriosis)

HIGH-YIELD FACTS

Cervical Dysplasia

Cervical Cancer

EPIDEMIOLOGY

Frequency

- Cervical cancer is expected to account for 12,800 new cancer cases in the United States in the year 2000.
- Cervical cancer is expected to account for 4,600 cancer deaths in the United States in the year 2000.

Age Affected

- Peak incidence between ages 45 and 55
- Fifteen percent of women develop it before age 30.
- Increasing percentage of women diagnosed before 20 years of age (perhaps due to early screening)

Race Prevalence

- More prevalent in African American (AA) women and urban Hispanic women than white women
- AA mortality rate = two times greater than whites

SYMPTOMS

Early Stages
- None
- Irregular/prolonged vaginal bleeding/pink discharge
- Postcoital bleeding (brownish discharge)

Middle Stages
- Postvoid bleeding
- Dysuria/hematuria

Advanced Stages
- Weight loss
- Bloody, malodorous discharge
- Severe pain, due to spread to sacral plexus

Cervical cancer is the third most common gynecologic malignancy (breast cancer is first; ovarian cancer is second).

Symptoms of cervical cancer become evident when cervical lesions are of moderate size; looks like "cauliflower."

- Eversions
- Polyps
- Papillary endocervicitis/papillomas

Tuberculosis, syphilitic chancres, and granuloma inguinale can also cause cervical lesions.

Cancer cells create foci of keratinization with cornified "pearls" that can be visible.

Adenocarcinoma is relatively resistant to radio- and chemotherapy compared to squamous cell carcinoma.

Cancers that metastasize to cervix:
Remember: **RIB E**ye steak.
Rectal
Intra-abdominal
Bladder
Endometrial

TYPES OF CERVICAL CANCER

Squamous Cell Cancer

- Accounts for **80%** of cervical cancer

Types of Squamous Cell Carcinoma
- Keratinizing
- Nonkeratinizing:
  - *Well-demarcated* tumor-stromal borders
- Small-cell carcinoma:
  - Small, round, or spindle-shaped cell with *poorly defined* tumor-stromal borders

Adenocarcinoma

- Accounts for **10 to 20%** of all invasive cervical cancers
- Arises from columnar cells lining the endocervical canal and glands
- **Early diagnosis is difficult → 80% false-negative rate with Pap smear**

Cancers Metastatic to Cervix by Direct Extension

Rectal
Intra-abdominal
Bladder
Endometrial

Occasionally (via hematogenous spread): Breast, lung

SITES OF DISTANT ORGAN METASTASES (IN ORDER OF FREQUENCY)

1. Lung
2. Liver
3. Bone

CLINICAL STAGING OF INVASIVE CERVICAL CANCER

Clinical staging of cervical cancer is important for prognosis and treatment.

Modes of Staging
- Pelvic and rectal exam (under anesthesia)
- Chest x-ray
- Liver function tests
- Evaluate genitourinary tract via intravenous pyelogram or computed tomography (CT) with intravenous contrast dye.
- Evaluate lymph node enlargements or abnormalities with external CT-guided biopsies.

TREATMENT OF INVASIVE CERVICAL CANCER

- **Radical surgery**—radical hysterectomy with lymph node dissection
- **Radiation therapy**—high-dose delivery to the cervix and vagina, and minimal dosing to the bladder and rectum:
  - External beam whole pelvic radiation
  - Transvaginal intracavitary cesium—transvaginal applicators allow significantly larger doses of radiation to surface of cervix.

> Radical hysterectomy requires removal of:
> Uterus
> Cervix
> Parametrial tissue
> Upper vagina
> + Pelvic lymphadenectomy from the bifurcation of the iliac vessels to the level of the inguinal ligament

TREATMENT FOR BULKY CENTRAL PELVIC DISEASE

- Hysterectomy after radiation therapy
- Tumor cytoreduction:
  - Use of cytotoxic chemotherapy before definitive treatment with radiation or radical surgery

RECURRENT CERVICAL CARCINOMA

- Recurs within 2 to 3 years of primary treatment

Screening for Recurrent Cancer

Look for:
- Vaginal bleeding
- Hematuria/dysuria
- Constipation/melena
- Pelvic and leg pain
- Fistulas
- Sacral backache or pain in sciatic distribution
- Costovertebral angle and flank pain

Cause of Death

- Uremia and pyelonephritis are major causes of death in cervical cancer.
- Found in 50% of patients

Excretory urogram can identify periureteral compression by tumor.

Treatment of Recurrent Cancer

- Patients may only be treated for cure if disease is confined to pelvis.
- Patients with central recurrence after radical hysterectomy are treated with **radiation.**
- Patients previously treated with radiotherapy are only treated by **radical pelvic surgery.**
- Chemotherapy:
  - Response rates higher with combination therapy
  - Most combinations include platinum.
  - Response rates = 50 to 70% for 4 to 6 months of life.

CLEAR CELL ADENOCARCINOMA OF CERVIX

- Incidence in women exposed in utero to diethylstilbestrol (DES) = 1:1000
- *Who?* Ages 16 to 27; median age = 19 years
- Overall survival rate—80%
- 5-year survival rate for stage I disease—> 90%

Women who took DES themselves during pregnancy have a 1.35% increased relative risk of breast cancer.

Screening of DES-Exposed Women

- Annual Pap smear
- Careful palpation of vaginal walls to rule out adenosis or masses

Treatment

- Similar to treatment of squamous cell carcinoma of cervix
- Preferred treatment is radical hysterectomy and pelvic lymph node dissection for stage I or IIA.
- Vaginectomy if vagina is involved

Disease Recurrence

- Most DES-related clear cell carcinomas recur ≤ 3 years of initial treatment.
- Pulmonary and supraclavicular nodal metastasis common → yearly screening chest x-ray recommended

TABLE 21-1. Staging of Invasive Cervical Cancer

International Federation of Gynecologists and Obstetricians (FIGO) Stage	Description of Carcinoma	5-Year Survival Rate Post Treatment
0	In situ; intraepithelial carcinoma	
I	Confined to cervix; preclinical IA Preclinical (Diagnosis only by microscopy) ■ Minimal microscopic invasion of stroma: ■ Max of 7-mm horizontal spread	65–90%
	IA-1 ≤ 3-mm depth	
	IA-2 > 3-mm to ≤ 5-mm depth from the base of the epithelium	
	IB ■ Clinically confined to cervix ■ Preclinical greater than IA-2	85%
	IB-1 Clinical lesion ≤ 4 cm in diameter	
	IB-2 Lesion > 4 cm in diameter	
II	■ Carcinoma extends beyond cervix ■ Has not extended to pelvic wall ■ Involves upper two thirds of vagina, but not lower 2	45–80% 30–40% if adenocarcinoma
	IIA No parametrial involvement	
	IIB Obvious parametrial involvement	
III	■ Carcinoma extended to pelvic wall ■ No cancer-free space between the tumor and the pelvic wall (on rectal exam) ■ Tumor involves lower one third of vagina ■ Hydronephrosis or nonfunctioning kidney	< 60% 20–30% if adenocarcinoma
	IIIA Does not involve pelvic wall	
	IIIB Involves pelvic wall	
IV	Carcinoma extends beyond true pelvis or Clinically involves mucosa of bladder or rectum	< 15%
	IVA Spread to adjacent organs	
	IVB Spread to distant organs	

TABLE 21-2. TNM Category Staging

T		First Resection of Primary Tumor
	TX	Primary tumor cannot be assessed
	T0	No evidence of primary tumor
	T1	Confined to cervix
	T2	Beyond cervix Upper two thirds vagina but not lower one third
	T2a	No parametrium
	T2b	Parametrial involvement
	T3	Tumor extends to pelvic wall Involves lower one third vagina Kidney dysfunction
	T3a	Pelvic wall not involved
	T3b	Pelvic wall involved
	T4	Distant metastasis
	T4a	Adjacent organs
	T4b	Distant organs
N		**Regional Lymph Nodes**
	NX	Regional lymph nodes cannot be assessed
	N0	No regional lymph node metastasis
	N1	Regional lymph node metastasis
M		**Distant Metastasis**
	MX	Presence of distant metastasis cannot be assessed
	M0	No distant metastasis
	M1	Distant metastasis (excludes peritoneal metastasis)

TABLE 21-3. Grading of Cervical Carcinoma

Grade	Invasive Squamous Tumor	Adenocarcinoma
X	Cannot be assessed	
1	Well differentiated	■ Small component of solid growth and nuclear atypia ■ Mild to moderate
2	Moderately differentiated	Intermediate-grade differentiation
3	Poorly differentiated	■ Solid pattern ■ Severe nuclear atypia predominate
4	Undifferentiated	

Endometrial Cancer

GENERAL FACTS

An **estrogen-dependant neoplasm** that begins as proliferation of normal tissue: Over time, chronic proliferation becomes hyperplasia (abnormal tissue) and, eventually, neoplasia. Endometrial cancer is the most common gynecologic cancer. Most cases (> 75%) are diagnosed in *postmenopausal* women.

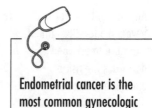

Endometrial cancer is the most common gynecologic cancer.

CLINICAL PRESENTATION

Abnormal bleeding is present in 90% of cases:
  - Bleeding in postmenopausal women (classic)

or
  - Meno/metrorrhagia (in premenopausal cases)

or
  - Abnormal Pap smear: 1 to 5% of cases

Pap smears are *not* diagnostic, but a finding of AGCUS (abnormal glandular cells of unknown significance) leads to further investigation.

DIFFERENTIAL DIAGNOSIS OF POSTMENOPAUSAL BLEEDING

  - Exogenous estrogens
  - Atrophic endometritis/vaginitis
  - Endometrial cancer
  - Endometrial/cervical polyps

Postmenopausal bleeding always requires an endometrial biopsy as the first step in the workup.

Etiologies of Endometrial Cancer

All etiologies (except radiation) result in **chronic elevations** in circulating levels of **estrogen:**
  - Ovarian failure (i.e., polycystic ovarian disease [PCOD])
  - Exogenous estrogens
  - Estrogen-producing tumors (i.e., granulosa cell tumors)
  - Liver disease (a healthy liver metabolizes estrogen)
  - Previous radiation (leading to sarcomas)

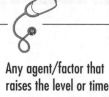

Any agent/factor that raises the level or time of exposure to estrogen is a risk factor for endometrial cancer.

Risk Factors

- Obesity
- Early menarche/late menopause
- Nulliparity
- PCOD
- Diabetes mellitus
- Hypertension
- Endometrial hyperplasia
- Tamoxifen treatment for breast cancer (increases risk two to three times)

Protective Factors

- Combined oral contraceptives
- Cigarette smoking
- Multiparity

Any agent/behavior that lowers the level or time of exposure to estrogen decreases the risk of endometrial cancer.

Diagnosis of Endometrial Hyperplasia and Cancer

- **Biopsy** (gold standard)
- Pap smear (to evaluate cervical involvement)
- Endocervical curettage (specimens from endocervix and cervix must be examined separately to determine if there has been spread)

A positive finding would include endometrial hyperplasia or cancer.

ENDOMETRIAL HYPERPLASIA

Endometrial hyperplasia is a precancerous condition. Types include the following:

Simple (Cystic Hyperplasia Without Atypia)
- *Glandular and stromal proliferation:* 1 to 2% progress to cancer (this is the most differentiated and lowest risk of cancer)

Complex (Adenomatous Hyperplasia Without Atypia)
- *Only glandular proliferation* (both simple and complex are treated with progesterone)

Atypical
- Simple type of atypical
- Complex type of atypical
- Proliferation with **cytologic atypia**

In general, the most differentiated hyperplasia is the lowest risk of developing into cancer, and the least differentiated is the highest risk.

Twenty-nine percent of atypical endometrial hyperplasias progress to cancer:
- Simple type is treated by hysterectomy.
- Complex type is treated like cancer.

Workup for Endometrial Cancer

After diagnosis of endometrial cancer is made, the following should be performed to evaluate for possible metastasis:
- Physical exam

- Pathology
- Chest x-ray
- Labs
- CA-125

Histologic Subtypes of Endometrial Cancer

- **Endometroid** (ciliated adenocarcinoma)—75 to 80%
- **Papillary serous:**
  - *Poor prognosis*
  - No history of elevated estrogen
  - More common in blacks
  - Acts like ovarian cancer
  - Presents late (stage IV)
- **Sarcomas** (covered below)

STAGING OF ENDOMETRIAL CANCER

Staging is determined by the **extent of the tumor.** Therefore, **staging must be accomplished surgically,** not clinically, so the tumor can be visualized. This is always the first step in treatment.

I—only uterine involvement	IA—limited to endometrium IB—invasion < one half of myometrium IC—invasion > one half of myometrium	90% 5-year survival
II—cervical involvement	IIA—endocervical glands only IIB—invasion of cervical stroma	70% 5-year survival
III—local spread	IIIA—invasion of serosa and/or adnexa, and/or positive peritoneal cytology IIIB—invasion of vagina IIIC—mets to pelvic/para-aortic lymph nodes	40% 5-year survival
IV—distant spread	IVA—invasion of bladder and/or bowel IVB—distant invasion, including intra-abdominal and/or inguinal lymph nodes	10% 5-year survival

GRADING

Grading is determined by the tumor **histology:**

GI   Well differentiated—< 5% solid pattern

GII   Moderately differentiated—5 to 50% solid pattern

GIII   Poorly differentiated—> 50% solid pattern

Grade is the most important prognostic indicator in endometrial cancer.

Basic treatment for all stages (surgical staging is always the first step):
- Total abdominal hysterectomy (TAH)
- Bilateral salpingo-oophorectomy (BSO)
- Nodal sampling
- Peritoneal washings

Adjuvant Therapy

After the above steps in treatment, adjuvant therapy depends on the stage.

Stages I–II   **Brachytherapy** (intracavitary radiation)

Stages III–IV **External beam radiation**
Hormone therapy: Progestin therapy is often used as adjuvant hormonal therapy:
- If the cancer is progesterone receptor positive—70% have a 5-year survival.
- If the cancer is receptor negative—15 to 20% have a 5-year survival.

Chemotherapy is used only for *cancers that recur outside the pelvis.*
   Doxorubicin
   Cisplatin

Side effects:
Doxyrubicin—cardiotoxicity
Cisplatin—nephrotoxicity

Uterine sarcoma is classified separately from endometrial cancer:
- Presents as a rapidly enlarging mass with bleeding
- Not from fibroids (< 1% of fibroids progress to cancer)
- Poor prognosis

Most cases are diagnosed with exploratory surgery for what was thought to be a uterine myoma (fibroid).

Types

- Leiomyosarcoma (LMS)
- Mixed mesodermal (MMD)
- Endometrial stromal sarcoma (ESS)

Diagnosis

- ≥ 10 mitosis/high-power field
- Usually diagnosed from specimen sent after hysterectomy
- Staged just like endometrial cancer

Treatment

- Surgical (TAH/BSO, nodes, washings)
- Plus adjuvant:
  - **LMS**—doxorubicin and cisplatin
  - **MMD**—ifosphamide and cisplatin
  - **ESS**—progestin therapy

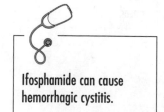

Ifosphamide can cause hemorrhagic cystitis.

Ovarian Cancer

There are two basic histologic types of ovarian cancer:
- Epithelial
- Nonepithelial

EPIDEMIOLOGY

- Second most common gynecologic malignancy
- Fifth most common cancer for women
- The deadliest gynecologic malignancy
- Seventy percent of patients are diagnosed as stage III or IV.
- 1 in 70 lifetime risk

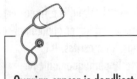

Ovarian cancer is deadliest gynecologic cancer because it is difficult to detect before dissemination. It is the second most common gynecologic cancer.

EPITHELIAL CELL OVARIAN CANCER

Ovarian cancer usually refers to epithelial cell type.

70% of cases of ovarian cancer are diagnosed at stage III or IV.

Histologic Subtypes of Epithelial Ovarian Cancer

Five subtypes arising from epithelial tissue:
- Serous   40%
- Endometroid   15%
- Mucinous   15%
- Undifferentiated   15%
- Clear cell   5%

Epithelial cell ovarian cancer accounts for 90% of all ovarian cancers.

Typical Clinical Presentation

Signs/symptoms are usually from metastasis. Ovarian cancer typically spreads by exfoliation of cancerous cells into the peritoneal fluid. The peritoneal fluid carries it to other structures in the abdomen.

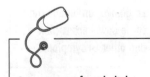

Serous type of epithelial ovarian cancer is the most common type of ovarian cancer and is bilateral 65% of the time.

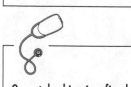

Typical scenario:
A postmenopausal woman with widening girth notices that she can no longer button her pants.
Diagnosis: Ovarian cancer.

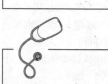

Omental caking is a fixed pelvic and upper abdominal mass with ascites. It is nearly pathognomonic for ovarian cancer.

Ovarian cancer spread is normally through the peritoneal fluid, which carries cancer cells to other abdominal structures.

Ovarian cancer metastasis to the umbilicus is "Sister Mary Joseph's nodule."

Large ovarian tumors can cause bowel obstruction and other GI symptoms.

About 25% of ovarian cancers occur in association with endometriosis.

Signs and Symptoms

- Pelvic mass
- Abdominal mass ("omental caking") (widening abdominal girth)
- Pleural effusion (dyspnea)
- Ascites
- Ventral hernia (due to ↑ intra-abdominal pressure)

CA-125

CA-125 is a tumor marker elevated in 80% of cases. It is useful in tracking the progression of the disease and the response to treatment.

Risk Factors

- Advanced age
- Family history
- Nulliparity
- Talc powder, high-fat diet, fertility drugs (data inconclusive on these)

Protective Factors

- Prolonged breast feeding
- Oral contraceptives
- Multiparity
- Reproductive surgery

HEREDITARY OVARIAN CANCER SYNDROMES

Five to 10% of cases occur in association with genetically predisposed syndromes called **hereditary ovarian cancer syndromes.** There are three types:

1. **Breast–ovarian cancer syndrome:** It involves cancer of the breast and ovary and is linked to the BRCA-1 gene, is autosomal dominant, is seen in younger women.
2. **Lynch II syndrome—hereditary nonpolyposis colon cancer (HNPCC):** It involves sites that may include breast, ovaries, uterus, and colon.
3. **Site-specific ovarian cancer:** It accounts for < 1% and has extremely strong genetic link. Usually two or more first-degree relatives have the disease.

OVARIAN CANCER WORKUP

1. As with any pelvic mass, the first step of evaluation is ultrasound.
2. Definitive identification of adnexal mass by laparoscopy/laparotomy follows.

Screening Recommendations

- Women with **standard risk** (fewer than two first-degree relatives with ovarian cancer): No routine screening recommended
- Women with **high risk** (two or more first-degree relatives with ovarian cancer): Genetic testing and counseling

If testing shows one of the hereditary syndromes, perform:

- Annual CA-125
- Annual transvaginal ultrasound
- Annual pelvic exam

STAGING

Ovarian cancer is staged surgically, not clinically.

Stage I—tumor limited to ovaries	IA—one ovary, capsule intact IB—both ovaries, capsules intact IC—tumor on ovary surface, capsule ruptured, ascites with malignant cells, or positive peritoneal washings	> 90% 5-year survival
Stage II—pelvic spread	IIA—involvement of uterus/tubes IIB—involvement of other pelvic structures IIC—IIA or IIB plus tumor on ovary surface, capsule ruptures, ascites with malignant cells, or positive peritoneal washings	70% 5-year survival
Stage III—spread to the abdominal cavity	IIIA—positive abdominal peritoneal washings *microscopic* IIIB—≤ 2-cm implants on abdominal peritoneal surface IIIC—> 2-cm implants on abdominal peritoneal surface and/or positive retroperitoneal or inguinal nodes	25% 5-year survival
Stage IV—distant metastasis	Parenchymal liver/spleen spread Pleural effusion, skin or supraclavicular nodes	5% 5-year survival

TREATMENT

Surgery is used to get rid of as much of the tumor as possible, as well as to biopsy like sites of spread. This always includes total abdominal hysterectomy/bilateral salpingo-oophorectomy and often includes lymph node sampling, omentectomy, and bladder and bowel resection. Debulking is the attempt to remove as much of the primary and metastatic tumor sites as possible and is employed in advanced disease.

Postop Management

First-line chemotherapy: Paclitaxel and cisplatin *or* paclitaxel and carboplatin:

Stage I–II   **Only chemotherapy** if stage I/IIC or high-grade tumor

Stage III–IV   **Chemotherapy,** plus:
Radiation if residual tumor < 2 cm
Interval debulking if tumor > 2 cm (internal debulking means additional surgery after chemotherapy)

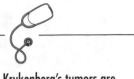

Krukenberg's tumors are ovarian tumors that are metastatic from another primary cancer, usually of colon, breast, or uterine origin.

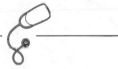

CA-125 is elevated in 80% of cases of ovarian cancer, but only in 50% of stage I cases. It is most useful as a tool to gauge progression/regression of disease.

Ovarian and endometrial tumors are staged surgically, whereas cervical cancer is staged clinically.

Poor Prognostic Indicators

- Short disease-free interval
- *Mucinous or clear cell tumor*
- Multiple disease sites
- *High CA-125*

NONEPITHELIAL OVARIAN CANCER

These account for roughly 10% of ovarian cancers.

Histologic Types

- Germ cell—8% of all ovarian cancers; include teratomas, dysgermino-mas, choriocarcinomas
- Gonadal–stromal—1% of all ovarian cancers; include granulosa–theca cell tumors, Sertoli– Leydig tumors

OVARIAN GERM CELL TUMORS (GCTS)

Eight percent of ovarian cancers are GCTs. GCTs arise from totipotential germ cells that normally are able to differentiate into the three germ cell tissues. Ninety-five percent are benign.

Clinical Presentation

- Abdominal pain with rapidly enlarging palpable pelvic/abdominal mass
- Acute abdomen
- Fever
- Vaginal bleeding
- Usually found in children or young women

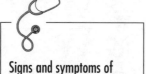

Signs and symptoms of GCTs are from the primary tumor, not mets (unlike epithelial ovarian cancer).

Types of Ovarian GCTs

Dysgerminoma (Most Common) (arises from totally undifferentiated totipotential germ cells)
- Affects women *in teens to early 20s*
- 20% bilateral
- 20% associated with pregnancy
- **LDH is the tumor marker.**

Endodermal Sinus Tumor (arises from extraembryonic tissues)
- 20% of GCTs
- Most aggressive GCT
- Characteristic **Schiller–Duval bodies**
- AFP is the tumor marker.

Immature Teratoma (arises from embryonic tissues)
- 20% of GCTs
- Mixture of cells representing all three germ layers

Embryonal and Choriocarcinoma (arise from trophoblasts)
- Rare
- Tumors may cause **sexual precocity** or abnormal uterine bleeding.
- **β-hCG is the tumor marker.**

Mixed GCTs
- 10% of GCTs
- Dysgerminoma and endodermal sinus tumor is the most common combination.
- **LDH, AFP,** and **β-hCG** may be elevated.

Treatment of Ovarian GCTs

- Surgery:
  - **Unilateral** adnexectomy and complete surgical staging
- Adjuvant chemotherapy:
  - Recommended for all but stage I, grade I immature teratoma

BEP Therapy	Side Effects
- Bleomycin	Pulmonary fibrosis
- Etopiside	Blood dyscrasias
- CisPlatin	Nephrotoxicity

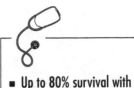

- Up to 80% survival with incomplete resection
- GCTs are very chemosensitive.

Prognosis of Ovarian GCTs

Prognosis is generally good because most are discovered *early*. Five-year survival is 85% for dysgerminomas, 75% for immature teratomas, and 65% for endodermal sinus tumors.

OVARIAN SEX CORD–STROMAL TUMORS

One percent of ovarian cancers: They arise from the sex cords of the embryonic gonad before they differentiate into male or female. They are functional tumors that secrete estrogen or testosterone. They usually affect older women.

Types of Sex Cord–Stromal Tumors

Granulosa–Theca Cell Tumor
- Secretes estrogens that can cause feminization, precocious puberty, or postmenopausal bleeding
- Association with endometrial cancer
- **Inhibin is the tumor marker.**

Sertoli–Leydig Cell Tumor
- Secretes testosterone
- Presents with *virilization, hirsutism, and menstrual disorders as a result of the testosterone*
- **Testosterone is the tumor marker.**

Treatment of Ovarian Sex Cord–Stromal Tumors

Surgical Treatment
- **TAH/BSO**
- **Unilateral** oophorectomy in young women with low-stage/grade neoplasia

Adjuvant Therapy
- Data are inconclusive, but chemotherapy and radiation play a small role at present.

TABLE 23-1. Ovarian Tumors and Their Serum Markers

Ovarian Tumor	Serum Tumor Marker
Dysgerminoma	LDH
Endodermal sinus tumor	AFP
Embryonal and choriocarcinoma	Beta-hCG
Epithelial ovarian tumor	CA-125
GCT	Inhibin
Sertoli–Leydig cell tumor	Testosterone

FALLOPIAN CELL CARCINOMA

Fallopian cell carcinomas usually are adenocarcinomas. They spread through the peritoneal fluid in a similar fashion to ovarian cancer. It is very rare and can affect any age.

Fallopian cell carcinoma is the least common gynecologic malignancy.

In any postmenopausal bleeding or discharge that cannot be explained by endometrial biopsy, fallopian cell carcinoma should be considered.

Classic Presenting Triad
- Pain
- Vaginal bleeding
- Leukorrhea

Many are diagnosed during a laparotomy for other indications.

Hydrops tubae perfluens is the pathognomonic finding, defined as cramping pain relieved with watery discharge.

Staging, Treatment, and Prognosis
- All similar to ovarian cancer

Vulvar Dysplasia and Cancer

VULVAR INTRAEPITHELIAL NEOPLASIA (VIN)

Dysplastic lesions of the vulva that have potential to progress to carcinoma: Etiology is unknown, although human papillomavirus (HPV) has been implicated because of similarity in pathology and often concomitant presence of cervical intraepithelial neoplasia (CIN).

Risk Factors

Like cervical cancer, vulvar cancer risk factors include HPV types 16, 18, 31, and 33, and the precancerous lesions are classified as intraepithelial neoplasia (termed VIN as opposed to CIN).

Presentation

Pruritus and/or irritation (recent or long-standing), raised white lesions

Diagnosis

- Biopsy
- Colposcopic exam (must include cervix, vagina, perineal and perianal skin)

Staging

As in cervical dysplasia, VIN is based on degree of epithelial spread:

VIN I—involvement of < ½ epithelium.

VIN II—involvement of > ½ epithelium

VIN III—full-thickness involvement (carcinoma-in-situ)

Treatment

Treatment is according to the size of the lesion:
- Small, well-circumscribed VIN → wide local excision
- Multifocal lesions → laser vaporization
- Extensive lesions → vulvectomy

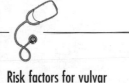

Risk factors for vulvar dysplasia include HPV, herpes simplex virus type II (HSV-II), lymphogranuloma venereum (LGV), pigmented moles, and poor hygiene.

Most common site of vulvar dysplasia is labia majora.

Vulvar cancer is a relatively rare gynecologic cancer (4 to 5% of all gynecologic cancers) and can arise as carcinoma of various types:
- Squamous (90%)
- Adeno
- Basal
- Melanoma
- Metastasis

Most often found in women 60 to 70 years old

Signs and Symptoms

- Pruritus (most common)
- Ulceration
- Mass (often exophytic)
- Bleeding

Risk Factors

Same as vulvar dysplasia (HPV, HSV-II, LGV, pigmented moles, and poor hygiene)

Diagnosis

Biopsy of the suspicious lesion

Staging

Stage I: < 2-cm tumor, no spread	Survival > 90%
Stage II: > 2-cm tumor, no spread	Survival > 90%
Stage III: Spread to unilateral nodes or vagina or anus or lower urethra	Survival rates correlate to number of positive nodes: 1 node ≈ 85%; ≥ 3 nodes ≈ 15%
Stage IV: Mucosa, bilateral nodes Stage IVa: Spread to upper urethra, rectal Stage IVb: Distant mets	Survival < 10%

Treatment

Stages I–II
Radical vulvectomy and lymphadenectomy (wide local excision is sometimes possible for certain small lesions < 1 cm)

Stages III–IV
As above, plus removal of affected organs and adjunct radiation therapy

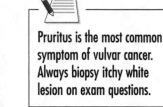

Pruritus is the most common symptom of vulvar cancer. Always biopsy itchy white lesion on exam questions.

HIGH-YIELD FACTS

Vulvar Dysplasia

- Vaginal cancer is a rare gynecologic malignancy (2% of gynecologic cancers).
- Usually presents in **postmenopausal women**
- Most common type is squamous cell carcinoma (others types are the same as vulvar cancer types).

Signs and Symptoms

- Ulcerated mass
- Exophytic mass
- Bleeding
- Asymptomatic

Adenocarcinoma of the vagina often correlates with in utero diethylstilbestrol exposure; these patients often present young.

Diagnosis

Biopsy of suspicious lesion

Staging

Stage I: Limited to vaginal mucosa   Survival ≈ 75%

Stage II: Beyond mucosa but not   Survival ≈ 70%
    involving pelvic wall

Stage III: Pelvic wall involvement   Survival ≈ 35%

Stage IV: Involvement of bladder,   Survival < 15%
    rectum, or distant mets

Treatment

Stages I–II
Surgical resection and radiation

Stages III–IV
Radiation only

Gestational Trophoblastic Neoplasias (GTN)

DEFINITION OF GTN

Gestational trophoblastic neoplasias are neoplasms arising from placental syncytiotrophoblasts and cytotrophoblasts.

The four tumors are:
- Hydatidiform mole (complete or partial)
- Invasive mole
- Choriocarcinoma
- Placental site trophoblastic tumor

HYDATIDIFORM MOLE

Complete Mole

A placental (trophoblastic) tumor forms when a maternal ova devoid of DNA is "fertilized" by the paternal sperm:

Karyotype: Most have karyotype 46XX, resulting from sperm penetration and subsequent DNA replication. Some have 46XY, believed to be due to two paternal sperms simultaneously penetrating the ova.

Epidemiology: Incidence is:
- 1 in 1,500 pregnancies in the United States
- 1 in 200 in Mexico
- 1 in 125 in Taiwan

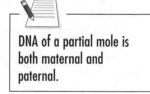

DNA of complete mole is always paternal.

Partial Mole

A mole with a fetus or fetal parts. Women with partial (incomplete) molar pregnancies tend to present later than those with complete moles:

Karyotype: Usually 69XXY, and contains both maternal and paternal DNA

Epidemiology: 1 in 50,000 pregnancies in the United States

DNA of a partial mole is both maternal and paternal.

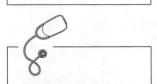

A young woman who passes grape-like vesicles from her vagina should be diagnosed with hydatidiform mole.

All early (< 20 weeks) preeclampsia is molar pregnancy until proven otherwise.

GTN secrete human chorionic gonadotropin (hCG), lactogen, and thyrotropin.

Ten to 15% of complete moles will be malignant. Two percent of partial moles will be malignant.

Any of the following on exam indicates molar pregnancy:
- Passage of grape-like vesicles
- Preeclampsia early in pregnancy
- Snow storm pattern on ultrasound

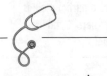

Nonmetastatic malignancy has almost a 100% remission rate following chemotherapy.

Invasive Mole

A hydatidiform mole that invades the myometrium: It is by definition malignant, and thus treatment involves complete metastatic workup and appropriate malignant/metastatic therapy (see below).

HISTOLOGY OF HYDATIDIFORM MOLE

- Trophoblastic proliferation
- Hydropic degeneration (swollen villi)
- Lack/scarcity of blood vessels

SIGNS AND SYMPTOMS

- Passage of vesicles (look like grapes)
- Preeclampsia < 20 weeks
- Abnormal painless bleeding in first trimester

DIAGNOSIS

- hCG > 100,000 mIU/mL
- Absence of fetal heartbeat
- Ultrasound- "snowstorm" pattern
- Pathologic specimen—grapelike vesicles
- Histologic specimen (see above)

Treatment of Complete or Partial Moles

- Dilation and curettage (D&C) to evacuate and terminate pregnancy
- Follow-up with the workup to rule out invasive mole (malignancy):
  - Chest x-ray (CXR) to look for lung mets
  - Liver function tests to look for liver mets
  - Weekly hCG level: The hCG level should decrease and return to normal within 2 months. If the hCG level rises, does not fall, or falls and then rises again, the molar pregnancy is considered malignant, and metastatic workup and chemotherapy is necessary.
- Contraception should be used during the 1-year follow-up.

Metastatic Workup

CXR, computed tomography (CT) of brain, lung, liver, kidneys

Treatment (For Nonmetastatic Molar Pregnancies)

- Chemotherapy—methotrexate or actinomycin-d (as many cycles as needed until hCG levels return to normal)

or

- Total abdominal hysterectomy + chemotherapy (fewer cycles needed)

Treatment for metastatic molar pregnancy is the same as for choriocarcinoma (see below)

CHORIOCARCINOMA

An epithelial tumor that occurs with or following a pregnancy (including ectopic pregnancies, molar pregnancies, or abortion):

Histopathology: Choriocarcinoma has characteristic sheets of trophoblasts with extensive hemorrhage and necrosis, and unlike the hydatidiform mole, choriocarcinoma has no villi.

Epidemiology: Incidence is about 1 in 40,000 pregnancies.

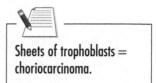

Sheets of trophoblasts = choriocarcinoma.

Diagnosis

- Increased hCG
- Absence of fetal heartbeat
- Uterine size/date discrepancy
- Specimen (sheets of trophoblasts, no villi)

As with invasive mole and malignant hydatidiform mole, a full metastatic workup is required when choriocarcinoma is diagnosed.

Treatment of Nonmetastatic Choriocarcinoma and Prognosis

- Chemotherapy—methotrexate or actinomycin-d (as many cycles as needed until hCG levels return to normal)

or

- Total abdominal hysterectomy + chemotherapy (fewer cycles needed)

Remission rate is near 100%.

Treatment of Metastatic Choriocarcinoma, Metastatic Invasive Mole, or Metastatic Hydatidiform Mole

Treatment is determined by the patient's risk (high or low) or prognostic score.

Prognostic Group Clinical Classification

Low risk:
- hCG < 100,000 IU/24-hr urine or < 40,000 mIU/mL serum
- Less than 4 months from antecedent pregnancy event or onset of symptoms to treatment
- No brain or liver metastasis
- No prior chemotherapy
- Pregnancy event is not a term pregnancy.

High risk: Opposite of above (i.e., hCG > 100,000 IU/24-hr urine, more than 4 months from pregnancy, brain or liver mets, etc.)

World Health Organization (WHO) Prognostic Scoring System

Risk Factor	SCORE			
	0	1	2	4
Age (years)	≤ 39	> 39		
Pregnancy	H. mole	Abortion	Term	
Interval from pregnancy event to treatment (in months)	< 4	4–6	7–12	> 12
hCG (IU/mL)	$< 10^3$	10^3–10^4	10^4–10^5	$> 10^5$
ABO blood group (female × male)		O × A A × O	B AB	
Number of metastases		1–4	5–8	> 8
Site of metastasis		Spleen Kidney	GI Liver	Brain
Size of largest tumor (cm)		3–5	> 5	
Prior chemotherapy agent		Single	Multiple	

Scores are added to give the prognostic score.

Treatment According to Score/Prognostic Factors

Low risk (score ≤ 4)	Single-agent therapy (methotrexate)	Remission rate 90 to 99%
Intermediate risk (score 5 to 7)	Multiple-agent therapy (MAC therapy—methotrexate, actinomycin, and cyclophosphamide)	Remission rate $\approx 50\%$
High risk (score ≥ 8)	Multiple-agent therapy (EMACO therapy—etoposide, MAC, and vincristine)	

HIGH-YIELD FACTS

GTN

PLACENTAL SITE TROPHOBLASTIC TUMOR (PSTT)

PSTT is a rare form of GTN. It is characterized by infiltration of the myometrium by intermediate trophoblasts, which stain positive for human placental lactogen. Unlike other GTN, hCG is only slightly elevated.

Treatment

Total abdominal hysterectomy: Prognosis is poor if there is tumor recurrence or metastasis.

Sexually Transmitted Diseases and Vaginitis

PELVIC INFLAMMATORY DISEASE (PID)

Definition

Inflammation of the female upper genital tract (uterus, tubes, ovaries, ligaments) caused by ascending infection from the vagina and cervix

Common Causative Organisms

- *Neisseria gonorrhoeae*
- *Chlamydia trachomatis*
- *Escherichia coli, Bacteroides*

Diagnosis

Physical Exam
- Abdominal tenderness
- Adnexal tenderness
- Cervical motion tenderness

Lab Results and Other Possible Exam Signs
- +/– Fever
- Gram-positive staining
- Pelvic abscess
- Elevated white count
- Purulent cervical discharge

Laparoscopy
This is the "gold standard" for diagnosis, but it is usually employed only in cases unresponsive to medical treatment.

Risk Factors

- Multiple sexual partners
- New sex partner(s)
- Unprotected intercourse
- Concomitant history of sexually transmitted disease

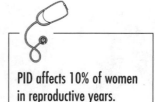

PID affects 10% of women in reproductive years.

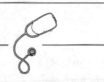

Rarely is a single organism responsible for PID, but always think of chlamydia and gonorrhea first.

Requirement for diagnosis of PID:
1) Abdominal tenderness
2) Adnexal tenderness
3) Cervical motion tenderness
Positive lab tests are not necessary for diagnosis.

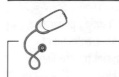

Chandelier sign—when you touch the cervix, there is so much pain that she jumps to the chandelier.

Criteria for Hospitalization

- Pregnancy
- Peritonitis
- Gastrointestinal (GI) symptoms (nausea, vomiting)
- Abscess (tubo-ovarian or pelvic)
- Uncertain diagnosis

Treatment

Inpatient
Cefotetan + doxycycline (preferred for chlamydia)
Clindamycin + gentamicin (preferred for abscess)

Outpatient
Ofloxacin + metronidazole
Ceftriaxone + doxycycline (preferred for chlamydia (because of doxycycline)

Sexual partners are treated also.

GONORRHEA

An infection of the urethra, cervix, pharynx, or anal canal, caused by the gram-negative diplococcus, *Neisseria gonorrhoeae*

Presentation

- Asymptomatic
- **Dysuria**
- **Endocervicitis**
- **Vaginal discharge**
- Pelvic inflammatory disease (PID)

Diagnosis

- Culture in Thayer–Martin agar (gold standard)
- Gonazyme (enzyme immunoassay)

Treatment

Ceftriaxone

or

Ciprofloxacin + doxycycline

or

Azithromax

Treat partners.

Sidebar notes:

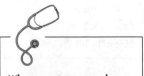

Criteria for hospitalization for PID:
GU PAP
GI symptoms
Uncertain diagnosis

Peritonitis
Abscess
Pregnancy

There is a 50 to 90% chance of transmission after one exposure to gonorrhea.

Fifteen percent of women with gonorrhea will progress to PID if untreated.

When treating gonorrhea, empirical treatment of chlamydial co-infection is also given.

Chlamydia is an infection of the genitourinary (GU) tract, GI tract, conjunctiva, nasopharynx, caused by *Chlamydia trachomatis*, an obligate intracellular bacteria.

Presentation

There are numerous serotypes of chlamydia generally speaking. Serotypes A–K cause more localized GU manifestations and the L serotypes a systemic disease (lymphogranuloma venereum).

Serotypes A–K

Serotypes A–K of *Chlamydia trachomatis* can have the following presentation:
- Asymptomatic
- **Mucopurulent discharge**
- **Cervicitis**
- **Urethritis**
- PID
- Trachoma—conjunctivitis resulting in eyelash hypercurvature and eventual blindness from corneal abrasions
- Fitz-Hugh–Curtis syndrome

Serotypes L1–L3

Serotypes L1–L3 of *Chlamydia trachomatis* cause **lymphogranuloma venereum.** This is a systemic disease that can present in several forms:
- Primary lesion—painless papule on genitals
- Secondary stage–lymphadenitis
- Tertiary stage—rectovaginal fistulas, rectal strictures

Diagnosis

- Microimmunofluorescence test (MIF)—measures antichlamydia immunoglobulin M (IgM) titers. Titer > 1:64 is diagnostic.
- Isolation in tissue culture
- Enzyme immunoassay

Treatment

Doxycyline or azithromycin/erythromycin

Syphilis is an infection caused by the spirochete *Treponema pallidum*.

Presentation

Syphilis has various stages of manifestation that present in different ways:
- Primary syphilis—**painless hard chancre** of the vulva, vagina, or cervix (or even anus, tongue, or fingers), usually appearing 1 month after exposure: Spontaneous healing after 1 to 2 months
- Secondary syphilis—**generalized rash** (often palms and soles), condyloma lata, mucous patches with lymphadenopathy, fever, malaise, usu-

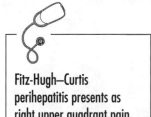

Chlamydia is twice as common as gonorrhea.

Fitz-Hugh–Curtis perihepatitis presents as right upper quadrant pain, fever, nausea, and vomiting. It can be caused by gonorrhea or chlamydia.

Use erythromycin rather than doxycycline for pregnant women or children with chlamydia.

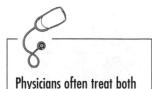

Physicians often treat both gonorrhea and chlamydia even if diagnosing only one.

ally **appearing 1 to 6 months after primary chancre:** Spontaneous regression after about 1 month
- Tertiary syphilis—**presents years later** with skin lesions, bone lesions (gummas), cardiovascular lesions (e.g., aortic aneurysms), central nervous system (CNS) lesions (e.g., tabes dorsalis).

Diagnosis

- Screening is done via rapid plasma reagin (RPR) or Venereal Disease Research Laboratory (VRDL). These are nonspecific and can give positive results for many conditions.
- Treponemal test (FTA-ABS) is a very specific test, performed if RPR is positive.
- Visualization of spirochetes on darkfield microscopy is an additional test available.

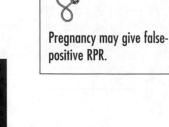

Pregnancy may give false-positive RPR.

Treatment

- **Penicillin G** for all stages, though in differing doses
- Doxycycline, if penicillin allergic

GENITAL HERPES

- Infection caused by herpes simplex virus type I (HSV-I) in 85% of cases, and by HSV-II in 15% of cases
- HSV is a DNA virus.
- Fifteen percent of adults have antibodies to HSV-II, most without history of infection.

Presentation

Patients with herpes can be asymptomatic, in addition to the following:
- *Primary infection:* **Painful multiple vulvar vesicles,** *associated with fever, lymphadenopathy, malaise,* usually 1 to 3 weeks after exposure
- *Recurrent infection:* Recurrence from viral stores in the sacral ganglia, resulting in a *milder version* of primary infection including vesicles.
- *Initial primary infection:* This is defined as **initial infection by HSV-II** in the presence of *preexisting antibodies to HSV-I.* The preexisting antibodies to HSV-II can make the presentation of HSV-I milder.

These patients present very ill.

Major Risks

- Cervical cancer
- Neonatal infection

Stress, illness, and immune deficiency are some factors that predispose to herpes recurrence.

Diagnosis

- Gross examination of vulva for typical lesions
- Cytologic smear—multinucleated giant cells (Tzanck test)
- Viral cultures

Treatment

Treatment for HSV is palliative and not curative.
- *Primary outbreak*—acyclovir
- *Recurrent infection*—one half original dose of acyclovir
- *Pregnancy*—acyclovir during third trimester

HUMAN IMMUNODEFICIENCY VIRUS (HIV) AND ACQUIRED IMMUNE DEFICIENCY SYNDROME (AIDS)

HIV is an RNA retrovirus and causes AIDS. The virus infects CD-4 lymphocytes and other cells and causes decreased cellular immunity.

Presentation

Initial infection: Mononucleosis-like illness occurring weeks to months after exposure—fatigue, weight loss, lymphadenopathy, night sweats. This is followed by a long asymptomatic period lasting months to years.
AIDS: Opportunistic infections, dementia, depression, Kaposi's sarcoma, wasting

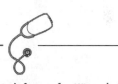

Treatment of AIDS is palliative and not curative.

Risk Factors

- Intravenous drug use
- Blood transfusions between 1978 and 1985
- Prostitution
- Multiple sex partners/unprotected sex
- Bisexual partners

Diagnosis

- **Enzyme-linked immunosorbent assay (ELISA)**—detects antibodies to HIV. It is sensitive but not as specific.
- **Western blot**—done for confirmation if ELISA is positive. It is very specific.
- **Polymerase chain reaction (PCR)**—an alternative means of testing

Risk factors for HIV include intravenous drug use, blood transfusions (1978–1985), multiple sex partners, unprotected sex, and sex with bisexual partners.

Treatment

Two antiretroviral agents plus one protease inhibitor has been common treatment.

HUMAN PAPILLOMAVIRUS (HPV)

HPV causes genital warts (**condylomata acuminata**):
- Subtypes 6 and 11 are not associated with cervical or penile cancer.
- Subtypes 16, 18, 31, and 33 are associated with cervical and penile cancer.

Presentation

Warts of various sizes (sometimes described as cauliflower-like) on the external genitalia, anus, cervix, or perineum

Diagnosis

- Warts are diagnosed by visualization.
- Cervical dysplasia caused by HPV infection is screened via Pap smear.

Treatment

- Condylomata acuminata are treated with cryosurgery, laser ablation, or trichloroacetic acid.
- See cervical dysplasia chapter for treatment of cervical dysplasia.

CHANCROID

Presentation

Chancroid presents as a papule on external genitalia that becomes a painful ulcer (unlike syphilis, which is painless) with a gray base. Inguinal lymphadenopathy also is possible.

Etiology

Haemophilus ducreyi

Diagnosis

Gram stain of ulcer or inguinal node aspirate showing gram-negative rods

Treatment

Ceftriaxone, erythromycin, or azithromycin

PEDICULOSIS PUBIS (CRABS)

Presentation

Pruritus in genital area from parasitic saliva

Etiology

Pediculosis is a parasite.

Diagnosis

Visualization of crabs, history of pruritus

Treatment

Permethrin cream or Lindane shampoo

VAGINITIS

Definition

Vaginitis is inflammation of the vagina, often resulting in increased discharge and/or pruritus, and usually caused by an identifiable microbe (see Table 26-1).

Lactobacillus, the normal flora in the vagina, creates an acidic environment that kills most other bacteria. Raising the pH allows other bacteria to survive.

Etiology

- **Antibiotics**—destabilize the normal balance of flora
- **Douche**—raises the pH
- **Intercourse**—raises the pH
- **Foreign body**—serves as a focus of infection and/or inflammation

There are several common organisms that cause vaginitis: Bacterial (*Gardnerella*), *Candida*, and *Trichomonas*. The distinguishing features are described with the following characteristics.

Diagnostic Characteristics

- **Clinical characteristics**
- **Quality of discharge**
- **pH**—secretions applied to test strip reveal pH of discharge.
- **"Whiff" test**—combining vaginal secretions with 10% KOH: Amines released will give a fishy odor, indicating a positive test.
- **Microscopic findings**

TABLE 26-1. Vaginitis

	Physiologic (Normal)	Bacterial Vaginosis	Candidiasis	Trichomoniasis
Clinical Complaints	None	Malodorous **discharge,** especially after menses, intercourse	**Pruritus, erythema, edema,** odorless discharge, dyspareunia	**Copious, frothy discharge,** malodorous, pruritus, urethritis
Quality of Discharge	Clear or white, no odor	Homogenous **gray** or white, **thin,** sticky	White, **"cottage cheese-like"**	Green to **yellow,** sticky, **"bubbly"** or "frothy"
pH	3.8—4.2	> 5.5	4–5	5–6.5
Microscopic Findings	Epithelial cells Normal bacteria include mostly *Lactobacillus*, with *Staphylococcus epidermidis*, *Streptococcus*, as well as small amounts of colonic flora	Visualize with saline **Clue cells** (epithelial cells with bacteria attached to their surface) Bacteria include *Gardnerella* (*Haemophilus*) and/or *Mycoplasma*	**In 10% KOH Budding yeast** and pseudohyphae	In saline Motile, **flagellated, protozoa**
"Whiff" Test	Negative (no smell)	**Positive** (fishy smell)	Negative	Positive or negative
Treatment		Oral or topical **metronidazole** or topical **clindamycin**	Oral, topical, or suppository **imidazole** (or other various antifungals)	Oral **metronidazole** (*Note:* Metronidazole has potential disulfiram-like rxn and has a metallic taste)
Treat Sexual Partners?		Not necessary	Not necessary	**Yes**

See Figure 26-1.

HIGH-YIELD FACTS

STDs and Vaginitis

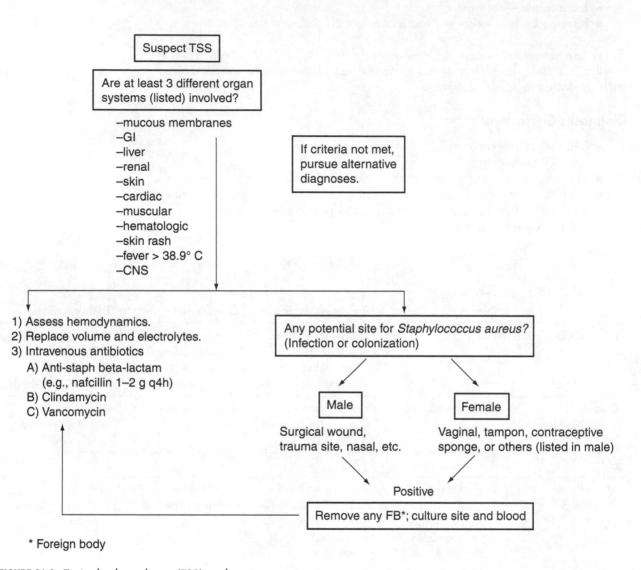

FIGURE 26-1. Toxic shock syndrome (TSS) workup.

(Redrawn, with permission, from Pearlman MD, Tintinalli JE, eds. *Emergency Care of the Woman.* New York: McGraw-Hill, 1998: 615.)

Vulvar Disorders

VULVAR DYSTROPHIES

Vulvar dystrophies are a group of disorders characterized by various pruritic, white lesions of the vulva. Lesions must be biopsied to rule out malignancy.

Lichen Simplex Chronicus (LSC)

LSC is a hypertrophic dystrophy caused by chronic irritation resulting in the raised, whitened appearance of hyperkeratosis. Lesions may also appear red and irritated due to itching. Microscopic examination reveals acanthosis and hyperkeratosis.

Lichen Sclerosis

An atrophic lesion characterized by paperlike appearance on both sides of the vulva and epidermal contracture leading to loss of vulvar architecture: Microscopic examination reveals epithelial thinning with a layer of homogenization below and inflammatory cells.

Lichen simplex chronicus and lichen sclerosis carry no increased risk of malignancy.

Treatment of Vulvar Dystrophies

- Steroid cream (hydrocortisone)
- Diphenhydramine at night to prevent itching during sleep

PSORIASIS

Psoriasis is a common dermatological condition that is characterized by red plaques covered by silver scales. Although it commonly occurs over the knees and/or elbows, lesions can be found on the vulva as well. Pruritus is variable.

Treatment

- Steroid cream
- Coal tar with ultraviolet light therapy or topical vitamin D

VESTIBULITIS

Inflammation of the vestibular glands that leads to tenderness, erythema, and pain associated with coitus (insertional dypareunia and/or postcoital pain): Etiology is unknown. Although the affected area turns white with acetic acid under colposcopic examination, these lesions are not dysplastic.

> The vestibular glands (Bartholin's glands) are located at the 5 and 7 o'clock positions of the inferolateral vestibule (area between the labia minora).

Treatment

- Temporary sexual abstinence
- Trichloroacetic acid
- Xylocaine jelly for anesthesia
- Surgery—if lesions are unresponsive to treatment, vestibulectomy is possible, though with risk of recurrence.

CYSTS

Bartholin's Abscess

Bartholin's abscesses occur when the main duct draining Bartholin's gland is occluded, which usually occurs due to infection. Inflammatory symptoms generally arise from infection and can be treated with antibiotics.

> Bartholin's glands are analogous to the male Cowper's gland (bulbourethral gland). It secretes a thick alkaline fluid during coitus.

TREATMENT

- Incision and drainage and marsupialization (suturing the edges of the incised cyst to prevent reocclusion)

or

- Ward catheter (a catheter with an inflatable tip left in the gland for 10 to 14 days to aid healing)

Sebaceous Cysts

Sebaceous cysts occur beneath the labia majora (rarely minora) when sebaceous gland ducts are occluded. Besides the palpable, smooth mass, patients are generally asymptomatic. Infection or other complications can be treated with incision and drainage.

Hidradenomas

Hidradenomas (apocrine sweat gland cysts) also occur beneath the labia majora as a result of ductal occlusion. These cysts tend to be more pruritic than sebaceous cysts. They are also treated by incision.

Other Rare Cysts

Cyst of canal of Nuck: A hydrocele (persistent processus vaginalis), contains peritoneal fluid

Skene's duct cyst: Ductal occlusion and cystic formation of the Skene's (paraurethral) glands

Pthirus pubis

Crab lice ("crabs") are blood-sucking parasites that are transmitted through sexual activity or fomites. Adults lay eggs, which hatch into the lice that cause intense itching.

DIAGNOSIS

A magnifying glass will aid in revealing small brown lice and eggs attached to hair shafts.

TREATMENT

Treat with Permethrin cream or Kwell shampoo (contraindicated in pregnant or lactating women), as well as washing all garments.

Sarcoptes scabei

"Scabies" are also parasitic infections (more contagious) spread by person-to-person contact or via fomites. Patients may present with papular and/or vesicular eruptions on genitals or extremities, as well as with intractable itching. Close observation reveals that the source of itching is the site where adult parasites have burrowed into skin and laid eggs. Adults, larvae, or eggs may be seen.

TREATMENT

Kwell cream or lotion from the neck down, overnight. Crotamiton is applied similarly in pregnant/lactating women and children under 10 years of age.

HIGH-YIELD FACTS

Vulvar Disorders

HIGH-YIELD FACTS

Vulvar Disorders

Menopause

DEFINITIONS

- **Menopause** is the *final menstruation* marking the termination of menses (defined as 6 months of amenorrhea).
- Menopause is preceded by the **climacteric** or **perimenopausal period,** the multiyear transition from optimal menstrual condition to menopause.
- The **postmenopausal period** is the time after menopause.

Average age of menopause in the United States is about 51 years.

FACTORS AFFECTING AGE OF ONSET

- Genetics
- Smoking (decreases age by 3 years)
- Chemo/radiation therapy

Cigarette smoking is the only factor shown to significantly reduce age of menopause (3 years).

PHYSIOLOGY DURING THE PERIMENOPAUSAL PERIOD

Oocytes Die

- Women's immature eggs, or **oocytes, begin to die** precipitously and become **resistant to follicle-stimulating hormone (FSH),** the pituitary hormone that causes their maturation.
- **FSH levels rise** for two reasons:

    1. Decreased inhibin (inhibin inhibits FSH secretion; it is produced in smaller amounts by the fewer oocytes)
    2. Resistant oocytes require more FSH to successfully mature, triggering greater FSH release.

FSH levels double to ≈ 20 mIU/mL in perimenopause and triple to ≈ 30 in menopause.

Ovulation Becomes Less Frequent

Women **ovulate less frequently,** initially one to two fewer times per year and, eventually, just before menopause, perhaps once every 3 to 4 months. This is due to **shortened follicular phase.** The luteal phase does not change.

Estrogen Levels Fall

Estrogen (estradiol-17β) levels begin to decline, resulting in **hot flashes** (may also be due to increased luteinizing hormone [LH]). Hot flashes usually occur on the face, neck, and upper chest and last a few minutes, followed by intense diaphoresis.

PHYSIOLOGY DURING THE MENOPAUSAL PERIOD

- **Levels of androstenedione** fall, a hormone that is primarily produced by the follicle.
- **Ovaries increase production of testosterone,** which may result in hirsutism and virilism.
- **Decrease in estradiol level** and decrease in estrone level
- **FSH and LH levels rise** secondary to absence of negative feedback.

The most **important physiological change** that occurs with menopause is the **decline of estradiol-17β** levels that occurs with the cessation of follicular maturation. Table 28-1 lists the organ systems affected by those decreased estradiol levels.

TABLE 28-1.

Organ System	Effect of Decreased Estradiol	Available Treatment
Cardiovascular	↑ LDL, ↓ HDL After two decades of menopause, the risk of myocardial infarction (MI) and coronary artery disease is equal to that in men.	■ HRT/ERT (see below) results in 50% reduction in cardiac death.
Bone	Osteoporosis. Estrogen receptors found on many cells mediating trabecular bone maintenance (i.e., ↑ osteoblast activity, ↓ osteoclast activity)	■ HRT/ERT ■ Calcitonin ■ Etidronate (a bisphosphonate osteoclast inhibitor) ■ Calcium supplementation 50% reduction in death from hip fracture with normal estrogen levels
Vaginal mucous membranes	Dryness and atrophy, with resulting dyspareunia, atrophic vaginitis	■ HRT/ERT pill or cream
Genitourinary	Loss of urethral tone, dysuria	■ HRT/ERT
Psychiatric	Lability, depression	■ HRT/ERT
Neurologic	Preliminary studies indicate there may be a link between low levels of estradiol and Alzheimer's disease.	■ HRT/ERT
Hair and skin	Skin—less elastic, more wrinkled Hair—male growth patterns	■ HRT/ERT pill or cream

LDL = Low-density lipoprotein
HDL = High-density lipoprotein
HRT = Hormone replacement therapy
ERT = Estrogen replacement therapy

Hormone replacement therapy (HRT) or estrogen replacement therapy (ERT) has been shown to counteract the complications of estradiol loss listed in Table 28-1.

Estrogen Replacement Therapy

ERT = estrogen only: Indicated in women status post hysterectomy

Hormone Replacement Therapy

HRT = estrogen + progesterone: The progesterone component is needed to protect the endometrium from constant stimulation and resultant increase in endometrial cancer. It is indicated for women who still have their uterus.

RISKS OF HRT/ERT

- Increase incidence in breast cancer
- Increase incidence in endometrial cancer (ERT only)
- Thromboembolism
- Cholecystitis/cholelithiasis

Risks can be reduced by beginning therapy years after menopause and/or treatment for only a few years.

CONTRAINDICATIONS TO HRT/ERT

- Unexplained vaginal bleeding
- Breast carcinoma (relative, not absolute, contraindication)
- Metastatic endometrial carcinoma
- Liver disease
- History of thromboembolic disease
- History of MI (ERT/HRT has not shown to be effective in cardioprotection after an MI has occurred)

HRT possibly increases the risk of breast cancer, but it definitely decreases the risk of coronary artery disease. Consider the following in assessing the risks and benefits of HRT:
Breast cancer is the most common female malignancy, accounts for about 50,000 deaths/yr.
Coronary artery disease is the most common cause of mortality, accounts for about 500,000 deaths/yr.

Estrogen creates a hypercoagulable state due to increased production of hepatic coagulation factors.

HIGH-YIELD FACTS

Menopause

233

HIGH-YIELD FACTS

Menopause

Pelvic Relaxation

ANATOMY OF PELVIC FLOOR SUPPORT

Several crucial structures make up the support of the female pelvic floor. Disturbance of any of the following can result in prolapse:

- Bony structure
- Broad and round ligaments
- Endopelvic fascia
- Pelvic diaphragm
- Urogenital diaphragm
- Perineum

> The pelvic diaphragm is made up of the levator ani and coccygeal muscles.

PROLAPSE

Prolapse is the downward displacement of an organ from its normal position. There are several types.

Types of Prolapse

Prolapses can be classified according to the location of the protruding structure: Anterior, apical, and posterior.

Anterior
- Cystocele (bladder)—see Figure 29-1
- Cystourethrocele

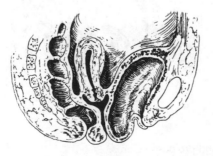

FIGURE 29-1. Cystocele.

(Reproduced, with permission, from Pernoll ML. *Benson & Pernoll's Handbook of Obstetrics and Gynecology*, 10th ed. New York: McGraw-Hill, 2001: 807.)

FIGURE 29-2. Rectocele.
(Reproduced, with permission, from Pernoll ML. *Benson & Pernoll's Handbook of Obstetrics and Gynecology,* 10th ed. New York: McGraw-Hill, 2001: 807.)

Apical
- Uterocele
- Vaginal prolapse

Posterior
- Rectocele—see Figure 29-2
- Enterocele (intestine)—see Figure 29-3

Grading of Prolapse

Organ displacement:

▪ To the level of the ischial spines	Grade I
▪ Between ischial spines and introitus	Grade II
▪ Within introitus	Grade III
▪ Past introitus	Grade IV

Risk Factors for Prolapse

Many conditions can cause prolapse by disturbing the anatomical supports (childbirth), disrupting the innervations, or increasing the pressure load. The following are some examples:
- Increased load—obesity, cough (e.g., chronic obstructive pulmonary disease)

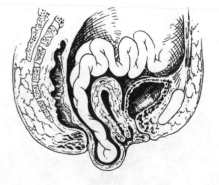

FIGURE 29-3. Enterocele and prolapsed uterus.
(Reproduced, with permission, from Pernoll ML. *Benson & Pernoll's Handbook of Obstetrics and Gynecology,* 10th ed. New York: McGraw-Hill, 2001: 808.)

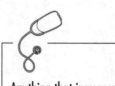

In general, think of prolapse as either limited to the upper vagina, to the introitus, or protruding from the body.

Anything that increases pelvic pressure can cause a prolapse:
- Constipation
- Chronic obstructive pulmonary disease
- Tumor/mass

- Loss of levator ani function—postpartum
- Disturbance of parts—postsurgical
- Loss of innervation—amyotrophic lateral sclerosis (ALS), paralysis
- Loss of connective tissue—spina bifida, myelomeningocele

Signs and Symptoms of Prolapse

- Feeling of "pressure"
- Organ protrusion, especially upon exertion
- Incontinence
- Groin pain
- Dyspareunia
- Spotting

Symptom alleviation/exacerbation is often related to pelvic effort (i.e., better when prone, better in the morning, worse with standing, worse in evening).

Diagnosis

Diagnosis is made by direct visualization of prolapsed organ during complete pelvic examination: Patient should be examined in the standing position.

Treatment of Prolapse

Asymptomatic Prolapse
- Usually requires **follow-up** but no immediate intervention
- Pelvic-strengthening exercises (i.e., **Kegel** maneuvers) and/or HRT/ERT may benefit.

Symptomatic Prolapse
Can be treated with a pessary or surgically

Pessary
A **pessary** is an object placed in the upper vagina designed to help maintain support of the pelvic organs. Types include:

Smith-Hodge—an oval ring
Doughnut (ring)
Inflatable
Gehrung—U-shaped

Surgical Treatment

These are several types of surgical repairs for each type of prolapse.

CYSTOCELE

Kelly plication (anterior vaginal repair)—endopelvic fascial reinforcement via vaginal approach
Lefort procedure/colpocleisis—surgical obliteration of the vaginal canal
Burch/Marshall–Marchetti–Krantz procedures—urethrovescicular suspension via abdominal approach
Sling procedure—elevation of bladder neck and urethra via vaginal and abdominal approaches

RECTOCELE

Posterior repair—posterior vaginal wall reinforcement with levator ani muscles via vaginal approach

ENTEROCELE

Moschovitz repair—approximation of endopelvic fascia and uterosacral ligaments via abdominal approach to prevent an enterocele

UTERINE PROLAPSE

Hysterectomy—a uterine prolapse often occurs in conjunction with another prolapse, and so combined repairs are usually performed.

URINARY INCONTINENCE

Definition

Involuntary loss of urine that is a symptom of a pathological condition. Incontinence can be due to reversible or irreversible (but treatable) causes.

Reversible Causes of Urinary Incontinence

Delerium, infection, atrophic vaginitis, drug side effects, psychiatric illness, excessive urine production, restricted patient mobility, and stool impaction are *reversible* causes of urinary incontinence.

It is helpful to search out these easily correctable causes before moving on to the more expensive and invasive workup for the irreversible causes.

Irreversible Types of Urinary Incontinence

STRESS INCONTINENCE

Loss of urine (usually **small amount**) only *upon increased intra-abdominal pressure* (i.e., with coughing, laughing, exercise): Caused by **urethral hypermotility** and/or **sphincter dysfunction** that maintains enough closing pressure at rest but not with exertion

URGE INCONTINENCE

Sudden feeling of **urgency** followed by **complete emptying** of bladder: Caused by **unopposed detrusor contraction**

OVERFLOW INCONTINENCE

Constant **dribbling** +/− urgency with **inability to completely empty the bladder:** Caused by **detrusor underactivity** (due to a neuropathy) or **urethral obstruction**

MIXED INCONTINENCE

Combinations of above

Evaluation

HISTORY

Ask about aforementioned symptoms, medications, medical history (diabetes mellitus, neuropathies)

PHYSICAL

Pelvic exam: Check for cystoceles, urethroceles, and atrophic changes.
Rectal exam: Check for impaction, and rectocele; assess sphincter tone.
Neuro exam: Assess for neuropathy.

LABS

Urinalysis and culture to rule out urinary tract infection

Q-TIP TEST

A cotton swab is placed in the urethra. The change in angle between the Q-tip and the woman's body is measured upon straining. Normal upward change is < 30°, and a **positive test** is one with **> 30° change. A positive test indicates stress incontinence.**

CYSTOMETRY

Cystometry provides measurements of the **relationship of pressure and volume in the bladder.** Catheters that measure pressures are placed in the bladder and rectum, while a second catheter in the bladder supplies water to cause bladder filling. Measurements include residual *volume, pressures at which desires to void occur, bladder compliance, flow rates,* and *capacity.* Diagnoses: Stress, urge, and overflow incontinence.

URODYNAMIC STUDIES

A set of studies that evaluate lower urinary tract function. Studies may include **cystometry** (see above), **bladder filling tests, cystoscopy, uroflowmetry leak-point pressure tests,** to name a few. Can help diagnose all types of incontinence.

Treatment

STRESS INCONTINENCE

- **Kegel exercises** strengthen urethral muscles.
- **Estrogen therapy**
- **Alpha-adrenergic drugs**
- Surgical repair (usually Burch procedure or Kelly plication)

URGE INCONTINENCE

- **Medications:**
  - Anticholinergics
  - Calcium channel blockers
  - Tricyclics
- **Timed voiding:** Patient is advised to urinate in prescribed hourly intervals before the bladder fills.
- Surgery is rarely used to treat urge incontinence.

OVERFLOW INCONTINENCE

Due to Obstruction
Relieve obstruction.

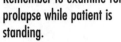

Remember to examine for prolapse while patient is standing.

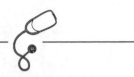

Q-tip test: Increased upwards motion of the Q-tip is caused by loss of support from the urethrovesicular (UV) junction, indicating stress incontinence.

Pelvic Relaxation

Due to Detrusor Underactivity

Treat possible neuro causes:

- **Diabetes mellitus**
- B_{12} deficiency

Women's Health

This chapter focuses on women's health, ages 13 through the postmenopausal years.

HEALTH MAINTENANCE AND SCREENING TOOLS

Pap Smear

- Yearly beginning at age 18 or when sexually active
- After three consecutive normal Paps in a healthy, low-risk female, screening may be done every 2 to 3 years.

Manual Breast Exams

- An annual breast exam should be performed on all women beginning at age 13.
- *All women, especially by age 30, should perform self-breast exams once per month (e.g., premenopausal women should examine their breasts one week after their menstrual period).*

Mammography

- Annually beginning at age 35 if there is family history of breast cancer
- Annually beginning at age 40 for all others

Colon Cancer Screening

- Fecal occult blood testing beginning at ages 40 to 50 years
- Sigmoidoscopy starting at age 50, every 5 years (if higher risk, start earlier)

or

- Colonoscopy every 10 years (especially if inflammatory bowel disease, colonic polyps, colon cancer, or a family history of familial polyposis coli, colorectal cancer, or cancer family syndrome)

Laboratory Testing

THYROID-STIMULATING HORMONE (TSH)

Test:
- At age 65 and older, check every 3 to 5 years
- Periodic screening (age 19 to 64) if strong family history of thyroid disease and if autoimmune disease

CHOLESTEROL

Test:
- Every 5 years beginning at age 20
- Every 3 to 5 years between ages 65 and 75

Periodic screening if:
- Familial lipid disorder
- Family history of premature coronary artery disease (CAD) (< 55 years)
- History of CAD

LIPIDS

Periodic screening if:
- Elevated cholesterol
- History of parent or sibling with blood cholesterol ≥ 240 mg/dL
- History of sibling, parent, or grandparent with premature (< 55 years) CAD
- Diabetes mellitus (DM)
- Smoker
- Obese

FASTING GLUCOSE

Test:
- Every 3 years beginning at age 45
- Every 3 to 5 years if:
  - Family history of DM (one first- or two second-degree relatives)
  - Obese
  - History of gestational DM
  - Hypertension
  - High-risk ethnic group

Tuberculosis (TB) Skin Testing

Recommended for:
- Regular testing for teens
- Human immunodeficieny virus–positive (HIV+) people should be tested regularly.
- Exposure to TB-infected person requires testing.
- Medically underserved/low-income populations

Sexually Transmissible Infection Testing

Recommended for:
- History of multiple sexual partners
- History of sex with a partner who has multiple sexual contacts
- Partner has a sexually transmitted disease (STD)
- History of STD

Routine screening for chlamydial and gonorrhea infection is recommended for all sexually active adolescents and high-risk females, even if they are asymptomatic.

HIV Testing

Recommended for:
- Women seeking treatment for STDs
- History of prostitution/intravenous drug abuse
- History of sex with an HIV+ partner
- Women whose partners are bisexual
- Women transfused between 1978 and 1985
- Women in an area of high prevalence of HIV infection
- Women with recurrent genital tract disease
- Women < 50 years of age who have invasive cervical cancer
- Women who are pregnant or planning to become pregnant

BACTERIURIA TESTING/URINALYSIS

- Periodically for women with DM and women ≥ 65 years of age
- During routine prenatal care

Immunizations

- Tetanus–diphtheria booster once between 13 and 16 years
- Tetanus–diphtheria booster every 10 years
- Measles, mumps, rubella (MMR) for all nonimmune women
- Hepatitis B vaccine for those not previously immunized
- Varicella vaccine if not immune
- Hepatitis A vaccine if at high risk
- Influenza vaccine annually beginning at age 55
- Give influenza vaccine prior to age 55 if:
  - Residents of chronic care facilities
  - Immunosuppression
  - Hemoglobinopathies
  - **Women who will be in T2 or T3 during the endemic season**
- Pneumococcal vaccine if 65 years of age or sooner if:
  - Sickle cell disease
  - Asplenia
  - Alcoholism/cirrhosis
  - Influenza vaccine risk factors

PREVENTIVE HEALTH INFORMATION

Nutrition and Exercise

The issues of nutrition and body weight should be emphasized during the three major transitional periods in a woman's life:

1. Puberty
2. Pregnancy
3. Menopause

One's body weight is determined by three major factors:

1. Genetics and heredity, which control:
   - Resting metabolic rate
   - Appetite
   - Satiety
   - Body fat distribution
   - Predisposition to physical activity

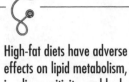

High-fat diets have adverse effects on lipid metabolism, insulin sensitivity, and body composition, even in the absence of weight gain.

Exercise will increase the body's metabolic rate and prevent the storage of fat.

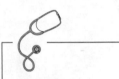

Alcohol:
- Accounts for 100,000 deaths per year in the United States.
- Excessive use for women is about one half the quantity considered excessive for men.
- When compared to men, women have relatively reduced activity of gastric alcohol dehydrogenase to begin alcohol metabolism and have less body water in which to distribute unmetabolized alcohol.

2. Nutrition
3. Physical activity and exercise

GOALS

1. Maintain a healthy diet consisting of small frequent meals (i.e., four to six instead of two to three):
   - Utilize the Food Guide Pyramid as a tool in making food choices in daily life.
   - Adjust caloric intake for age and physical activity level:
     - As one ages, there is a decrease in resting metabolic rate and loss of lean tissue.
     - Older women who are physically active are less likely to loose lean tissue and can maintain their weight with higher caloric intake.
2. Physical activity during all stages of life should include exercise at moderate intensity for 30 minutes on most days of the week.

SUBSTANCE ABUSE

Alcohol

Women experience more accelerated and profound medical consequences of excessive alcohol than men (a phenomenon called "telescoping"):
- Cirrhosis
- Peptic ulcers that require surgery
- Myopathy
- Cardiomyopathy
- When combined with cigarette smoking → oral and esophageal cancers
- Fetal alcohol syndrome:
  - Teratogenic effects are dose related.
  - Includes growth retardation, facial anomalies, mental retardation

Cigarettes

- Linked to lung cancer and CAD
- Most common factor in chronic obstructive pulmonary disease
- *Endocrine effects:* Smokers reach menopause earlier and have increased risk of osteoporosis.
- *Obstetric effects:* Reduced fertility, increased rates of spontaneous abortion, premature delivery, low-birth-weight infants, reduced head circumferences
- Children who grow up exposed to secondhand smoke have higher rates of respiratory and middle ear illness.

SEAT BELT USE

- Deaths due to accidents are greatest in women ages 13 through 39.
- Accidents cause more deaths than infectious diseases, pulmonary diseases, diabetes, and liver and kidney disease.
- Motor vehicle accidents account for 50,000 deaths per year and > 4 to 5 million injuries per year.
- Seat belts decrease chance of death and serious injury by > 50%.

SAFER SEX PRACTICES

Improved and successful prevention of pregnancy and STDs by more adolescents requires counseling that includes:

- Encouragement to postpone sexual involvement
- Provision of information about contraceptive options, including emergency contraception and side effects of various contraceptive methods

FEMALE SEXUAL RESPONSE AND SEXUAL EXPRESSION

Female Response Cycle

Consists of:

Desire

- Begins in the brain with perception of erotogenic stimuli via the special senses or through fantasy

Arousal

- Clitoris becomes erect.
- Labia minora become engorged.
- Blood flow in the vaginal vault triples.
- Upper two thirds of the vagina dilate.
- Lubricant is secreted from the vaginal surface.
- Lower one third of vagina thickens and dilates.

Plateau

- The formation of transudate (lubrication) in the vagina continues in conjunction with genital congestion.
- Occurs prior to orgasm

Orgasm

- Rhythmic, involuntary, vaginal smooth muscle and pelvic contractions → pleasurable cortical sensory phenomenon ("orgasm")

Sexuality During Prenatal Through Childhood

Resolution

- Sexual development begins prenatally when the fetus differentiates into a male or female.
- Sexual behavior, usually in the form of masturbation, is common in childhood.
- As children grow older, they are socialized into cultural emphases on privacy and sexual inhibition in social situations.
- Between ages 7 and 8, most children engage in childhood sexual games, either same-gender or cross-gender play.

Adolescence

Gender identity and sexual preferences begin to solidify as puberty begins.

- Lung cancer is the most common cause of cancer death in women.
- Related to 400,000 deaths per year

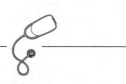

Adolescent pregnancy and abortion rates in the United States are higher than in any other developed country.

It is normal for children < 6 years of age to be curious about their own or others' bodies, and they may engage in observable sexual behaviors.

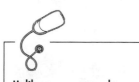

Unlike men, women have no refractory period and can experience multiple orgasms without a time lag in between.

HIGH-YIELD FACTS

Women's Health

After somatosensory stimulation, orgasm is an adrenergic response.

Menstrual Cycle

The menstrual cycle can affect sexuality (i.e., in some women, there is a peak in sexual activity in the midfollicular [postmenstrual] phase).

Pregnancy

For some women, intercourse is avoided during pregnancy due to fear of harming the baby or a self-perception of unattractiveness.

Postpartum

- Women often experience sexual problems within the first 6 months of delivery.
- Problems may include:
  - Perineal soreness
  - Excessive fatigue
  - Disinterest in sex

Menopause

A decrease in sexual activity is most frequently observed.

Advancing age is associated with decreased:
- Intercourse frequency
- Orgasmic frequency
- Enjoyment of sexual activity:
  - Sexual enjoyment may also be decreased with the increased duration of the relationship and with the partner's increasing age.

Decreased sexual responsiveness may be reversible if caused by reduction in functioning of genital smooth muscle tissue.

Psychosocially, middle-aged women often feel less sexually desirable.

Hormonal Changes

Estrogen decrease → decreased vaginal lubrication, thinner and less elastic vaginal lining

Estrogen decrease → depressive symptoms → decreased sexual desire and well-being

DISORDERS OF SEXUAL DYSFUNCTION

It is important to first clarify whether the dysfunction reported is:
- *Lifelong or acquired?*
- *Global* (across all partners) *or situational?*

General Evaluation Strategies

Differentiate between the following possible etiologies:
- Medical illnesses
- Menopausal status
- Medication use (antihypertensives, cardiovascular meds, antidepressants, etc.)

Rule out other psychiatric/psychological causes:
- Life content (stress, fatigue, relationship problems, traumatic sexual history, guilt)
- Major depression
- Drug abuse
- Anxiety
- Obsessive–compulsive disorder

General Management Strategies

- Medical illnesses need evaluation and specific treatment.
- Screen for and treat depression with psychotherapy or medication.
- Reduce dosages or change medications that may alter sexual interest (i.e., switch to antidepressant formulations that have less of an impact on sexual functioning such as bupropion [Wellbutrin] or nefazodone [Serzone]).

or

- Combine buspirone (Buspar), an antianxiety agent, with a selective serotonin reuptake inhibitor to counteract the sexual side effects.
- Address menopause and hormonal deficiencies.

Sexual Desire Disorders

- **Hypoactive sexual desire disorder**—persistent or recurrent absence or deficit of sexual fantasies and desire for sexual activity
- **Sexual aversion disorder**—persistent or recurrent aversion to and avoidance of genital contact with a sexual partner

Sexual Arousal Disorder

- Partial or total lack of physical response as indicated by lack of lubrication and vasocongestion of genitals
- Persistent lack of subjective sense of sexual excitement and pleasure during sex

MANAGEMENT

- Treat decreased lubrication with KY Jelly or Astroglide.
- Menopausal symptoms may respond to oral or topical estrogen.
- Sildenafil (Viagra) may be helpful.
- Referral for psychosocial consultation or therapy if psychological issues exist

Sexual intercourse during pregnancy is NOT related to bacterial vaginosis or preterm birth in normal, healthy pregnancies. But there are certain obstetrical conditions in which coitus should be avoided (i.e., placenta previa, abruptio placentae, premature labor, and premature rupture of membranes).

Little is known about how being a new mother affects sexual desire and response.

Complaints of sexual arousal disorder are typically accompanied by complaints of dyspareunia, lack of lubrication, or orgasmic difficulty.

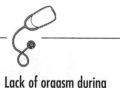

Lack of orgasm during intercourse is considered a normal variation of female sexual response if the woman is able to experience orgasm with a partner using other, noncoital methods.

HIGH-YIELD FACTS

Women's Health

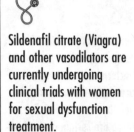

Sildenafil citrate (Viagra) and other vasodilators are currently undergoing clinical trials with women for sexual dysfunction treatment.

Atrophic vaginitis → coital pain → decreased sexual desire

Exogenous administration of estrogen improves vaginal lubrication, atrophic conditions, hot flashes, headaches, and insomnia.

Orgasmic Disorder

Persistent delay or absence of orgasm

EVALUATION

Differentiate between the following:
- Take sexual experience into account—women often become more orgasmic with experience.
- Physical factors that may interfere with neurovascular pelvic dysfunction (i.e., surgeries, illnesses, or injuries)
- Psychological and interpersonal factors are very common (i.e., growing up with messages that sex is shameful and men's pleasure only).
- Partner's lack of sexual skills

MANAGEMENT

For lifelong, generalized orgasmic disorder, there is rarely a physical cause. Treat with masturbation programs and/or sex therapy.

Sexual Pain Disorders

DYSPAREUNIA

Recurrent genital pain before, during, or after intercourse

Evaluation

Differentiate between:
- Physical disorder
- Vaginismus
- Lack of lubrication

Management

- If due to vaginal scarring/stenosis due to history of episiotomy or vaginal surgery, vaginal stretching with dilators and massage
- If postmenopausal, vaginal estrogen cream to improve vaginal pliability
- Low-dose tricyclic antidepressants may be helpful.
- Pelvic floor physical therapy (Kegel exercises)
- Coital position changes

VAGINISMUS

Recurrent involuntary spasm of the outer third of the vagina (perineal and levator ani muscles) interfering with or preventing coitus

Evaluation

- Obtain history.
- Rule out organic causes (i.e., vaginitis, endometriosis, pelvic inflammatory disease, irritable bowel syndrome, urethral syndrome, interstitial cystitis, etc.).
- Examine the pelvis for involuntary spasm.
- Rule out physical disorder or other psychiatric disorder.

Management

- Treat organic causes.
- Psychotherapy
- Provide reassurance.
- Physical therapy (i.e., Kegel exercises, muscle relaxation massage, and gradual vaginal dilatation) (the woman controls the pace and duration)

DOMESTIC VIOLENCE

Domestic violence refers to a relationship in which an individual is victimized (physically, psychologically, or emotionally) by a current or past intimate or romantic partner.

Recognition of the Occurrence of Domestic Violence

- Injuries to the head, eyes, neck, torso, breasts, abdomen, and/or genitals
- Bilateral or multiple injuries
- A delay between the time of injury and the time at which treatment is sought
- Inconsistencies between the patient's explanation of the injuries and the physician's clinical findings
- A history of repeated trauma
- The perpetrator may exhibit signs of control over the the health care team, refusal to leave the patient's side to allow private conversation, and control of victim.
- The patient calls or visits frequently for general somatic complaints.
- **In pregnant women:** Late entry into prenatal care, missed appointments, and multiple repeated complaints are often seen in abused pregnant women.

Assessment

See Table 30-1.

TABLE 30-1. Abuse Assessment Screen

1. Have you ever been emotionally or physically abused by your partner or someone important to you?

2. Within the last year, have you been hit, slapped, kicked, or otherwise physically hurt by someone?

3. Since you've been pregnant, have you been hit, slapped, kicked, or otherwise physically hurt by someone?

4. Within the last year, has anyone forced you to have sexual activities? Has anyone in the past forced you to have sexual activities?

5. Are you afraid of your partner or anyone you listed above?

Source: Nursing Research Consortium on Violence and Abuse, 1989. Reproduced, with permission, from Seltzer VL, Pearse WH. *Women's Primary Health Care,* 2nd ed. New York: McGraw-Hill, 2001: 659.

Menopause and sexual dysfunction: Menopause → vaginal atrophy and lack of adequate lubrication → painful intercourse → decreased sexual desire

Many antidepressants alter sexual response by increasing the availability of serotonin and decreasing dopamine.

Estrogen improves overall sense of well-being—probably secondarily improves sexual desire.

HIGH-YIELD FACTS

Women's Health

Reaction to Domestic Violence

- Listen in a nonjudgmental fashion, and assure the patient that it is not her fault, nor does she deserve the abuse.
- Assess the safety of the patient and her children.
- If the patient is ready to leave the abusive relationship, connect her with resources such as shelters, police, public agencies, and counselors.
- If the patient is not ready to leave, discuss a safety or exit plan and provide the patient with domestic violence information.
- Carefully document all subjective and objective findings. The records can be used in a legal case to establish abuse.

SEXUAL ASSAULT

Sexual assault occurs when any sexual act is performed by one person on another without that person's consent.

Rape is defined as sexual intercourse without the consent of one party, whether from force, threat of force, or incapacity to consent due to physical or mental condition.

Rape-Related Post-Traumatic Stress Disorder (RR-PTSD)

A "rape-trauma" syndrome resulting from the psychological and emotional stress of being raped

SIGNS AND SYMPTOMS

Acute Phase
- Eating and sleep disorders
- Vaginal itch, pain, and discharge
- Generalized physical complaints and pains (i.e., chest pain, backaches, and pelvic pain)
- Anxiety/depression

Reorganization Phase
- Phobias
- Flashbacks
- Nightmares
- Gynecologic complaints

MANAGEMENT

Physician's Medical Responsibilities
- Obtain complete medical and gynecologic history.
- Assess and treat physical injuries in the presence of a female chaperone (even if the health care provider is female).
- Obtain appropriate cultures.
- Counsel patient and provide STD prophylaxis.
- Provide preventive therapy for unwanted pregnancy.
- Assess psychological and emotional status.
- Provide crisis intervention.
- Arrange for follow-up medical care and psychological counseling.

Physician's Legal Responsibilities

- Obtain informed consent for treatment, collection of evidence, taking of photographs, and reporting of the incident to the authorities.
- Accurately record events.
- Accurately describe injuries.
- Collect appropriate samples and clothing.
- Label photographs, clothing, and specimens with the patient's name; seal and store safely.

TREATMENT

Infection Prophylaxis

- Gonorrhea, chlamydia, and trichomonal infections:
  - Ceftriaxone 125 mg IM + azithromycin 1 g PO in a single dose

or

  - Doxycycline 100 mg PO bid for 7 days + metronidazole 2 g PO in a single dose
- Offer the hepatitis B vaccine.
- Administer tetanus–diphtheria toxoid when indicated.

Postcoital Regimen

- **Combined estrogen–progestin pills:** Ovral (50 ug ethinyl estradiol, 0.5 mg norgestrel): 2 tabs PO STAT, then 2 more tabs 12 hours later:
  - 75% effective
- **Mifepristone (RU 486):** A single dose of 600 mg PO:
  - 99.9% effective

ETHICS

It is the physician's responsibility to:
- Determine the patient's preferences.
- Honor the patient's wishes when the patient can no longer speak for herself.

End of Life Decisions

- *Advanced directives* (**living will and durable power of attorney for health care**) allow patients to voice their preferences regarding treatment if faced with a potentially terminal illness.
- In the **living will,** a competent, adult patient may, in advance, formulate and provide a valid consent to the withholding/withdrawal of life-support systems in the event that injury or illness renders that individual incompetent to make such a decision.
- In the **durable power of attorney for health care,** a patient appoints someone to act as a surrogate decision maker when the patient cannot participate in the consent process.

Life-Sustaining Treatment

Any treatment that serves to prolong life without reversing the underlying medical condition

In general, where the performance of one duty conflicts with the other, the preferences of the patient prevail.

Sexual abuse occurs in approximately two thirds of relationships involving physical abuse.

Any injury during pregnancy, especially one to the abdomen or breasts, is suspicious for abuse.

Because abuse may begin later in pregnancy or after the baby is born, pregnant women should be questioned about abuse during each trimester and postpartum.

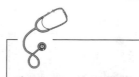

Physicians are not obligated to perform procedures if they are morally opposed to them or give advice on sexual matters that they are ignorant of, but should refer patients as necessary.

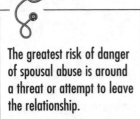
Reproductive Issues

The ethical responsibility of the physician is:

- To identify his or her own opinions on the issue at hand
- To be honest and fair to their patients when they seek advice or services in this area
- To explain his or her personal views to the patient and how those views may influence the service or advice being provided

Informed Consent

A legal doctrine that requires a physician to obtain consent for treatment rendered, an operation performed, or many diagnostic procedures

Informed consent requires the following conditions be met:

1. Must be **voluntary**
2. **Information:**
   - **Risks and benefits** of the procedure are discussed.
   - **Alternatives** to procedure are discussed.
   - **Consequences** of not undergoing the procedure are discussed.
   - Physician must be willing to **discuss the procedure** and answer any questions the patient has.
3. The patient must be **competent.**

Exceptions

The following are certain cases in which informed consent need not be obtained:

1. Lifesaving medical emergency
2. Suicide prevention
3. Normally, minors must have consent obtained from their parents. However, minors may give their own consent for certain treatments, such as alcohol detox and treatment for venereal diseases.

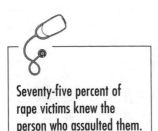
Patient Confidentiality

The information disclosed to a physician during his or her relationship with the patient is confidential.

The physician should not reveal information or communications without the express consent of the patient, unless required to do so by law.

Exceptions

- A patient threatens to inflict serious bodily harm to herself or another person.
- Communicable diseases
- Gunshot wounds
- Knife wounds

MINORS

When minors request confidential services, physicians should encourage minors to involve their parents.

Where the law does not require otherwise, the physician should permit a competent minor to consent to medical care and should *not* notify the parents without the patient's consent.

If the physician feels that without parental involvement and guidance the minor will face a serious health threat, and there is reason to believe that the parents will be helpful, disclosing the problem to the parents is equally justified.

OFFICE HEALTH MAINTENANCE TESTS

Starting Age	Test	How Often?
Age 13–16	■ Tetanus–diphtheria booster	Once
> Age 16	■ Tetanus–diphtheria booster	Every 10 years
≥ Age 18 (*or before if sexually active*)	■ Pap ■ Manual breast exams ■ CBC, BUN, creatinine, hemoglobin	Annually Periodically
≥ Age 20	■ Cholesterol	Every 5 years
≥ Age 40	■ Mammogram ■ Fecal occult blood testing	Annually
≥ Age 45	■ Fasting glucose	Every 3 years
≥ Age 50	■ Sigmoidoscopy or ■ Colonoscopy if high risk	■ Every 5 years ■ Every 10 years
≥ Age 55	■ Influenza vaccine	Annually
≥ Age 65	■ TSH ■ Cholesterol ■ Urinalysis ■ Pneumococcal vaccine	Every 3–5 years Periodically Once

HIGH-YIELD FACTS

Women's Health

Awards for Obstetrics and Gynecology

General Awards
Web Sites of Interest

Emory University Program in Family Planning and Human Sexuality

Ten-week internship offering research and providing educational and clinical experiences in the field of reproductive health. $1,500 stipend. March 1 deadline.

MARCH OF DIMES SUMMER SCIENCE RESEARCH

A program designed for medical students willing to spend 3 months working in a laboratory or clinical setting devoted primarily to research in birth defects. The first step is for the Dean's office to submit to the March of Dimes one or two names of individuals on the staff who are actively engaged in birth defects research. These staff people will be requested by the March of Dimes to provide the names of two students each. Although a maximum of four names will be provided, only two can be selected from each school. Stipend is $1,000 per student. Deadline: January 15.

March of Dimes Research Support on Reproductive Hazards in the Workplace

A program designed to recognize and ultimately detect adverse reproductive effects in occupationally exposed women and men. Deadline: February 1.

National Osteoporosis Foundation Student Fellowship

Eight-week to 4-month fellowship for research related to the causes and prevention of osteoporosis. The research may be either clinical or basic under the supervision of an established investigator. Maximum award $4,000. Deadline: March 31.

AMWA STUDENT LOAN FUND

This fund with lenient payback terms continues to provide AMWA member medical students with financial help when they are most in need. With the escalating costs of a medical school education, AMWA's loans provide students with much-needed financial assistance when they face huge resource needs. Women who are enrolled in accredited U.S. medical or osteopathic medicine schools, who are U.S. citizens or permanent residents and who are student members of national AMWA are eligible to apply for a loan. For an application or additional information, contact Marie Glanz, at (703) 838-0500 or e-mail mglanz@amwa-doc. org.

AMWA WILHELM-FRANKOWSKI SCHOLARSHIP

This scholarship was offered for the first time in 1996 and was made possible through the generous bequests of Drs. Hazel Wilhelm and Clementine Frankowski. The $4,000 medical student scholarship, awarded for community service, activity in women's health issues, and participation in AMWA and other women-in-medicine groups, is now awarded annually to an AMWA student member. Medical students attending an accredited U.S. medical or osteopathic medicine school in their first, second, or third year are eligible to apply. Applications are mailed from January through mid-April of each year. Contact AMWA at <amwa-doc.org> for additional information and to be placed on the mailing list to receive a scholarship application. Deadline for receipt of completed applications is April 30. Supporting documentation deadline is May 15.

COUNTRY DOCTOR SCHOLARSHIP PROGRAM

$10,000 annually, $40,000 aggregate

Georgia residents qualify for funding to obtain primary care medical degrees such as IM, General Surgery, OB/GYN, Peds, and FP. In return, the student must practice in a Georgia board-approved town of 15,000 or less population. APPLICATION DEADLINE: May 15. Contact: Joe B. Lawley, PhD, State Medical Education Board, 270 Washington St SW, 7th Floor, Room 7093, Atlanta, GA 30334.

AWHS OVERSEAS ASSISTANCE GRANT

The American Women's Hospitals Service provides assistance

with transportation costs (airfare, train fare, etc.—up to $1,500) connected with pursuing medical studies in an off-campus setting where the medically neglected will benefit.

Grants are awarded to national AMWA members completing their second, third, or fourth year at an accredited U.S. medical or osteopathic medicine school or a resident who will be spending a minimum of six weeks and no longer than one year in a sponsored program, which will serve the needs of the medically underserved.

The program must be sponsored by your school, another school, or an outside agency or, if there is no sponsor, it must be a program for which your school takes responsibility and provides academic credit.

Contact Marie Glanz at (703) 838-0500 or mglanz@amwa-doc. org to obtain further details about this opportunity and request an application.

BPW CAREER ADVANCEMENT SCHOLARSHIP FOR WOMEN

$500 to $1,000 grants for women over 25 in their third or fourth year of studies with critical need for assistance. APPLICATION DEADLINE: April 15. Contact: Scholarships/Loans Business and Professional Woman's Foundation, 2012 Mass Ave NW, Washington, DC 20036. Tel: (202) 293-1200 ext. 169.

Alpha Omega Alpha Research Fellowships

The purpose of the fellowships is to stimulate interest in re-search among medical students. Areas of research may include clinical investigation, basic research, epidemiology, and the social sciences, as related to medicine. The program is designed to stimulate students who have not had prior research experience. Fellowship is for $2,000. Deadline: January.

AMA-MSS Councils

The Medical student section of the AMA (AMA-MSS) has several councils for which it seeks medical students.

Application involves a current curriculum vitae, an essay on why you want to be a member of an AMA Council, which Council(s) you prefer, what you consider to be your major strengths and qualifications for the position, and what benefits you feel are likely to result from your participation.

- Council on Constitution and Bylaws
- Council on Ethical and Judicial Affairs
- Council on Legislation
- Council on Long Range Planning and Development
- Council on Medical Education
- Council on Medical Service
- Council on Scientific Affairs

AMA-MSS Committee Application

Medical students are sought to serve on the following AMA-MSS committees:

- Committee on Computers and Technology (formerly Computer Projects Committee)
- Committee on Long Range Planning
- Legislative Affairs Committee
- Minority Issues Committee
- Ad Hoc Committee on Community Service and Advocacy
- Ad Hoc Committee on Membership Recruitment and Retention
- Ad Hoc Committee on MSS Programs and Activities
- Ad Hoc Committee on Scientific Issues Committee (CSI)
- Ad Hoc Committee on International Health and Policy

All applications must be completed and submitted with a CV to American Medical Association, Department of Medical Student Services, 515 North State Street, Chicago, IL 60610. Fax: (312) 464-5845.

AMA POLITICAL ACTION COMMITTEE (AMPAC)

AMPAC is a bipartisan group that serves to advance the interest of medicine within Congress, specifically by supporting candidates for office that are friendly to medicine. They also provide numerous programs to educate physicians, medical students, and their families on political activism. The Board directs the programs and activities of this extremely important political action committee. Adding medical students to the leadership of this group will provide for better medical student representation within the group, as well as greater student involvement in this important process. Terms are for two years.

Editorial Positions with Medical Student JAMA

MS/JAMA is the seven- to eight-page medical student section of the Journal of the American Medical Association (JAMA) that appears in the first JAMA of every month, September through May, and is also produced each month on the MS/JAMA Web site. As a regular section of a major medical journal, produced by and for medical students, MS/JAMA represents a unique opportunity to train to become journal editors, writers, and contributors. The MS/JAMA Web site is located at www.ama-assn.org/msjama.

AMA Foundation Leadership Award Program

This award is an exciting opportunity to advance your leadership skills within organized medicine. Medical students who have demonstrated strong nonclinical leadership skills in med-

icine or community affairs and have an interest in further developing these skills within organized medicine are eligible. The objective of the award program is to encourage involvement in organized medicine and continue leadership development among the country's brightest and most energetic medical students and residents. Twenty-five medical students will be selected. Travel expenses for award winners, including airfare and three nights' hotel accommodation, will be paid for directly by the AMA Foundation to attend the 2001 AMA National Leadership Development Conference. For applications call (800) AMA-3211, ext. 4751 or 4746.

GOVERNMENT RELATIONS INTERNSHIP PROGRAM APPLICATION

The Department of Medical Student Services, in conjunction with the Washington office of the American Medical Asso-

ciation, is pleased to offer assistance to students seeking to increase their involvement and education in national health policy and in the national legislative activities of organized medicine.

Through the Government Relations Internship Program, stipends of $2,500 are available to assist selected students who are completing health policy internships in the Washington, DC area. To be eligible for the program, students must be AMA members who have secured a policy internship in the Washington, DC area. Through the program, students may also apply for an internship at the AMA's Washington office (two positions available) or at the Health Care Financing Administration in Baltimore, Maryland (one position available). Students participating in the program generally arrange their internships with Congressional offices, specialty societies, or federal agencies in the DC area. A list of possible internship contacts is available.

WEB SITES OF INTEREST

ACOG.org

ACOG.org is the official Web site for the American College of Obstetrics and Gynecology. The Web site has several items of interest to medical students, including a career guide for medical students interested in the specialty.

<www.som.tulane.edu/student/t_3hints/OBGYN.HTM>

Some nice tips from Tulane medical school on how to impress during your OB/GYN rotation.

Medical student membership in ACOG

A one-time $10 fee includes:
- ACOG publications
- Reduced meeting fees

- Entry into their member-only Web site
- Updates in the specialty

JOIN AMWA (American Medical Women's Association)

For a one-time fee of $52, you can become a medical student life member of AMWA. Membership benefits include:

REVIEW RESOURCES

Awards and Opportunities

- Networking opportunities at the national and local levels—60 physicians branches and 120 student branches
- Continuing Medical Education (CME) programs
- Leadership and mentoring opportunities
- Professional and personal development programs
- AMWA's legislative network
- AMWA's Annual, Interim, and Regional Meetings offering career and personal development curricula
- Gender Equity Information Line to assist you with concerns on sexual harassment, gender bias, racial discrimination, and other matters
- Women's Health Advocacy
- Subscription to the *Journal of the American Medical Women's Association* (JAMWA), a quarterly peer-reviewed scientific publication
- AMWA Connections, a bimonthly newsletter keeping you connected to your colleagues
- Women's health projects and innovative "Train-the-Trainer" programs
- Discounts for AMWA publications such as *The Women's Complete Healthbook, The Women's Complete Wellness Book,* and *Developing a Child Care Program*
- Advanced access and reduced fees to AMWA's Career Development Institute
- Members-Only sections on the AMWA Web site

www.obgyn.pdr.net

An online journal that features News from the Literature, Malpractice Update, Controversies in OB/GYN, and a Path Quiz.

ms4c.org

Medical Students for Choice (MSFC) is dedicated to ensuring that women receive comprehensive reproductive health care, including abortion. One of the greatest obstacles to safe, legal abortion is the absence of trained providers. The more than 6,000 medical students and residents of <ms4c.org> are committed to ensuring that medical practitioners are prepared to provide their patients with the full range of reproductive health care choices.

ama-assn.com

- FREIDA Online—computer access to graduate training program data (members receive up to 30 free mailing labels)
- Airline discounts for travel to residency interviews (graduating seniors only)
- USP Drug Information for the Health Care Professional (free 1998 benefit for three and four multiyear membership options)
- Discounts up to 35% in AMA's Medical Student Catalog
- PaperChase—discounted online subscription to MEDLINE searches (free access after 5 P.M.)
- Policy Promotion Grants for chapter and community projects
- Educational loans consolidation thru Mellon Bank (888) 867-2116

medscape.com

This site's medical student section includes features such as "today's headlines," a medical student discussion forum to vent and exchange study tips, a weekly "focus" story from a med student's perspective, free tools for your palm pilot, test-taking skills, study tips, and a "clerk-shop clues" section that summarizes the latest advances relevant to OB/GYN, Medicine, Surgery, and other clerkships.

Index

Fluid balance
acute pyelonephritis, 104
methyldopa, 113
prolactin, 39
puerperium of the normal labor and delivery, 84
septic abortion, 131
Fluorescent in situ hybridization (FISH), 47
Fluorescent treponemal antibody-absorbed (FTA-ABS), 222
Fluoxetine, 97
Folate, 97
Foley catheter, 123
Folic acid, 95, 97, 102
Follicle-stimulating hormone (FSH)
amenorrhea, 160
anovulation, 154
endometriosis, 179
menopause, 231, 232
menstrual cycle, 159
oral contraceptives, 145
pregnancy, physiology of, 32
Follicular cysts
diagnosis, 182
physiology, 182
signs/symptoms, 182
treatment, 182
Fontanel, anterior/posterior, 59
Food and Drug Administration, U.S. (FDA), 96
Food Guide Pyramid, 89
Footling breech, 61
Forceps delivery, 67, 73, 77
Frank breech, 61
Frankenhäuser ganglion, 77
Frank goiter, 33
Fundal height, 20, 43, 44
Fundus, 14, 86

G

Galactorrhea, 162
Gallbladder, 29
Gallium, 90
Gallstones, 104
Gamete intrafallopian transfer (GIFT), 155
Gametogenesis, 128
Gastrointestinal system
anesthesia, general, 78
medical conditions in pregnancy
appendicitis, 104
cholelithiasis and cholecystitis, 105
differential, 104
milk helping the, breast, 90
pelvic inflammatory disease, 220
pelvic pain, 173
pregnancy on the mother, general effects of
gallbladder, 29
liver, 29
reflux esophagitis, 29
Gastroschisis, 43
Gehrung pessary, 237
Genetics
abortion, induced, 137, 138
abortion, spontaneous, 128, 131
fetal death, 134
hereditary nonpolyposis colon cancer, 204
hereditary ovarian cancer syndromes, 204
menopause, 231
stillbirths, 135
testing, 47

Genital herpes
definition, 222
diagnosis, 222
presentation, 222
risks, major, 222
treatment, 223
Genitofemoral nerves, 14
Genitourinary system
menopause, 232
pain control during labor and delivery, 77
pregnancy on the mother, general effects of
bacteruria, asymptomatic, 29
bladder, 30
nocturia, 29
renal function, 30
renal tubule changes, 30
stress incontinence, 29–30
ureters, 30
urinary frequency, 29
urinary stasis, 29
Gentamicin, 116, 125, 220
Geophagia, 48
Germ cell tumors, ovarian
clinical presentation, 206
dysgerminoma, 206
embryonal and choriocarcinoma, 206
endodermal sinus, 206
mixed, 206–207
treatment, 207
Germinal epithelium, 17
Gestational age
assessment of
abdominal exam and fundal height, 43, 44
Nägele's rule, 43
definition, 23, 43
Gestational diabetes
classification, 99
definition, 99
effects of, 100
shoulder dystocia, 62
Gestational trophoblastic neoplasias (GTN)
choriocarcinoma
definition, 215
diagnosis, 215
prognostic group clinical classification, 215–216
treatment, 215
definition, 213
hydatidiform mole
complete mole, 213
diagnosis, 214
histology, 214
invasive mole, 214
metastatic workup, 214
partial mole, 213
signs/symptoms, 214
treatment, 214–215
placental site trophoblastic tumor, 217
Globulin, 29
Glomerular filtration rate (GFR), 30
Glucagon, 32
Glucocorticoids, 38
Glucose
challenge test, 99–100
human placental lactogen, 38
screening for intolerance to, 27
3-hour glucose tolerance test, 100
women's health, 242
Glycogen, 34
Glycosaminoglycans, 35
Gonadotropin-releasing hormone (GnRH), 32, 145, 157, 159, 164, 179

Gonazyme, 220
Gonorrhea
definition, 220
diagnosis, 220
ectopic pregnancy, 133
presentation, 220
rape-trauma syndrome, 250
treatment, 220
Gram-positive bacilli, 125
Gram-positive cocci, 125
Gram stain, 117, 126, 224
Grand mal seizures, 112
Granuloma inguinale, 192
Granulosa–theca cell tumor, 207
Graves' disease, 101
Gravidity, 41
Gravid uterus, 72
Groin pain, 237
Gynecoid pelvic type, 81

H

Haemophilus ducreyi, 224
Hair, 34, 157, 163, 232
Hallucinogens, 94
Head, fetal
cephalopelvic disproportion, 75
compression, 73
crystal methamphetamine, 95
forceps delivery, 77
head-to-abdominal circumference ratio, 47
Ritgen maneuver, modified, 65
Headache
contraceptives
injectable, 146
oral, 145
hydralazine, 113
hypertension in pregnancy, 111
labetalol, 113
postspinal puncture, 87
preeclampsia, 112
tocolytic therapy, 114, 115
Health. *See* Women's health
Health and Human Services, U.S. Department of, 89
Heart
induction of labor, 74
murmurs, 28
palpitations, 113
postpartum care, routine, 86
pregnancy-induced hypertension, 111
tachycardia, 73, 103, 114, 116
See also Cardiovascular system; Fetal heart *listings*
Heartburn, 29, 49–50
Height, fundal, 20, 43, 44
HELLP syndrome, 111
Hemarthrosis, 170
Hematocrit, 85, 184
Hematologic disease and induced abortion, 137
Hematuria, 30, 194
Hemodilution, 30
Hemoglobin, 31, 85
Hemorrhage
cerebral, 111
choriocarcinoma, 215
coitus in postpartum, 88
corticosteroids, 115
epidural analgesia, 81
epilepsy, 102
indomethacin, 115

278